Avoiding the Output Blues

A Digital Publishing Primer

Taz Tally
Ph.D.

ISBN 0-13-084876-X

Prentice Hall PTR
Upper Saddle River, NJ 07458
www.phptr.com

Library of Congress Cataloging-in-Publication Data

Tally, Taz.
Avoiding the output blues: a digital publishing primer /Taz Tally.
p.   cm.
Includes bibliographical references and index.
ISBN (invalid) 0-13-084876-X
1. Printing--Data processing. 2. Desktop publishing.
I. Title.
Z249.3.T355   1999
686.2'2544--dc21   99-23834
                                                         CIP

Editorial/production supervision: *Nicholas Radhuber*
Manufacturing manager: *Alexis Heydt*
Acquisitions editor: *Tim Moore*
Editorial assistant: *Bart Blanken*
Marketing manager: *Bryan Gambrel*
Cover design: *Anthony Gemmellaro*
Cover design director: *Jerry Votta*
Interior design: *Meg VanArsdale*
Book production: *Taz Tally and Jazmine Saige*

© 1999 by Prentice Hall PTR
Prentice-Hall, Inc.
Upper Saddle River, New Jersey 07458

Prentice Hall books are widely used by corporations and government agencies for training,
marketing, and resale. The publisher offers discounts on this book when ordered in bulk quantities.
For more information, contact:
Phone: 800-382-3419, Fax: 201-236-7141
E-mail: corpsales@prenhall.com
or write:
Corporate Sales Department
Prentice Hall PTR
1 Lake Street
Upper Saddle River, NJ 07458

Printed in the United States of America
10 9 8 7 6 5 4 3 2 1

ISBN 0-13-084876-X

Prentice-Hall International (UK) Limited, *London*
Prentice-Hall of Australia Pty. Limited, *Sydney*
Prentice-Hall Canada Inc., *Toronto*
Prentice-Hall Hispanoamericana, S.A., *Mexico*
Prentice-Hall of India Private Limited, *New Delhi*
Prentice-Hall of Japan, Inc., *Tokyo*
Prentice-Hall (Singapore) Pte. Ltd., *Singapore*
Editora Prentice-Hall do Brasil, Ltda., *Rio de Janeiro*

DEDICATION

To Rae Tally and Sid Tally, my Mom & Dad, for all the opportunities, advantages, encouragement, love, and support they have always provided me.

Table of Contents

DTP 101 – The Big Picture   1

Chapter 1: Pressing Problems   3

The basic challenge of printing • New language skills • New technical challenges • Image reproduction challenges • Text and line art • Tonal images • The challenge of color • Changing printing technologies • Reduce & simplify: Making RIP-ready files

Chapter 7: Basic Computer Skills & Habits   69

Chapter 8: Resolving Resolution   79

DTP 301 – Project Construction   145

Chapter 12: Taming Your Scanner   147

Chapter 13: Document Construction 185

DTP 401 – Finishing The Project

Chapter 16: Screening Your Images

Acknowledgements

APPRECIATIONS

Many people have contributed to the completion of this book, but there are some who I would like to particularly recognize. First, I want to thank my brother, Sid, for his love and support in so many ways, for so many years, through so many episodes of may life. I thank my friend and business partner, Marcia Morgan, for her unflagging faith, encouragement and support, as well as her many suggestions during this entire project. I want to recognize Howie Fenton for his friendship and encouragement as well as his invaluable professional insight and recommendations which lead to dramatic improvements in the first draft of this book. I also thank my good friend, Lee Altman, who helped with many aspects of this book, including the planning, design, and initial editing, and who provided the printing support which helped us launch the project. I am also in debt to my good friend, Frank Elge, for his kind encouragement and suggestions, as well as his efforts and insights into marketing and sales. To a loyal friend, Paul Williams, who helped me get started in this business, a heartfelt thank you. A special thanks to Mario Macari for the great book cover artwork and to Ella Mills-White for her nifty cartoon figures.

And finally, a loving thank you for so many things, to my fabulous Jaz, without whom this book would never have been finished. Through a time when there were not enough resources to have others help, Jaz labored with editing changes, unflagging support, and many suggestions, and most of all her love, to help bring this book to completion.

Overview

The title of this book, *Avoiding The Output Blues,* tells the tale of what this book is about, preventing, or at least mitigating, as many problems as possible when it comes to creating and printing documents with desktop publishing equipment and software.

Most of us who are using desktop publishing equipment today are doing so without the benefit of any formal or professional training. Many of us have been thrust, dropped, dragged, pulled, pushed or otherwise cajoled into the world of desktop publishing. Many of us have also come to enjoy the art and technology of the desktop, once we figured out how to make it work for us rather than struggle against it. *Avoiding the Output Blues* is an attempt to provide fundamental background information, as well as a myriad of tips and tricks, about desktop publishing won through many years of mistakes and trial and error. I hope it helps.

Enjoy!

Meet the bits & bytes Players
Stars of
"As the BYTE Turns"

Danny D'Ziner

Danny is a very bright, creative artist and designer. Although he never intended to, Danny has started working on a computer. Now Danny does nearly all his work on a computer. Danny bought a great system and started to work. All was rosy until Danny started sending out his files to a printer to have them output at high resolution for printing. Danny was used to having everything he handed to the printer work. He was soon to find out that not everything he created on the computer could be output through a high resolution Postscript RIP. Danny had to learn how to avoid the perils and pitfalls of Postscript. He needed help.

Sam E. Sales

Like Danny, Sam E. was educated in the old school. He was used to picking up art boards from his clients and delivering them to scheduling, and then on to prepress. He had been doing most of Danny's printing for several years now, and they had a good relationship with few problems. Sam E. Sales has started having problems with client files, though. He gets more disks, and he has no idea what's on them. Prepress has even sent back some clients' disks with strange instructions about parent EPS files and missing fonts. Sam E. no longer feels comfortable answering client questions or even presenting quotes for these electronic jobs. He might just have to learn about that computer after all.

Pauline E. PrePress

Pauline has been with the same printing company for over ten years. She started out in typesetting and then learned stripping (no, not in a night club) and had become quite proficient at assembling film. Pauline likes technology, so when her printing company started getting computers to do typesetting, she learned to use them. Over time Pauline has graduated from typesetting to page layout and, finally, on to scanning and electronic stripping. Pauline's responsibilities now include pre-flighting incoming client files. Problems with client files have become the biggest bottleneck in prepress. In fact, the problems have become more numerous and severe as clients send in increasingly complex files and more "finished jobs." Sam E.'s problems were coming to her, and worse, he usually refused to inform his clients about their file preparation problems, so the same mistakes reoccurred. Now, Pauline had a secret crush on one of Sam E.'s clients, Danny D'Ziner, but he is one of the worst offenders! Maybe she could help.

DTP 101

The Big Picture

THE ORIGINAL DTP SYSTEM!

1
Pressing Problems

Will Danny D'Ziner and Pauline E. Prepress be able to PICT their way through the Perils of Postscript, or will they have one Tiff too many?

Many items on my document look different from the originals, including the photographs, colors, and where images overlap. Why?

That's a good question, but the answer is complicated.

Where do I start? I know part of the answer!

Let's ask Pauline. She can help explain the details.

Many variables affect the printing process. The differences you see boil down to changes in media, image format, and reproduction techniques.

THE PRINTING CHALLENGE

Pressing problems of putting ink on paper

The basic challenge of printing

The printing process is a challenge in reproduction. There are three challenges. The first is to reproduce a document so that it looks as close to the original image fidelity as possible. The second challenge is to provide consistent reproduction of that document over a high volume of prints. The third challenge is to perform the first two challenges in an economically affordable fashion. The second and third requirements, volume and affordability, make the first challenge, image fidelity, most difficult. If price were not an issue, we could reproduce all images as continuous tone photographs. But even then volume would be a problem. How do we quickly create one million photographic copies of a 400-page catalog and then bind it all together for ready distribution and use? Traditional printing technologies employ many time-consuming steps involving many skills, including: typesetting, photography, engraving, mechanical pasteup, and stripping. These skills demand many people with high skill levels to compose and/or reproduce high quality pages. Many of these processes have been changed and simplified with electronic preparation of documents, but much skill is still required, although not always brought to bear. Along with process changes have come changes in people's jobs. Some jobs have changed, others have been eliminated, and new ones have appeared. Chapter 3, "Peaceful Coexistence," Chapter 4, "Electronic Publishing Systems," and Chapter 13, "Document Construction," address how the printing business and process have changed, some of the new tools we are using, and how the nature of the printed document has changed.

▼ *Figure 1.1 The Original Desktop Printing Press*
Getting many kinds of ideas and information across to many people has always been the role and the challenge of the printing press. New electronic technologies are changing the way we create and produce printed materials. These same technologies are also fundamentally changing the ways in which we communicate and even what we communicate.

New language skills

Along with the new tools and documents, an entirely new language and set of skills has evolved. Terms like "rubylith" and "PMTs" have given way to a digital lexicon which is more concerned with megabytes, Postscript, and file formats. Discussions of photography, film, and enlargers have given way to debates about scanners, Photoshop software, and pixel depth. Chapter 2, "Terms of Endearment," Chapter 5, "Software," Chapter 6, "bits & Bytes,"

Chapter 7, "Basic Computer Skills and Habits," and Chapter 11, "Tales Of True Typesetting" address the fundamentals of the new languages and skills required to operate an electronic publishing system effectively. Chapter 18, "The Proof Is In The Separation," and Chapter 19, "Managing the Mess," cover some of the new responsibilities which document creators have.

New technical challenges

While the age-old considerations of line screen and dot gain are still with us, a whole new raft of technical issues have appeared which needs to be mastered. The designer and artist and even the secretary now responsible for the monthly newsletter never used to worry about line screens and trapping. Now, they too are having to worry about scanning resolutions, file formats, file preparation, and color calibration. Chapter 8, "Resolving Resolution," Chapter 9, "Grappling With Graphics," Chapter 14, "Color Me Right," Chapter 16, "Screening Your Images," and Chapter 17, "Feeling Trapped?" cover most of the fundamental technical issues involved with producing electronic documents for print.

Image reproduction challenges

We can divide image reproduction challenges into four basic categories: text, line art, tonal (particularly continuous tone), and color images. Of these four, text and line art are the easiest to tackle. The ability to reproduce text was initially solved with the invention of the printing press and later facilitated by the invention of movable type. Text has been the easiest of the image reproduction challenges because there are a finite number of character shapes which are constantly reproduced. Both line art and text reproduction were greatly aided through the invention and adaptation of photography to the printing process. Basic text and line art images, because they are constructed out of only black or white areas, can be faithfully reproduced through the photographic process and then directly transferred, again through photography, to plates for high volume reproduction on a printing press. Tonal images, by contrast, are images constructed from shades of gray and (in the case of continuous tone images) constantly varying shades of gray. Shades of gray which characterize tonal images are much more difficult to reproduce than the solid black and white areas inherent in text and line art images. Chapter 13, "Taming Your Scanner," takes you through the depths of image acquisition and editing.

▼ Figure 1.2 Text Images
In an electronic document, type is one of the three kinds of images which need to be reproduced in print. There are literally thousands of varieties of type. As you will see, type, which is created with resources called font files, are special kinds of graphics which need to be carefully managed in order to get them to reproduce correctly. Typesetting has become easier with electronic publishing, but considerable skill is still required in order to set type properly.

Text and line art

Most graphic images, both line art and tonal, are by their very nature unique. Graphic images, unlike text, cannot be faithfully reproduced through the combination of a set number of basic forms. Words, sentences, and paragraphs are formed through the construction of various combinations of a basic set of characters. In English, we have a basic set of 52 alphabetic characters (upper and lower case), 10 numeric characters, and a variety of punctuation marks: 126 characters in all. These 126 characters are the basis for the ASCII character set discussed in Chapter 3, "Peaceful Coexistence," and listed in the Appendix. So, due to the lack of basic repeatable building blocks, unique graphic image reproduction is, by its very nature, more challenging than reproducing type. Line art reproduction used to be a very time-consuming process because the original image had to be laboriously redrawn by hand. Line art (as well as text reproduction) has been greatly aided through the invention and adaptation of photography to the printing process. Basic line art and text images, because of the continuity of their shapes and their single tone nature (they are either black or white), can be faithfully reproduced through the photographic process and then directly transferred, again through photography, to plates for high volume reproduction on a printing press.

▼ Figure 1.3 Line Art Images
Line art images used to be reproduced with cameras and film. Today line art images are routinely captured with digital scanners. Line art images are often the least demanding form of graphic to reproduce because they only have two tonal values which need to be copied. In electronic imaging, issues like path lengths and flatness ratios often need to be addressed.

Tonal images

The reproduction of tones in general and continuous tone images (contones) in particular has always been a daunting challenge. The challenge has always been how to create a tone or continuous tone out of a solid ink. In screen printing this is accomplished by essentially smearing the ink out into layers of various thicknesses to create tones or continuous tones. This technique is effective but is a relatively slow process which does not lend itself to economic high volume reproduction. The solution to economic, high volume tonal reproduction has been to simulate rather than actually reproduce tones. There have been numerous ingenious methods of tone simulation. Many of the initial contone reproductions were created through the use of line art simulations of contones. Through the use of varying line lengths, thickness, and spacing, the appearance of tone and continuous tone was created. This technique was very effective and many of these original prints are highly valued today. However, this line art technique is very time consuming and requires considerable creative as well as technical skills.

The traditional technique which has been developed to reproduce contone images economically is called halftoning screening, halftoning, or AM (Amplitude Modulation) screening. In AM screening the size or amplitude of evenly spaced dots is varied to simulate different tones. Patterns of dots of various sizes are created to simulate the appearance of continuous tone. More recently, a process known as FM (Frequency Modulation) screening has been developed. In FM screening, the position instead of the size of a dot is varied in order to create a contone image. Some screening technologies vary the position as well as the size of the dots to simulate tones. At a distance these dot patterns or screens have the appearance of tones to the human eye. This screening process used to be accomplished photographically and is now performed by a Postscript RIP. Chapter 10, "Ripping Up Your Files," and Chapter 16, "Screening Your Images," tackle the challenges of reproducing contone images on a press.

The problem of dot gain, where the size of a printed dot expands as it is applied during the printing process, is still with us. Instead of adjusting for this ink spread photographically as we used to, we now apply tone correction curves to our images through applications like Photoshop. Refer to Chapters 12, 16, and 18, "Taming Your Scanner," "Screening Your Images," and "The Proof Is In The Separation" for treatment of dot gain issues.

▼ *Figure 1.4 Contone Images*
Continuous tone (contone) images are some of the more complex images to reproduce. Contones have a wide range of tonal values which need to be reproduced. Color contone has the additional burden of color as well as tone reproduction. Low cost, easy-to-use desktop scanners have made acquiring these images easy. However, considerable knowledge and skill are required in order to produce a faithful reproduction of an original.

The challenge of color

The final print reproduction challenge has been and remains the reproduction of color. Similar and related to the challenge we face with reproducing tonal shades, color tests the need to reproduce a very wide range, essentially an infinite one, of colors. If we need to reproduce a solid color, we have the ability to mix up an exact match and print that color separately on the press. This is an effective and even economical solution if we have only one or two colors to reproduce. We do this when we print spot colors. However, every separate color which we print requires its own cylinder on a printing press to apply that color. Once we start printing more than six colors, the cost of doing so becomes prohibitively expensive in all but the most demanding color applications. So the real color reproduction challenge becomes apparent when we need to reproduce continuous tone (contone) color which would require the use of dozens or even hundreds or thousands of individual colors in order to reproduce all of the variations of colors in any standard contone image. This practice would clearly involve astronomical costs and is therefore an untenable solution. What is clearly called for is a solution which requires mixing some basic colors to produce a wide variety of other colors. This is precisely the approach which has been taken in the printing process. We use the colors Cyan (C), Magenta (M), Yellow (Y), and Black (B) in various combinations to attempt to reproduce the range of colors contained in natural scenes and art productions. This solution is very satisfactory for a wide range of applications. However, there are many colors, particularly those which are bright and rich in white, which cannot be reproduced in the CMYK color gamut. (See Chapters 14, 16, and 18, "Color Me Right," "Screening Your Images," and "The Proof Is In The Separation" for more detailed information.)

It is important to keep in mind that in the case of both tonal and process color reproduction, the results are cost effective approximations of characteristics of the original images. The various screening technologies merely create the appearance of tones and are not actually tonal in nature like the original images they represent. Process color recreations of original colors are approximations and not identical reproductions. The commercial printing process, in an effort to keep the reproduction process affordable, dramatically alters the content and the media of the original image. Hence, even though we have refined and will continue to refine the print reproduction process, and even though there is much we can do to assure as close a match as possible, we should not expect the end results to be identical to the original. Chapter 14, "Color Me Right," covers a wide gamut of issues relating to color reproduction.

Changing printing technologies

So we see that our solutions to these three basic printing challenges of high volume, reasonable cost, and consistent, high fidelity image reproduction have been the development and evolution of three interrelated printing technologies: the offset printing press, screening technologies, and process color. The ways in which these technologies have been implemented have changed only incrementally in the past 200 years – that is, until the advent of open architecture Postscript-based publishing systems. And that is what this book attempts to address: the fundamental challenges of and solutions to preparing Postscript files for print.

Reduce & simplify: making RIP-ready files

All of the various page elements we create electronically and want to reproduce on a press, including text, line art, and contone images, must be processed through a device called a RIP or Raster Image Processor. The job of the RIP is to take your electronic document data and convert it into a form, often some kind of a dot pattern, which can be reproduced on a print device. We must always be cognizant of the fact that there are many items which we can create on a computer which are difficult or impossible to print. Any print-bound document we are creating on a computer must ultimately be processed through a Postscript RIP, and this RIP is often a tight funnel through which our electronic files must fit before we can image them onto a piece of film or paper. The main emphasis of this book is to help you understand the concepts and help you master the techniques necessary to create RIP–ready files, that is, files which are compatible with processing through a Postscript RIP. Our battle cry for this book, then, is to REDUCE & SIMPLIFY all of our documents and images as much as possible. We want to reduce the file size of our graphic files and simplify our designs and graphics whenever we can to make them more Ripable. Off we go…charge!

PAULINE'S FILE PREP TIPS

File Prep Hint # 1

Take a field trip to your favorite printing company or service bureau and have them take you through and explain the production and printing process in detail. This will be an enlightening experience. Have them show you how they handle customer files and what they check for. By doing this activity you will more fully understand the challenges printers face when they try to reproduce your work. When you are on your tour, don't be afraid to ask plenty of questions. Make sure you understand the entire production process. This is also a good way to establish a relationship with the folks in the electronic prepress production department, the people who actually output your work!

2
Terms Of Endearment

As the Byte Turns continues…

Will the language barrier of Postscript keep Danny and Pauline at odds forever? Or will they both learn Spanish, move to Costa Rica, and live happily ever after? Hmmm . . . maybe a glossary would help!

What do you mean, your production department told me to save my 1 bit tiffs as vector graphics so that they will RIP faster. What are you talking about???

Well, Er, Ah…

Oh dear, I don't have the foggiest idea!!

Help !!!

This is difficult – not being able to communicate effectively about these files. Perhaps we should sponsor a seminar on basic Postscript terminology, invite our clients, and have the sales staff sit in too.

ELECTRONIC PUBLISHING TERMS

Half the battle

Half of winning the battle in mastering any new discipline is learning the language. The lexicon of desktop or electronic publishing is as specialized and filled with acronyms as any you will encounter. Hell, we even have acronyms which can have several different meanings depending upon the context. For instance, ATM may refer to Adobe Type Manager, Asynchronous Transfer Mode, or Automatic Teller Machine, depending upon whether we need to manipulate a font, send it over a network, or purchase something! Our catalog of terms is also very new and rapidly evolving. Many of the basic terms such as resolution, screening, pixel, vector, and halftone are not well understood by most of those who use them. Communication and understanding are not aided when the "experts" misuse terms as well. Confusion about the meaning and use of dpi, ppi, and lpi is a primary example. It is no wonder we are confused about resolution; we can't even agree to use the proper terms!

An increasing number of us in the world of DTP are non-specialists; that is, we use the technology, but our primary job is not publishing. Even if our primary job is publishing, few of us have been afforded the basic training we need to master the all-important fundamentals. With this in mind, I offer up a primer on electronic publishing terms. I have placed it in the beginning of the book, instead of the usual practice of placing it at the end, because of its primary importance in helping us master the fundamental tools of our trade.

Active: Currently usable window, application, or document.

AppleShare: Mac-based network file sharing software.

Application: A computer program with a specific set of capabilities (e.g., page layout, drawing, word processing).

Backup and archiving: Creating copies of files on separate storage devices or media as a means of protection against lost, damaged, or destroyed files.

Bitmapped Image: A graphic image constructed out of dots, also known as a raster image, in contrast to vector images, which are constructed out of lines.

Bitonal Image: Another name for black and white images; meaning two tones, black and white.

Built Color: Color created and printed using screened combinations of colors rather than a single solid color. Traditionally, built colors have been constructed, or built, from combinations of the basic CMYK process colors. Recently, additional colors, known as Hi-Fi colors, have been added to the four standard process colors (see process color, spot color, and Hi-Fi color).

Calibration: Matching of input, display, proof, and final production, especially with regard to color (see WYSIWYG).

CD-ROM: Compact Disk - Read Only Memory. An optical disk which contains up to 600 MB of information. This information can be accessed (read or copied) but cannot be edited.

Choke: A color trapping term used to indicate that a surrounding background area containing one color will be overlapped, or choked, into another foreground area containing another, usually darker, color which it encloses (see Spread).

Clear: Remove a selection without placing a copy of the selection on the clipboard.

Clipping path: Vector edge added to bitmapped contone images in order to create a clean sharp edge. Often used when creating hard edged silhouettes.

Close: Closing a document.

Clipboard: Short-term pasteable storage of copied or cut selections.

Color:
8 bit color = 256 colors or shades of gray
24 bit color = 16.7 million colors
32 bit color = 4.3 billion colors

Color Assignment: Various ways of designating how a color should be created and reproduced. In printing, colors are usually designated as either spot, process builds, or tints of spot colors (see color matching systems, spot color, process color, built color, and tint).

Color Matching Systems: Color assignment and matching systems which utilize specific mixtures of spot and/or process colors to create and reproduce colors. Several of the most common systems include Pantone®, Trumatch®, Focaltone®, and Toyo® (see PMS Color).

Color Space or Model: Systems for defining and/or describing a spectrum or range of colors:
RGB = Red, Green, Blue, Transmissive, or additive color space
CMYK = Cyan, Magenta, Yellow, and Black, reflective or subtractive color space
CIE = Commission International de l'Eclairage

HSV = Hue, Saturation, and Value

HSL = Hue, Saturation, and Lightness or Luminance

YCC = Luminance Chrominance, Chrominance

Compression: The reduction in the size of a file by reducing, through the use of shortcut data recording methods, the space required for storing the information contained in a file (see JPEG, Lossy compression, and Lossless compression).

Continuous Tone / Contone: An image which contains gradually changing shades of gray. A gradation or blend, and a photograph of a face are examples of contones. A contone is simulated in printing by the creation of a pattern of various-sized halftone dots.

Copy: Copy a selection; places a copy of the selection on the application clipboard.

CPU: Central Processing Unit. The primary computing chip in a computer. Speed of a CPU is determined by clock speed and MIPS of the CPU.

CREF Guidelines: An extensive set of file prep guidelines produced by the Scitex Users Group.

Cut: Copies and removes a selection while placing the copy of the selection on the clipboard.

Desktop: Virtual working or desktop surface on a Mac screen; what you see on your screen.

Digital: Any equipment, process, or media which utilizes sequences of 0s and 1s, binary numbers, or some facsimile, to create, store, transport, reproduce, or present information, hence the name "digital computer."

Digitize: Convert an analog or continuous format set of data such as a photograph, video, or sound clip to a digital file format.

Dialog Box: A pop-up window, such as a print dialog box, which provides response choices.

Document: A file created while working in an application containing pages of text and/or graphic elements.

DPI: Dots Per Inch. A linear measurement of resolution which refers to the number of image dots or spots which a printer can create per linear inch (for example, 300 dpi or 1200 dpi).

DPI^2: Dots Per Square Inch. An area measurement of resolution which refers to the number of image dots or spots which a printer can create per square inch (for example, a 300 dpi laser printer creates 90,000 dpi^2, a more accurate and useful measurement of resolution than dpi).

Electronic Publishing: 1) A general term which refers to the use of electronic (usually digital) equipment to create and reproduce text and graphic images of all kinds and combinations. 2) A specific term which refers to the use of digital media, or non-printed media, as the final communication format, examples of which include CD-ROM documents, Acrobat documents, on-line publications, and presentation documents.

Finder: Macintosh system-based application which allows the user to use the operating system and navigate around (Create, Name, Locate, Move, Throw Away, & Duplicate Files).

Folder: Virtual storage space for icons of applications, documents, and other items.

Font: Typeface of a specific style and size.

• Screen font -Font resource used for viewing type on a monitor.

• Printer font - Font resource used for sending type to a printer.

Graphic Formats:

• TIFF - (Tagged Image File Format) Used for high resolution bitmapped graphics and scanned images.

• PICT - Apple's quick drawing screen display language.

• PCX - MS DOS/Windows-based bitmapped graphic file format.

• EPS - (Encapsulated PostScript) Object oriented or vector based.

• PAINT- Low resolution (72 dpi) bitmapped.

• POSTSCRIPT - Uneditable (unless you speak Postscript) text-based page description file. This type of file cannot be opened and edited within a page layout or graphics program; Postscript files are downloaded directly to a printer.

• DCS - Desktop Continuous Scan.

• ScitexCT - Continuous Tone format developed by Scitex Corporation.

• Windows Metafile - File used for screen views with windows operating system.

• YCC - PhotoCD native file format.

Halftone: Or digital halftone. The pattern of dots, usually created by a laser printer or imagesetter, which is meant to produce the effect of a continuous tone image. Halftone dots are built out of smaller image dots or spots. The size of the halftone dot varies with the grayscale percentage it is simulating. Traditional halftones were created by taking a high contrast photograph of a continuous tone image through a screen. Digital halftones are created during the RIPing or rasterizing process on a printer or computer (see Raster Image Processor).

Halftone Dot: A composite dot created out of one or more image dots or spots. A halftone dot is created to serve as a simulation of grayscale or continuous tone. Larger halftone dots are used to create the impression of darker shades of gray and smaller halftone dots are used to simulate lighter shades of gray. A continuous area filled with halftone dots of the same size is known as a tint or screen.

Halftone Screening: A method of screening for reproducing a continuous tone image which varies the size of the halftone dots to simulate changes in grayscale value (also known as AM (amplitude modulation) screening). With this traditional, nonstochastic method, halftone dots are located in a rigid pattern and only the dot size is varied (see Stochastic Screening).

HI-Fi Color: High Fidelity Color. A color printing system which uses three or four colors in addition to the standard four-color process to produce color images on a printing press. The use of these additional colors dramatically increases the color gamut or range of colors which a printing press can reproduce using built colors.

Icon: Symbol for an item. It can be type or graphic (e.g., Disks, Folders, Applications, Documents).

Image Dot or Spot: The dot or spot which is generated and imaged on film, paper, or plates by a printing device such as a laser printer or imagesetter. Image dots are combined on film, paper, or plates to create images. The size of the image dot depends upon the resolution of the printing device. For instance, a 600 dpi laser printer creates an image dot which measures $1/600$ inch square, while a 2400 dpi imagesetter creates an image dot which measures $1/2,400$ inch square. Image dots are combined to create halftone dots (see resolution and halftone dots).

Imagesetter: High resolution (1200 dpi – 5000 dpi), laser-based photographic output device. Imagesetters can often produce both film and paper output. There are basically two types of imagesetters: Capstan imagesetters, in which the film is transported during imaging, and Drum imagesetters, in which the imaging laser is transported during imaging. Drum imagesetters are considered to be more precise and therefore higher quality and more suitable for reproducing large format and high quality color images.

JPEG: (Joint Photographic Expert Group). A standard Lossy compression scheme used with print images. JPEG compression provides a variety of compression ratios ranging from 2/1 to 40/1 (see Compression and Lossy compression).

Knockout: A color trapping term used to indicate that a background area equal to the size and shape of a foreground area containing a specific color will be removed, or knocked out, during the printing process. This allows the foreground area and color to print without contamination of the background color (see Overprint).

LAN: Local Area Network. Connection of computers and peripherals within a local environment such as within one building.

Laser Printer: Relatively low resolution (300 dpi-1200 dpi) black and white or color desktop printers, which usually print on paper but sometimes on film. Laser printers use toner, a magnetic thermoplastic, rather than a photographic image, which is fused onto the print surface as an imaging medium. Laser printers are generally used as proofing devices in high quality work, but can be used as final output for lower quality work (see Imagesetter).

Launch: Start-up/Activate an application.

Lossless compression: Compression of a file which *does not* result in the loss of some image data (see Compression, Lossy compression, and JPEG).

Lossy compression: Compression of a file which results in the loss of some image data (see Compression, Lossless compression, and JPEG).

LPI: Lines Per Inch. Resolution term used in printing which designates the number of halftone dots per inch which are printed horizontally and vertically. LPI differs from dpi in that dpi refers to image dots per inch (see Halftone dot, Image dot, and DPI).

Master page: A page formatting tool in a page layout application which serves as a template for document pages. Text and graphics items, such as logos and page numbers, which occur repetitively on document pages and are placed on master pages so that they will automatically be placed on the document pages. Master pages dramatically simplify the creation and editing of multipage documents and help maintain consistency from page to page. Master pages are often used along with style sheets to construct a document (see Style sheets).

Menu: Pop-up and pull-down lists of choices (e.g., application headers, dialog boxes, palettes).

Moiré Pattern: A repeating geometric pattern of dots produced when multicolor screened images are printed. This pattern is generated as the result of two colors being printed with slight misregistration at nearly the same angle.

Modem: Computer peripheral device used for connecting computers via phone lines. The term "modem" is a compound word derived from the two words "modulate" and "demodulate" (mo-dem), which is what a modem does. The sending computer modulates a digital signal from a computer into an analog signal for transfer over the phone lines. The receiving modem then demodulates the analog signal into a digital signal again for transfer into the receiving computer.

Multitasking: Performing more than one function simultaneously (e.g., printing and typesetting).

Native File: An original editable document file produced by an application; in contrast to some EPS and all Postscript files which are not easily editable within the application which produced them.

Network: A collection of interconnected devices such as computers, printers, modems, etc.

• AppleTalk: Low speed (270KB/sec) network protocol.

• Ethernet/EtherTalk: Medium Speed (10 MB/sec) network hardware and protocol.

OCR: (Optical Character Recognition: Digital). Conversion, through scanning, of text as editable characters rather than as graphics.

One Bit Graphic: Graphic file composed of only two values, usually either black or white.

Open: Refers to activating or opening a closed disk or folder.

Overprint: A color trapping term used to indicate that a foreground area containing a specific color will be printed directly on top of a background area or color without the removal of any of the background color (see Knockout).

Orphans: Single line sections of paragraphs occurring at the beginning or end of pages. These should be avoided.

PostScript: EPS page description language standard. This language is particularly useful for describing complex page elements such as scaled text and rotated and/or skewed graphics, or for producing high quality halftones of continuous tone images.

Paste: Place a copied or cut selection from the clipboard.

PhotoCD: A range of technologies and services related to a process of scanning, formatting, storage and saving, in a special digital format (YCC), images which have been captured by a camera on film. The PhotoCD process produces a range of image resolutions which can be used for different purposes such as TV, video, and printing at various sizes.

Pixel: Dot which is used to construct a graphic image. A pixel can be of various shapes and sizes. Pixels may be round, square, elliptical, or a custom shape. The size of a pixel depends upon the resolution of the graphic image. In a 300 dpi image each pixel is $1/300$ inch square. Pixels may contain one or more bits of graphic information.

Pixel Depth: The number of bits per pixel (b/p) a graphic image contains. B&W images have 1 b/p; grayscale images typically contain 8 b/p; RGB color images typically contain 24 b/p; and CMYK images typically contain 32 b/p.

PMS Color: (Pantone Matching System color). A color assignment and matching system developed by Pantone, Inc., which utilizes specific mixtures of spot and/or process colors to create and reproduce colors. The term PMS is often misused as a general term for spot color (see Color Matching Systems).

PostScript File: A uneditable, nondocument file which contains all text, graphics, and format information, created specifically to aid in the printing of complex files on a wide variety of PostScript compatible systems. Postscript files are downloaded directly to RIPs without opening the files.

PreFlight: Check or prepare an electronic file for output on a printer. At a minimum, it involves checking for the presence of all the high resolution graphic files and fonts which will be necessary to properly print a file.

Printer Description Files: Small files which contain information about page geometry (size and margins) and sometimes screen angle and frequency for a specific printer. This file is accessed when the "Printer Type" is selected in the "Page Setup" or "Print" dialog boxes.

Printer Driver: Files used to access printers from a computer. Also contains information about page geometry (size and margins) and screen angle and frequency for a specific printer. This file is accessed when the "Printer Type" is selected in the "Page Setup" or "Print" dialog boxes.

Proof printer: Low resolution B&W or color output device.

Process Colors: The four standard colors, Cyan, Magenta, Yellow, and Black (CMYK) which create, or build, a wide range of other colors (see Built Colors, Hi-Fi Color, and Spot Color).

Quicktime: A multimedia file format and compression scheme used in video and multimedia files.

Quit: Close an application.

Radio Button: A virtual button often contained in dialog buttons.

RAM (Random Access Memory). Fast, short-term volatile memory stored in RAM chips called SIMMS (Single Inline Memory Modules). Serves as fast, active desktop-like work area.

Raster: A dot. Generally used to describe the nature of a graphic, i.e., a raster graphic is one which is composed of dots.

Resolution: Number of dots per unit length (e.g., dots per inch, dpi) or dots per square area (e.g., pixels per square inch) at which an image is either captured (scanned) or printed. Scan resolution is generally stated in dots per inch (dpi), printing resolution is generally referred to as lines per inch (lpi), and image resolution in pixels per square inch (ppi^2). Some scanning equipment uses the term RES which refers to pixels per mm (Res 12 = 12 pixels per mm or 12p/mm) (see Image Dot, Halftone Dot, LPI, and Pixel).

Res: A resolution term which is shorthand for pixels per mm. More commonly used in place of dpi in high-end scanning systems.

RIP / Raster Image Processor: An electronic processor attached to an output device, such as a laser printer or imagesetter, which converts the Postscript description of a page to dots which will be used to compose the image on the printer's paper or film. It is the RIP that creates the digital halftone of a continuous tone image.

Router: Device used to connect dissimilar networks (e.g., to connect to AppleTalk and Ethernet).

Save: Moving document data from volatile RAM memory to a safer storage memory location on a disk, usually an internal hard drive.

Save As: Creating a new copy of a currently active document.

Scanners: Image capture devices.

•Transparency Scanner: Scans film (Drum and CCD).

• Reflective Scanner: Scans reflective art (Handheld, Flatbed, and Drum scanners).

• CCD Scanner: Charge Coupled Device, low to medium resolution, generally flatbed scanner.

• PMT Scanner: (Photo Multiplier Tube) High resolution, generally drum scanner.

Scratch disk: Photoshop's term for virtual memory, which is storage memory used as RAM space. Scratch disk memory use is much slower than normal RAM memory.

Screen: A pattern of dots created to simulate a shade of gray in a tint or a continuous tone image.

Scrapbook: Permanent storage of copied or cut selections. Can cut, copy and paste Scrapbook items.

Scroll: Used to view the contents of windows which display too small an area to view entire contents.

SCSI: (Small Computer System Interface). High speed peripheral interface standard.

SCSI2: Improved, faster high-speed peripheral interface standard.

Select: Choose an element or object by pointing and clicking.

Spot Color: A single, solid color, usually a custom color, used to create and print an image (see Process Color and Built Color).

Spread: An object-trapping term used to indicate that a foreground area containing one color will be overlapped by expanding or spreading that color into a surrounding background area containing another, usually darker, color (see Choke).

Stochastic Screening: A method of screening for reproducing a continuous tone image which varies the placement, and sometimes the size, of the halftone dots to simulate changes in grayscale value. Also known as FM (frequency modulation) screening. With traditional, nonstochastic, halftone screening techniques, halftone dots are located in a rigid pattern and only the dot size is varied. Stochastic screening eliminated moiré patterns and produces more pleasing tonal gradations in some images.(see Halftone Screening).

Storage Memory: Long term safe memory (e.g., hard drives, optical disks, floppy disks). Storage memory is slower but more secure than RAM.

Style sheet: A formatting template for type. Style sheets contain a complete set of character and/or paragraph formatting information such as typeface, type style, tracking, leading, and justification instructions. Style sheets are used to format type quickly and consistently in a document. Style sheets are often used along with Master Pages to construct a document (see Master Pages).

System Software: Background software which helps control the interaction of hardware, software, and operator (e.g., System 7.5 and Windows).

SWOP: (Standards For Web Offset Press). A series of standard specifications such as dot gain and screen angles used to create films and plates.

Trap: There are two types of traps, ink traps and object traps.

•Ink trapping refers to the propensity of one ink to stick to another ink when it is applied on a printing press.

• Object trapping refers to the amount of overlap assigned to two adjacent or touching object colors, a foreground and a background color, which will be printed on a printing press. There are several basic object trapping terms:

- Spread: Color overlap achieved by expansion of a foreground object color into a surrounding background object color.

- Choke: Color overlap achieved by the constriction of a surrounding background color around a foreground object color.

- Knock out: Removal of a background color from underneath a foreground object when no trap is formed.

- Overprint: The direct printing of one color on top of another.

- Trap Zone: The area of overlap between two trapped adjacent colors.

Tint: A screen of a spot color. In printing, a tint is created by a regularly spaced pattern of equal-sized halftone dots.

Typesetting: The placement and formatting of type on a page

• Justification: Formatting of lines of text either vertically or horizontally.

• Kerning: Space between two characters.

• Leading: Space between lines of text.

• Tracking: Space between characters and words.

Vector Graphic: A graphic image constructed from lines, also known as an outline graphic. In contrast to a Bitmapped or Raster Image, which is constructed from dots. Also known as an outline graphic.

Virtual memory: Passive storage memory, usually hard drive space used as active RAM space (see Scratch Disk).

Virus: An exotic, potentially destructive, self-replicating file.

WAN: (Wide Area Network). Connections of computers and peripherals over a large area such as between buildings, cities, or countries.

Window: Viewing area which appears on the desktop.
• There are two types of windows on a Mac: Finder Windows and Document Windows. Finder Windows contain icons of folders, applications, and documents. Document Windows contain actual text and graphics.

Widow: Single word sentences at the end of paragraphs. These should be avoided.

Windows Operating System: Graphically-oriented system software for IBM/Intel-based computers.

WYSIWYG (What You See Is What You Get). The promise of having what you view on your monitor matching what comes out of your printing device.

PAULINE'S FILE PREP TIPS

File Prep Hint # 2

It is important to learn the fundamental terms and concepts associated with electronic publishing. Knowing the terms will help you to communicate more effectively with your service companies as well as your colleagues. Knowing the concepts will make you a more effective creator and preparer of electronic documents. Some of the key terms and concepts you need to understand include: resolution, dpi vs. ppi vs. lpi, spot vs. process colors, color gamuts, RIPing, RAM vs. virtual memory, image spot vs. halftone dot, halftone cell, AM vs. FM screening, raster vs. vector, pixel depth, master pages, style sheets, preferences, Postscript, Postscript files vs. document files, paths and clipping paths, flatness and tolerance, splitting paths, Tiff vs. EPS vs. JPEG vs. PhotoCD, document vs. native file, halftoning, screen vs. print fonts, tracking, leading and kerning, compression, SWOP and trapping, and preflighting.

3
Peaceful Coexistence

As the Byte Turns continues…

Will Danny D'Ziner find true happiness with Pauline E. PrePress or will the perils of Postscript keep them apart?

ELECTRONIC PUBLISHING CULTURE

▼ *Figure 3.1 Stripping Table Method*
The conventional way of compositing film for plate production. With this method, clients would deliver print documents to printers on full-sized mechanical boards. Composite films would then be generated by the printer and assembled on flats. With this method of producing composite films, the full time printing professional had complete control over the construction of the print document. This generally meant less control for the creator of the document, the client, but far fewer production problems.

Effect of the postscript revolution

The 10 year period from 1985 to 1995 has been a period of revolution in the graphic arts industry. This revolution, referred to as the digital revolution, involves a shift from analog to digital treatment of information. This is a genuine revolution, a paradigm shift, and not merely a sequence of incremental changes. In 1995, we are still in the throes of this revolution with all of the attendant challenges and opportunities which are inherent in any drastic change. The digital revolution involves a fundamental change in how we create, capture, manipulate, store, transfer, and transform information. Indeed, it is forcing us to entirely rethink the ways in which we communicate. For many of us it has even changed how we view and interpret the world around us. To fully understand, adapt to, and take advantage of these changes, one must understand the basic concepts of digital information.

The digital revolution has brought about changes in nearly every aspect of our business. Some of the most obvious changes can be seen in the very tools we use to create, recreate, and reproduce images. The pencil, pen, brush, crayon, ruler, X-acto knife, camera, engraving tools, rubylith, drafting table, easel, art board, and waxer have all been replaced by digital equipment and software tools. Not only have our tools changed, but entire job titles, job descriptions, and responsibilities have been altered. Entire job categories and skill requirements have been changed and, in some cases, have vanished, while new ones have been added. Some jobs and skill sets such as typesetting and mechanical art have made the transition to the new tools, while others such as photo engraving have completely disappeared. Many of the jobs which used to be performed by specialists have been melded into other roles. For example, few current positions involve straight typesetting anymore. Most people who are setting type are also performing page layout and a variety of prepress functions as well. Prepress is rapidly becoming primarily electronic as more and more of the prepress functions such as stripping are performed digitally. The advent of the electronic document has not only changed the tools of prepress, but has in fact spread the functions and responsibilities of prepress to everyone involved in the creation and processing of a document. This responsibility includes the client who originally creates the document as well as the sales and customer service personnel of the service companies which handle and process these electronic documents. And nearly everyone's job is becoming more technically oriented as a whole new digital awareness and skills sets have to be adopted and mastered. Everyone has been going through retraining, and that retraining will continue.

Typically, when a company or individual begins to adopt an electronic-based publishing system, they focus primarily and often exclusively on short term individual hardware and software requirements and solutions. The question "What size computer and which software do I need to complete a particular job or set of jobs?" is usually the first and often the last question asked. This is a serious mistake. First, there are many issues which need to be addressed which are often overlooked, such as work flow, backup and archiving needs, file management and proper networking, electrical and lighting requirements, and the mix of conventional vs. digital prepress work. Additionally, the viability, productivity, and overall success of an electronic publishing system is dependent upon many variables. Proper integration of compatible hardware and software components, future needs, system expandability and upgradability, and the training needs of production staff members must be addressed early in the planning process.

Equally important is the thorough orientation and proper training of all personnel who will be associated with the electronic publishing system. One of the most important and often overlooked areas of concern is the knowledge, capabilities, and requirements of your publishing business partners, your clients, and service companies. Ultimately, after you have addressed, organized, and streamlined your own in-house electronic publishing skills and procedures, your prepress or publishing productivity will be largely affected by how well you and your partners understand and comply with each other's electronic publishing requirements.

All of these factors contribute to what I call Electronic Publishing (ETP) Culture. The continuing change in communications technology has had a profound effect on our business. These changes affect the products we produce and how we produce them and the entire nature of the service company/client relationship. A smooth transition to, and continued productivity with, an electronic publishing production system requires that all of these variables (equipment and software, people, and procedures) be changed, revised, and updated regularly.

You and/or your company's commitment to electronic publishing means not only substantial additions of equipment and changes in the production processes, but some significant adjustments in the way everyone who is even remotely involved in the production process

▼ *Figure 3.2 The Postscript Method*
With the advent of desktop Postscript- based systems, print documents are created and composited on a computer by a client and supplied to the printer as completed documents. Postscript systems have dramatically increased the control and flexibility which clients have in creating documents. But this increase in client control has not always been matched by client acceptance or even realization of their responsibility to produce print-ready documents. This situation has led to a wide variety of production problems for printers who must output these files.

perceives and performs jobs. Everyone from the sales and marketing and customer service representatives to press operators to clients must make the adjustment to a new "Electronic Publishing Culture." One of the consequences of the development and widespread acceptance and use of digital publishing is that customers now have more involvement and control than ever in the publishing process. An increasing percentage of business will involve direct client input into jobs. This involvement started initially with customers beginning to perform their own typesetting and has progressed through page layout. It now includes scanning, manipulation, and placement of final versions of line art and gray scale images and increasingly includes color images as well.

The rapid development of affordable, high-quality digital cameras will guarantee that clients will have even more input and control of their files in the future. The production process used to refer to image and film preparation which occurred once client-created art boards and related pieces reached a printing company or service bureau. Now production starts when a client sits down to work at a computer. Anyone who works with customer-generated files is familiar with the challenges involved. Indeed, solving customer file problems has become a significant production issue both in terms of time and technical expertise. Everyone's job has become more technical. Properly trained sales and customer service people are crucial to developing smooth production links between the in-house production staff and customers. Increasingly, there also needs to be direct communication between production staff members of a service company and the clients who generated the documents. And those of us who generate the original files, whether we are designers, photographers, mechanical artists, or desktop publishers working in a bank, all have the responsibility to create files which are appropriately constructed and formatted for their final use.

Like most cultural adjustments, these adjustments will not be made overnight. A progressive process, which gives everyone a chance to learn the opportunities and responsibilities of their new culture, is a prudent course to follow. But the changes must be made. Electronic publishing is a rapidly evolving collection of technologies. The envelope of capabilities is being constantly expanded. As new products and processes evolve along the way, everyone involved must also make adjustments.

▼ *Figure 3.3 Whose Responsibility?*
The pointing match. All too often, when roles and responsibilities for file preparation are not well defined, the client and the printing company end up pointing fingers at each other. This is an unhappy circumstance which can often damage relationships. All three parties – the client , the sales person, and the production staff – need to be well informed. It is the client's job to create and prepare and preflight the files properly. It is the printing company's

File preparation: whose responsibility?

Simply stated, it is we, the generators of electronic files, who are largely responsible for preparing our files for their final purpose, be that print or any other media. Preparing files for print is one of the most demanding file preparation challenges due to the technical requirements and restricted nature of printed media. Our design capabilities on a computer are far greater than our printing capabilities. This means there are a great many documents and designs which can be created on a computer which cannot be printed. Examples of issues which affect the printability of electronic files include graphics file size, the complexity of graphics, multiple layers, and improper formatting. In addition to these basic technical issues, there are component problems involved with files which travel away from their computer of origin. In fact, a large percentage of electronic prepress problems and delays stem from files which are sent to service companies with missing components.

There are still some among us who resist the notion that we should be responsible for preparing our files for output. This is a mistaken notion. The increased control and creative freedom which Postscript grants us also means that we have enlarged responsibilities for preparing the files which we construct. We must keep in mind the final use of a file when we construct that file. File content and construction requirements for a document which will be shown onscreen are quite different if that same file is to be printed. In the old days of art board preparation, printers were largely in control of the construction of the final composite layout and the content and organization of the production process. Within the Postscript realm, much of the construction of the final document is now in the hands of those who originally created that file: we, the clients. How we construct and prepare our documents therefore largely determines how printable a file is. Responsibilities throughout the production process have changed.

responsibility to inform and educate their clients as to how best to prepare files for their specific electronic prepress system. It is the responsibility of the sales and customer service representatives to facilitate this communication and to be well enough informed on electronic prepress issues that they may serve as useful conduits for at least basic information. Many successful printing companies employ a technical liaison whose primary responsibility is to help clients with job planning, technical questions, and file prep problems.

It is in our best interest to prepare our files properly for the media on or in which they will be ultimately produced. If we are ignorant of the requirements, then we should ask for those requirements. The better we prepare our files, the faster and easier our files will be processed. Sales and customer service representatives for service companies have an enhanced role as well. Sales and CSR staffs need to be knowledgeable about their company's electronic publishing capabilities and limitations. They need to be thoroughly steeped in the file prep requirements which their clients should follow, and they need to be able to interpret those requirements well enough to guide the client through filling out the EFIS (Electronic File Information Sheet). Production staff members also have new roles in this process. Production's responsibilities include providing regularly updated information and guidelines on supported equipment and software and file prep issues to both the sales and customer service staff as well as to their clients. Production personnel need to communicate more directly with clients, especially with regard to more technical file preparation issues. In general, service companies need to adopt the role of educator. It is in their best interest to do so.

> *"I never planned on becoming a color separator or a scanner operator, but the technology really allows the individual artist to regain control of their work. Of course, with the control comes an awful lot of responsibility."*
> Steve Johnson, Digital Photographic Pioneer

Partnering

The result of all this role and relationship migration is that clients and service companies need to work together, each with the new and changing responsibilities. Savvy clients will place a high value on service companies which are technically competent, communicate their needs, and are oriented toward education. These clients will also recognize and accept their own need to be technically competent. The best and most successful service companies will promote interactive relationships with their clients and will communicate well and often with their clients about capabilities and requirements. All parties must accept the need for continuing education as technology continues to evolve.

Another type of partnering becoming increasingly common is business-to-business partnerships. Technology is changing so fast that it is impossible for most companies to acquire all of the expertise and equipment necessary to offer all of the services which they might like to. A solution is to partner with another communications company which offers different but complimentary capabilities and products. A good example of this type of partnering is the emerging relationship between printing companies and service bureaus which offer PhotoCD services. PhotoCD service bureaus can offer inexpensive scanning services for clients, while the printing company can offer the print services from the digital PhotoCD files. Either the service bureau or the printing company can produce the film, depending upon which is better prepared to perform the output, or the files can go directly to plate or press. Myriad partnering opportunities are available and are limited only by our imaginations and our will.

Convergent technologies

Once disparate fields of communications (such as the print, photography, and video industries) which traditionally employed completely separate sets of tools are now beginning to use the same tools to produce their products. The common tools revolve around computer hardware and software. Digital technology is having the same revolutionizing effect on these other areas of communications as it has been having on print. Grand opportunities, along with startling adjustments, are the norm. Whole new technologies such as CD-ROM, PhotoCD, and online publishing are emerging to expand and complement our communications tools. The computer chip has been and will continue to be the basic enabling technology in these rapidly evolving and converging revolutions. As other portions of communications industries increasingly utilize these same basic tools, we will experience increasing integration of communications data. The sharing of print, sound, video, animation, and photographic files will become commonplace. Already, electronic documents are being prepared for non-print media distribution and viewing. The development and application of nonspecific file formats such as Acrobat and Common Ground, the evolution of more capable and easier to use telecommunications networks and equipment, and the growth of non-print media such as CD-ROMs have opened up whole new channels for communications and business opportunities.

Entire industries are blossoming from these revolutions in communications technology. The opportunities presented by this technological juggernaut are exciting, while at the same time the resources required to keep abreast are daunting. This rapid evolution does not, however, mean that what you learn today will be obsolete in six months to a year. Quite the contrary. After you learn the fundamentals they will provide you with a solid foundation on which you can continually add new information. Digital literacy is a must for anyone involved in the communications industry. Mastering the basics is the first and most important step in the process. Once you have a strong grasp of digital fundamentals, you will have the context within which to place all the refinements which you will continually need to learn. It is these digital fundamentals, and a few refinements, that this book addresses.

Happy bits & Bytes!

PAULINE'S FILE PREP TIPS

File Prep Hint # 3

Communicate with your printer. Work with this person during planning and construction phases of your job, not just when your job is completed. You will want to ask about items such as the press sheet size, which will affect the size and dimensions of your designs, the lpi at which they print (which will determine the resolution at which you scan images), and the file formats which the printer prefers, which will determine how you save your digital files. Working with your printer throughout your job design and creation will help avoid output problems and having to redo things later. In fact, if you have any questions about how to construct your file, ask at any time. An ounce of prevention is truly worth several pounds of cure in the digital world. The Postscript business is a constantly changing environment with new information becoming available all the time. Ignorance is not a sin, but staying that way is.

4

Electronic Publishing Systems

As the Byte Turns continues…

Will Pauline have time to help Danny with his conflict and find out that she has interests other than just fixing his SCSI chain?

I just bought a CD-ROM drive, but it won't work. Someone said I might have a SCSI ID conflict with my scanner or my external Syquest. What do you think?

Huh!!!

What the heck did he just ask me?

Can you please take this call?

Sure, and I don't mind helping our clients out, especially when they are willing to ask questions. But I have my hands full just doing production. We really should look into having a technical liaison to work with customers.

DTP HISTORY

Back in the dawn of the desktop publishing age – way back in 1985 – there were only a couple of hardware components and a mere handful of software components from which to choose. The hardware choices included the original compact Macintosh complete with a 8Mhz cpu, a built-in 9-inch B&W screen, 128K of RAM, a 400KB floppy disc drive, and no internal hard drive. For peripheral devices we had a choice of two printers, a 144dpi Imagewriter and the original 300 dpi LaserWriter (complete with 11 fonts). Application software for the original Mac counted three: MacWrite and MacPaint initially, followed quickly by the first page layout application, PageMaker 1.0. The combination of the Mac, the first LaserWriter, and Pagemaker constituted the first complete desktop publishing system. This was the first giant step in the democratization of publishing and the first step in the complete revamping of how print and other documents are created and prepress production is performed. A new language called Postscript had even been developed and many of us have had to learn how to understand and speak this language. This digital revolution has since spread to many other forms of communications media such as photography and video, as well as new forms of communication such as multimedia. But the foundation for the revolution has been laid in print.

The rapid evolution of technology since 1985 has been astounding. Today the range and depth of the tools available for capturing and processing images and the creation, distribution, and reproduction of electronic documents is stunning. Shown here in this section are some of the wide variety of these tools. The digital computers, which are the core of this communications technology, have evolved into very different machines with far greater capabilities than their bold but limited ancestors. Today's computers, which can process millions of instructions per second instead of a few thousand per second (typical of the computers in 1985), now boast 150Mhz+ processors, accelerated 21-inch 24-bit color monitors, 500+MB of RAM, multigigabyte hard drives, and a dizzying array of high resolution scanners, cameras, and printers for capturing and reproducing the images processed on these amazing computers. What is additionally amazing and sobering is that this technological juggernaut shows no signs of abating. Just five years from now all the seemingly incredible capabilities which we currently have will pale in contrast to the capabilities we will have then. Tomorrow, our currently impressive equipment will appear to be weak pretenders by comparison. Today's rapidly evolving communications business is not for the weak of heart or for those who resist change.

A modern electronic publishing system can be as simple as one computer, a single page layout application, and a laser printer, or it may contain a network of dozens of image capture and creation devices connected to various types of computer systems which provide for the processing, manipulation, and storage of electronic images and documents. These image creation and manipulation devices can in turn be attached to a wide array of output equipment for either the distribution or viewing of documents.

Image capture devices include a spectrum of scanners, which are used primarily to digitize images which have previously been captured or reproduced on either film (slides) or paper (photographs). They include flatbed CCD scanners and PMT drum scanners as well as dedicated slide scanners. Increasingly, images are being captured directly in digital format through the use of digital cameras. Analog video and direct capture digital video are additional tools for image capture. Original fine art art image creation is being increasingly performed directly on computers with the aid of marvelous pressure-sensitive pen tools attached to digitizing tablets.

Computers themselves have become more specialized. The original DTP systems were single station affairs. Today's sophisticated publishing systems consist of networks of computers designated for specific functions such as preflighting, scanning, image editing, page layout, trapping, imposition, and ripping. Systems involving many operators with many files often require computers which are dedicated to controlling the flow and management of documents across networks both local and distant. These file management computers are called servers and they come in many flavors including file servers, print servers, fax and modem servers, Bulletin Board Servers (BBS), and Web servers. All of these various types of computer stations can be fitted with a variety of storage devices including fixed internal and external hard drives, removable drives such as Syquest, Bernoulli, and optical mechanisms, CD-ROMs, and various tape mechanisms and formats.

Output devices span a wide variety of choices ranging from B&W lasers to digital presses. We can choose from among more than a half dozen types of desktop color printer technologies including thermal wax, four-color laser, dye sublimation, phase change, and several varieties of ink jet printers. For high resolution prepress output there is an impressive array of imagesetter devices and sophisticated press proofing systems. Direct to plate and even direct to press imaging is now common. Computers attached to four-color laser printers are increasingly being used as short run on-demand color printing presses.

Although you will read more about technology trends in later chapters, I will mention here that the same personal computer-based open architecture hardware and software systems which have led to the democratization of print-oriented publishing is in the process of opening up a wide variety of other communication technologies to all of us. These technologies include a range of audio, video, and animation, as well as type-oriented media.

Computers revealed: parts and functions

Motherboard (green)

Main circuit board that all other components and peripherals plug into and transmit and receive data through ="Skeleton," "nervous," and "circulatory" systems of the computer.

RAM (Random Access Memory)

Fast, short term, active work space memory = desktop work space. More RAM means larger work space. All system and application software launch into and operate within RAM. Adding RAM is like adding extra leaves to a work table.

Storage memory (large)

Medium to large volumes of permanent storage = file cabinets in an analog office. Examples include Hard Drives, Optical Disk Drives, Syquest, and Bernoulli cartridges and CDs.

Storage memory (small)

Small volume, portable storage devices (Diskette) = briefcase.

Expansion slot

Plug-in slots which allow for addition of other circuits boards (known as cards), such as video and network cards, which expand a computer's capabilities = adding a radio or air conditioner to your auto.

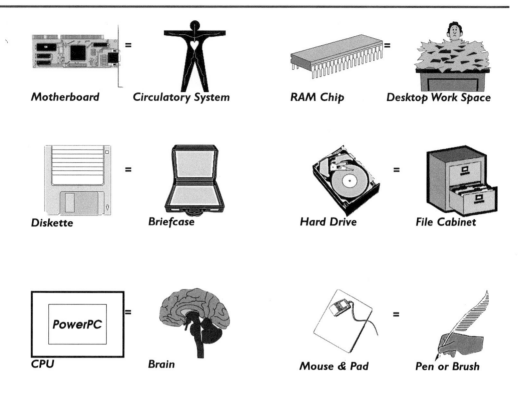

Motherboard	**Circulatory System**	**RAM Chip**	**Desktop Work Space**
Diskette	**Briefcase**	**Hard Drive**	**File Cabinet**
CPU	**Brain**	**Mouse & Pad**	**Pen or Brush**

CPU (Central Processing Unit)

Main computer chip on motherboard = brains of the outfit. Most data manipulation occurs here.

Video board

Converts digital data to a signal which can be used to produce images for display on your monitor. Allows you to see information that is in RAM. Similar to your cable box, which converts unreadable data into readable data.

SCSI, printer, and modem ports

Allows you to communicate outside of your computer locally or over long distance = intercom and telephone connections.

Keyboard, mouse, digitizing tablet

Basic tools for entering information/data into your computer = typewriter keyboard, pen/pencil/brush.

ELECTRONIC PUBLISHING SYSTEMS

Desktop Drum Scanner
Extremely high quality image capture is accomplished through the use of PMT drum scanners, such as this Optronics ColorGetter, which scans at resolutions up to 8000 dpi.

Flatbed Scanner
Increasingly higher quality image capture can be performed on low cost CCD flat bed scanners such as this Apple ColorOne scanner. A wide range of image types and media can be scanned with these low cost versatile machines.

Slide Scanner
Some scanners such as this Polaroid Sprintscan 45 slide scanner are dedicated to capturing images off of one type of media, in this case 35mm to 4 x 5 transparencies.

Digital Camera
Increasing numbers of images are being captured directly in digital form using cameras such as this Polaroid PDC 2000 digital camera. Digital image capture allows for the bypassing of traditional image capture on film and chemical processing.

Disk–Based Storage Systems
A wide variety of disk–based storage technologies are available including in rough order of capacity, (from L– R): "Floppy Disks" (400K – 1.2MB) of information can be stored and transported); ZIP disks (100MB – 200MB); Optical/CD disks (230MB – 1.3GB); and fixed Hard drives (500MB – Multi GB–TB+). Capacities of these various media are constantly increasing.

PhotoCD Image Disk
New technologies for capturing, storing, and transporting digital data, such as the very flexible PhotoCD technology, continue to develop and mature. One PhotoCD disk can store up to 100 images saved at five or six different resolutions.

Fax/Modem
With a modern modem and appropriate software, files can be sent and received across standard phone lines.

The Core Machine
The lion's share of image and document capture, creation, editing, printing, and storage and retrieval is controlled at desktop computers like this Macintosh PowerPC. Recent advances in technology have brought affordable desktop computers into the same realm of performance as more expensive proprietary systems.

Telephony
An increasing number of telephone systems and peripherals plug directly into computers providing both data and voice communication capabilities.

Mobile Computing
Decrease in size and increase in performance of laptop computers like this Apple PowerBook have made publishing on the road an increasingly viable activity.

Mainframe Computer
Networks have evolved so that files can be readily exchanged between desktop systems and large mainframe computers like this IBM AS400. Online services such as AOL and Compuserve use mainframes.

Intel Computer
In today's world of electronic communications, a wide variety of computers can be used to create electronic files. It is becoming increasingly easier for different types of computers to communicate over networks. Many applications operate on multiple platforms.

COMPONENTS
&
CAPABILITIES

B&W Proof Printer

B&W proofing, and in some cases final output, is handled by toner based laser printers such as this Apple LaserWriter NTX. Formats range from 8.5" x 11" up to 11" x 17" and resolutions from 300 dpi 1800 dpi.

Fax Machine

With current desktop computer systems and the appropriate software, faxes can be sent directly from design stations to fax machines.

Projector

The computer video signal can be sent directly to LCD-based projectors for the generation of extremely high quality presentations.

Color Proof Printer

Producing color prints on the desktop used to be an expensive, slow, and low quality exercise. No longer! There are a growing number of affordable, high quality desktop color printers such as this Polaroid dye sublimation PolarPrint printer.

B&W and Four Color Copiers/Printers

Through the use of an intermediary, Postscript RIPs documents can be sent directly from computers to "copy" machines. These machines are rapidly replacing offset presses in the low quality and volume markets.

Film Recorder

Direct final output from computer to film is available through the use of film recorders like this ProPalette 8000 film recorder from Polaroid.

Fast RIPs & Large Format Imagesetters

Fast RIPs and larger format imagesetters, like this combination of a Linotronic RIP60 RIP and 3060 Imagesetter, allow for the creation of fully imposed film and even plates directly off the imagesetter. This can save time and money.

Conventional Four–Color Press

Images placed on plates either directly from a computer or created via intermediate film production are placed on press cylinders and used for the reproduction of those images.

Direct Digital Presses

The last few years have seen the introduction of direct imaging presses in which images are sent directly to the press from the computer, thereby skipping the film and plate production steps. The next five years will be a time of rapid proliferation of this direct digital technology.

The RIP

The RIP (Raster Image Processor) is the business end of a Postscript publishing system. A RIP translates all file information into a printable format. RIPs can be stand-alone hardware modules or software versions which operate on computers like this Macintosh workstation.

Banner Printer

Previously available from machines costing over $100,000, high quality large format prints can now be quickly and affordably made from the desktop using FM screening technologies and inkjet printers like this 50 inch NovaJet pro printer from NCAD.

TYPES OF COMPUTER SYSTEMS

Central computers

Mainframes

▼ *Figure 4.1 Mainframe Computer*
Mainframe computers with their centrally located computing capabilities used "dumb" terminals for access to their power. Mainframes, which are large, expensive, and proprietary, dominated computer use until the 1980s, when the first personal computers arrived on the market.

For many years the original computing paradigm included a core or central computer to which were connected a number (sometimes hundreds) of "dumb" terminals which operators used to access the computing and storage power of the core or central computer. These types of computers are called "mainframes." Mainframe computer systems have all of their computing capabilities located at the central or mainframe computer. Operators access this computing capability from their "dumb" terminals, which have no computational capabilities of their own, over network lines. Mainframes are still heavily used, and some are even used for publishing. But mainframe computers are very expensive and require the operator to be part of a large organization which can afford to purchase one. Each mainframe computer manufacturer also has its own proprietary operating system and application software, which means that software development and utilization of files is restricted to that particular system.

Desktop computers

In the late 1970s, the paradigm of the mainframe computer was challenged by the introduction of the first personal computer by IBM, the IBM AT. These were and are called personal computers because they are small (hence the name "desktop") individual computers which have their computational (cpu), workspace (RAM), storage (disk drive), and communication (ports) capabilities built in. These machines are not only small and self contained, but also affordable for individual users. Another major change which occurred with the advent of the personal computer is the development and evolution of what is commonly called Open Architecture hardware and software. In the previous mainframe model of computing, each manufacturer had its own hardware, operating system, and application software, and there was little if any interchangeability. With open system architecture, many different manufacturers can make competitive hardware and software products to use interchangeably on the same machines. This competition and interchangeability has given consumers much lower costs and a wider range of choices for both hardware and software. Not long ago, computing was accessible only to a few of the technical elite. Computing has now become accessible to almost anyone who has a modest amount of money to spend and the desire to learn.

Macintosh

The first personal computers, the IBM ATs, were designed primarily for manipulating text and numbers; graphics were not a major consideration. The first computer manufacturer to create a personal computer designed specifically for graphics applications was Apple. The first affordable and available personal graphics computer was the 128K Macintosh. This machine had 128K of RAM, a 400K floppy disk drive, a 9-inch 72 dpi screen, and no hard drive. While this is almost unbelievably weak by today's standards, it was a milestone in personal computing. Prior to the first Macintosh, most computers used 64K or less RAM and had monitors with resolutions below 60 dpi.

Macintosh computers use Motorola CPU (central processing units) chips as their main "brains." Examples of these chips and computer models in which they were used include 68000 (used in the first Macs and MacPluses), 68020 (MacII), 68030 (MacIIci), 68040 (Quadras), and PowerPC (used in PowerMacs). Each progressive generation of chips represents a faster and more capable chip. The early CPU chips performed thousands of instructions per second at clock speeds of 8MHz. Today's machines perform millions of instructions per second (MIPS) at clock speeds of over 300 MHz and growing faster by the month. Each succeeding generation of chip and computer also sported other improvements and capabilities, most notably increases in RAM and disk storage space. The first Macs supported only 128K of RAM and had no internal hard drives. These capabilities have evolved into today's PowerMacs which now address up to 1GB (GigaByte) of RAM and multiple GBs of storage space. And these capacities will continue to grow. Soon we will be addressing multiple GBs of RAM and accessing TeraBytes of storage space.

Early on, most of the Motorola CPU chips were CISC (Complex Instruction Set Computing), the older generation of chips. The PowerPC (or PowerMac computers, as they are sometimes called) use RISC (Reduced Instruction Set Computing) chips, which are the newer and faster generation of chips. These RISC chips are similar to the RISC chips which have long been used by high performance graphics workstations such as Sun Spark stations and Silicon Graphics Indigos (Indys).

▼ Figure 4.2 Macintosh PowerPC
Significant improvements in performance were realized when Apple adopted for use in their PowerPC computers the same type of RISC (Reduced Instruction Set Computing) chips used by traditional high performance computers such as Sun and Silicon Graphics workstations.

Apple currently has a consumer line of Macintoshes called iMacs. These are sold through retail stores like Sears and Best Buy. They are equivalent to other PowerPC Macs, but have names deemed more suitable for the retail market.

PCs (personal computers)

"PC" or "Personal Computer" is a term coined in the 1980s by IBM for their desktop computers. Although all Macintoshes and computers made by IBM, Dell, Compac, and others are literally personal computers, IBM coined the name and registered it as a trademark. At this point in time, however, the colloquial usage of the term "PC" is generally used to refer to all those computers (IBM, Compac, Dell, etc.) which are based upon the Intel standard CPU chip and use DOS, Windows, or OS2 as an operating system. This distinguishes them from the Macintosh, which uses a Motorola CPU chip and the Mac operating system (OS). And while this distinction may seem arbitrary and somewhat vague, it will become more so as IBM begins producing computers using the same PowerPC chip as that used by the Apple Macintosh, and will in fact operate using the Mac OS as well as its own OS2.

▼ Figure 4.3 Pentium PC
The Pentium-based computer represents the highest performance "PC" type of computer. The Pentium replaced the previous 286, 386, and 486 machines.

As mentioned above, there is a wide variety of "PC" manufacturers, including IBM (the original), Compaq, Dell, and H, (non-IBM PCs are typically called IBM clones). PCs use Intel CPU (central processing unit) chips as their main "brains" rather than the Motorola CPU chips used in Macs. Examples of these chips include the 8086, 286, 386, 486, and Pentium. Like the Macintosh, each progressive generation of chips represents a faster and more capable chip. To date, all of the Intel CPU chips are CISC (Complex Instruction Set Computing), which are the older generation of chips. Newer generation PCs use Intel Pentium processors, which like their Mac cousins operate in the 300MHz+ range. Successive generations of Pentium processors are labeled Pentium I, II, III, etc.

PCs use a variety of operating systems. The early computers, 8086s and 286s, used one called DOS (short for Disk Operating System), which was a text based OS. DOS was developed by the now famous and titanic Bill Gates of Microsoft Corp. (hence, the term MS-DOS). Later, Windows, Windows NT, and OS2, which are GUIs (graphical user interfaces), were developed to make use of these computers easier. IBM makes the OS2 operating system and puts it on their computers. Microsoft makes DOS and Windows which is used by most clone manufacturers. There will be more on operating systems in the next chapter.

Peripheral devices and software

Along with the evolution of computers themselves, we have seen a parallel evolution of their associated peripheral devices. A peripheral device is one which adds specific capability to your electronic publishing system, such as scanning or printing. The most fundamental of all peripheral devices, the monitor, has gone though a dramatic evolution. Those first built-in 9-inch black and white Mac screens have evolved into 21-inch, 24-bit color monitors supported by 4MB+ of video RAM. Scanners which started out as 200 dpi, 1-bit B&W add-ons to pin printers now boast 8000 dpi of 30-bit color capture capabilities. Storage device choices have evolved from single option 400K floppies to removable storage. Printing device options which began as 180 dpi dot matrix printers are now available in a dizzying array of B&W and color printers spanning a range of resolutions from 300 dpi to 3600 dpi, with a wide choice of output technologies to suit almost any need including laser, die sublimation, thermal wax, phase change ink jet, and electrostatic, in formats ranging from letter to poster size. Telecommunications, while still in its infancy, has already made some dramatic progress as well. Initial modem capabilities included modem to modem speeds of only 300bps (bauds per second). We now have 56Kb (kilobit) network modems which access on-line services and a worldwide telecommunications system. Our image capture capabilities have moved beyond the scanner and now include professional quality direct image capture with digital still and video cameras.

▼ Fiure. 4.4 A Server
Servers are the key to controlling the access to and the storage and distribution of the enormous volumes of information which is being constantly accumulated. Servers often function as the traffic cops for controlling the flow of information around a network of independent electronic publishing stations.

Software has gone through an evolution similar to hardware's. Our initial DTP applications, PageMaker 1.0 and MacPaint, provided us with very basic page layout and painting capabilities without the benefits of sophisticated type controls or color capabilities. We now have very sophisticated typesetting and graphics applications which give us type controls to within $1/_{10,000}$ of a point and color graphics tools which exceed many of our traditional capabilities. We now also have access to sophisticated digital presentation, animation, sound, and multimedia tools. In addition, we have developed software which affords us complete control over production chores such as trapping, imposition, and work flow.

Servers

Initially, our electronic publishing systems consisted of one computer station attached to a variety of peripheral devices including a scanner and a printer. As we have been asking our publishing systems to perform an even greater number of sophisticated publishing chores, our system have evolved into more complex systems. On larger systems with large work flows, individual tasks such as scanning, page composition, image editing, file management, trapping, imposition, and even telecommunications chores are assigned to individual stations which are all connected by a network. The core computer in this type of system is the server. The server controls the ebb and flow of information around a network and often acts as a repository for large volumes of information such as databases of text and graphic files. There are even specific types of servers such as file severs, print servers, fax servers, and telecommunications servers like the computers which run the global telecommunications network we refer to as the Internet. On larger systems there are even servers to control systems of servers. Servers are becoming the key to the strength of modern electronic publishing systems.

The trend toward the use of servers is somewhat of a return to the original computing paradigm when the computing work was being done on a remote mainframe computer. The difference is that in modern electronic publishing each individual station remains independently capable, turning over only that work which is related to storage or movement of information around a network.

Others: Silicon Graphics and Suns

There are a variety of less common but important high-performance graphics-oriented computers known as "workstations." Two of the better known ones are Silicon Graphics "Indy" and Sun "Spark" stations. The Indy has been used extensively for 3-D modeling and the movie industry, while the Spark stations have long been a mainstay of the engineering CAD/CAM community. Both use very fast RISC-based CPUs, similar to the PowerPC chip discussed above, and are known for their exceptional performance as well as their steep prices. Recently, Indy and Spark stations have been finding their way into electronic publishing systems as file servers and high speed graphic workstations.

Clones

A clone is a a copycat hardware manufacturer. Many of the components used in computers today, such as hard drives, floppy disk drives, motherboards, and monitors, are generic and made by many different manufacturers. Any individual with the proper basic knowledge and tools can build a computer by purchasing and assembling components. As mentioned above, the two key components or features which distinguish one computer from another are

▼ Figure 4.5 Sun Spark Station
The Sun Spark station is a very high performance computer workstation. Powerful workstations made by Sun and Silicon Graphics have long utilized RISC-chip technologies and powerful operating systems like UNIX, which offers advantages like multitasking, to provide improved performance over Macintosh and PC-based systems. This performance came with a price, however. Most of these system prices begin at $25,000 and go up, and the operating systems tend to be less user friendly.

its "brain" or CPU and the operating system (OS) used to operate and control that computer.

What to buy?

Although it is very difficult to make specific recommendations about which system to buy because there are so many variables, here are some general recommendations for a starter electronic system. Remember that a station which uses many graphics usually demands more capabilities than a system which works primarily with text and numbers. A good choice for a starter Mac or PC publishing system will be a 250-300 MHz PowerPC or Pentium CPU , 64MB RAM, 2GB+ MB HD, 15-17 inch monitor, 20x CD, extended keyboard, mouse, 56Kmodem, and page layout, drawing, and painting software, at a cost of about $2,500–$4,000. Add a scanner for $1,000 – $1500 and a letter size Postscript printer at a price ranging anywhere from $1500 – $3000. If you paint and/or draw or perform a lot of image editing functions, consider purchasing a digitizing tablet for ~$200. Your total cost for this type of system would be between $5000 and $8500.

PAULINE'S FILE PREP TIPS

File Prep Hint # 4

Purchase reliable hardware, and most importantly, keep the hardware up to date and tuned up. Make sure your power is clean. Install isolated lines. Use high quality cables from one manufacturer. Keep your publishing environment clean and cool. Imaging equipment hates dirt and high temperatures.

File Prep Hint # 5

Know the basic components of your electronic publishing system and how they operate. You definitely need to know what RAM and storage memory are and how to effectively manage both. Be sure that you keep at least 20 percent of the RAM that you assign to any application free so that your application has room into which it can expand. Never assign all of your RAM to open applications, as your system needs RAM space in which to expand. Optimally, your hard drive space should remain at least 50 percent free. The more you know about your system, the more effective an operator you will be and the more troubleshooting skills you will be able to develop.

5
Software

As the Byte Turns continues...

Will Danny find out that Pauline is both a source of Knowledge and love, or will she just ignore him like two ships passing through fog in the night?

Mac vs. PC, Windows vs. Mac OS vs. OS2, Pentium vs. Power PC, Syquest vs. Bernoulli, PageMaker vs. XPress. What do I buy?

Well, I'm not sure!!!

I wish I knew for myself!

Can you help??

Sure. Have Danny give me a call and I'll advise him. It would be great if Danny had the same type of system components as well as software that we have. That would make file transfer and printing much easier.

OPERATING SYSTEMS AND APPLICATIONS

Types of software

In the last chapter we explored some of the basics of the physical hardware which make up a modern electronic publishing system. The other key component of any electronic publishing system is software. Software is the list of instructions, called "code," which provide a computer operator with tools which allow the operator to perform tasks. Software is divided into basically four categories: system software, applications, resources, and utilities. System software provides for basic computer operations such as turning a computer off and on and the look and feel of the interface. Examples of operating systems include Windows, the Mac OS, and OS2 . Application software provides us with sets of creative tools and capabilities which allow us to create and manipulate text, graphics, and completed documents. Examples of applications include QuarkXpress, Photoshop, and Freehand. Resources are items such as fonts, sounds, and color palettes used within applications for the creation of documents. Utilities are really just small applications used for performing specific functions such as disk formatting, troubleshooting, virus protection, and management of resources such as fonts and sounds. The dividing line between applications and utilities is an arbitrary one, vaguely drawn on the basis of size and complexity of the software.

▼ Figure 5.2 Disk Icons
Here is a sampling for various disk icons. In the upper left is an icon for an internal hard drive which has been customized with my name. It is common practice to include the size of the disk in its name (as shown here) indicating a 210MB hard drive. The middle icon represents a floppy disk, while the third icon shows a syquest removable disk.

Operating systems

The most fundamental of all software applications is operating system software. Operating system (OS) software provides the basic tools which allow an operator to control the computer. Without an operating system, an operator would have no way to communicate with and control the computer. Most operating systems provide basic functionality tools such as booting (turning the computer on), application launching, disk formatting, file naming, copying, movement and organization, resource management for RAM, fonts, sounds and video, access to peripherals such as monitors, drives, and scanners, and basic communication capabilities such as printing and file sharing. Each operating system has its own specific interface, or way of getting things done. There have historically been two type of interfaces, text and graphic. With a text-based interface one uses sequences of text to complete tasks. With a graphic-based interface, affection-

▼ *Figure 5.1 The Mac Desktop*

This is an example of a GUI or Graphical User Interface. All items are represented by logical icons; controls are provided by mouse movements and activation of menu choices, in addition to optional keyboard commands. This is a view of the Macintosh "Desktop." This view all of the icons and menus is created by the Finder, a part of the operating system (Mac OS). The two icons labeled "Tazmanian I" and "Briefcase" in the upper right corner below the Day and Time indicator are the icons for disks. Tazmanian I is the primary or "Boot" internal hard drive where the active system software is installed. "Briefcase" is the name of a 200MB removable syquest cartridge which I use for transferring files between offices. The large open window in the center shows some of the contents of "Tazmanian I." A Finder menu appears on the left and various folders, documents, and Alias (in italics) icons are shown on the right side of the Desktop. The cursor control icon, which is controlled by mouse movements, can be found on the Desktop under the File menu. Microsoft Windows and IBM OS2 provide functionally similar, albeit different looking, GUIs. The development of GUIs such as these has greatly simplified the operation of complex and sophisticated computers.

▼ Figure 5.3 Application Icons
Shown here are a variety of application icons. Each application has a unique icon which generally bears some graphical resemblance to the purpose for which the application is used. For instance, Ofoto, which is a scanning application, is represented by an icon of a scanner.

▼ Figure 5.4 Document Icons
Document icons are distinguished from other icons by the little dog ear on the upper right hand corner. Note how each icon has a specific look to it. In order, from top to bottom, are document icons for: PageMaker 5.0, QuarkXPress, Illustrator, and a Photoshop document.

ately known as a GUI (Graphical User Interface), icons or symbols are manipulated in order to complete tasks. A common example of a text-based interface is the Microsoft Disk Operating System commonly known as MS-DOS or just plain DOS. MS-DOS was one of the first operating systems used on personal or desktop computers [a personal computer is generally defined as a small self-contained (it has its own RAM, CPU, storage disks and video) affordable computer]. In fact, DOS, while now largely obsolete, has been the most widely used operating system in the world. The problem with text-based operating systems is that they do not operate in the same manner or fashion in which most people think or work. Typing out codes to carry out tasks is foreign to most people's mode of operating. For this reason, text-based operating systems are not considered to be "user friendly." Because of this generally low quotient of "user friendliness," more human-oriented or user-friendly operating systems (such as GUIs) were developed.

The first commonly available GUI was the Mac operating system, or Mac OS. Later, Microsoft, the originator of the original DOS, developed the Windows and Windows NT GUIs. These GUI operating systems utilize icons to represent various parts of the system such as disks and files. Icons are manipulated to perform various tasks. A mouse rather than a keyboard is the standard general tool used to manipulate a GUI. A variety of menus as well as keyboard commands can be used to manipulate a GUI. A simple example will illustrate the operational difference between text and a graphic-based operating systems. To copy a file from one location on a drive to another would require a command code sequence similar to this: C/ ....COPY D/. The same task in a GUI would involve the operator pointing with a mouse at the file to be moved, clicking on the file to select it, holding the mouse down and dragging the file to the new location, then releasing the mouse button. This second GUI-based method is very similar to how an operator would move a physical file from one file cabinet to another and is therefore easier for most operators to relate to and learn, making the GUI more user friendly.

Desktop views

The desktop view of an operating system is the entry level view of the access and controls available with a particular operating system. Each operating system has its own look and feel. The desktop view shown in Figure 5.1 is that of the Macintosh. Various icons represent specific functions or features of the computer. For example, in this view, two disks, Tazmanian I and Briefcase, are shown in the upper right hand corner of the "Desktop." Tazmanian I is the primary internal

▼ Figure 5.5 Application Information

Knowing and communicating to your service bureau the versions of the applications you use to construct documents is an important help when they output your files.

If you are working on a Macintosh, choose "About the Application" under the Apple Menu. An information plate will appear on the screen showing the name and version of the application you are using. If you hold down the option key when you choose "About QuarkXPress," you will see an even more detailed information plate. Note that in the more detailed information plate it shows a patch level as well as a version number. Knowing this patch or revision level can be very important when trouble shooting specific document creation or output problems.

hard disk or "boot" disk which contains the active operating system as well as a variety of applications, utilities, and documents. The main window seen here shows some of the contents of Tazmanian I. Icons for documents, folders, and the Trash can be seen on the Desktop as well. A view of a menu can be seen on the left, as well as the icon for the arrow cursor which is controlled by the movement of a mouse.

Icons

Each operating system which utilizes a GUI uses icons or symbols to represent features and items such as software applications, documents, and storage locations. Following are some common icons you will find used in the Mac operating system.

Menus

Another control tool common to all GUIs are menus. The operating system, which is itself an application, and each document creation application has its own set of menus, and are used for utilizing and controlling that application. The file menu shown in Fig. 5.1 is one of the menus used in the Finder, which is part of the Mac OS. The Apple Menu, shown in Fig. 5.5, is used to access a variety of items and information, including the "About this 'Application Name' " and "About this Macintosh" dialog boxes. When you are working in an application, QuarkXPress, for instance, the first choice under the Apple Menu will be "About QuarkXPress."

When you are working in the Finder, the first choice under the Apple menu will be "About This Macintosh."

Windows

Another common feature of many GUIs are windows. Windows provide views of the contents of file storage locations, the contents of documents, and controls of computer functions. There are basically three kinds of windows: location windows, document windows, and dialog boxes. Windows are used extensively in Mac, Windows and Windows NT operating systems.

Location windows

The primary view which you have into the contents of a computer is provided through location windows. Location windows, provided by the Finder on a Mac and the File Manager in Windows 3.1 and the Explorer in Windows 95 & 98, contain icons of folders, documents,

▼ Figure 5.6 RAM Allocation
This Macintosh RAM infor-
mation dialog box, which is
accessed by selecting "About
This Macintosh" when you are
in the Finder, provides information on how much total
RAM a machine has, how
much RAM is allocated to
each application, and how
much is available for further
use. Note that in this case
there is 24.5MB of total RAM;
3.2MB is allocated to the operating system, 3MB is allocated
to QuarkXPress, and there is
16.5MB or RAM available for
further use. Note the RAM
allocation bar for XPress
shows about 20 percent free, a
good rule of thumb to follow.
Painting applications need 3x
the file size of free RAM.

and applications. An example of a location window can be seen in Fig.
5.1, where the Tazmanian I window shows the location of files on the
hard drive named Tazmanian I.

Document windows

Document windows are created within page or graphic generation
applications like Quark and Illustrator. Document windows contain
actual page elements of text and graphics. These windows are nearly
identical in both the Mac and Windows environments. This page was
created in a document window.

Information and dialog boxes

Information and dialog boxes, which often appear in response to a
menu choice or keyboard command, provide information and choices. Examples of strictly informational boxes are the "About
QuarkXPress" and "About This Macintosh" boxes shown in Figures
5.5 and 5.6. The "About QuarkXPress" boxes provide information
about the QuarkXpress application such as the version and patch or
revision numbers of the application being used. The "About This
Macintosh" information box supplies information about how much
RAM your computer has and how it is being allocated. An example of
a dialog box, which provide choices as well as information, is the
"QuarkXPress Information" dialog box shown in Figure 4.7. This dialog box not only shows you how much RAM is allocated to
QuarkXPress and recommends a suggested and minimum RAM allo-
cations, but also provides you with the response box "Preferred size"
which allows you to change the amount of RAM which will be allocated to QuarkXPress the next time it is launched. All of these dialog
boxes are important in electronic publishing. The two Quark XPress
information boxes provide you with the version and revisions numbers which you need to provide your printer or service bureau when
you send them a document created in Xpress. The RAM allocation
and setting information and dialog boxes provide you with the means
to monitor and control your RAM use. A good rule of thumb for
RAM allocation in a page layout application is to have about 20 percent of the "allocation" bar in the "About This Macintosh" information box free. Painting applications should have a RAM allocation
equal to about three times the size of the documents which will be
manipulated.

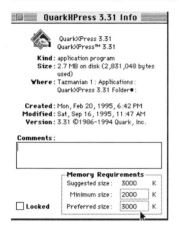

QuarkXPress 3.31 Info

QuarkXPress 3.31
QuarkXPress™ 3.31

Kind: application program
Size: 2.7 MB on disk (2,831,048 bytes used)
Where: Tazmanian 1 : Applications : QuarkXPress 3.31 Folder● :

Created: Mon, Feb 20, 1995, 6:42 PM
Modified: Sat, Sep 16, 1995, 11:47 AM
Version: 3.31 ©1986-1994 Quark, Inc.

Comments:

─── Memory Requirements ───
Suggested size:	3000	K
Minimum size:	2000	K
☐ **Locked** Preferred size:	3000	K

▼ *Figure 5.7 Application Information*
This Macintosh application information dialog box, which is accessed by selecting an application icon and choosing Get Info. under the File menu in the Finder, provides information on how much RAM should be and will be allocated to the application. Setting the "Preferred size" in this dialog box will determine how much RAM will be allocated to QuarkXPress when it is launched. Note that RAM sizes are measured in K (K=1000Bytes), so 3000K = 3MB.

Applications

Document creation

The primary tools used for creating, manipulating, and managing electronic documents are applications. Some applications are generalist applications such as Microsoft Works, sometimes referred to as "Swiss Army knife applications," which are designed to provide a wide range of capabilities such as text, graphics, spreadsheet, database, and telecommunications, in one application. Most professional electronic publishers work in applications which are more specific in orientation. Single or narrow focus applications tend to provide more depth and control than the Swiss Army knife applications. In addition, the more focused applications tend to print more easily at higher resolutions. At this point in time, if you are interested in producing professional quality work, you should generally work in more specific or focused applications. Examples of specific electronic publishing tasks and applications which are designed specifically to address those tasks include:

TASK	APPLICATION(S)	PLATFORM*
Painting	Photoshop, Painter	Mac & Windows
Drawing	Illustrator, Freehand	Mac & Windows
	Corel Draw	Mac & Windows
Page Layout	QuarkXPress, Pagemaker,	
	InDesign, Frame	Mac & Windows
Outlining	Streamline	Mac & Windows
Presentation	PDF, PowerPoint	Mac & Windows
Cross-platform	Acrobat PDF	Mac & Windows

*Note: Many of these applications also exist on other platforms such as Sun and Silicon Graphics stations.

It is generally a good idea to use an application for the primary purpose for which it was created. For example, you can set type and lay out pages in Drawing applications like Illustrator, Freehand, and Corel Draw, but typesetting and page layout functions are better handled in page layout applications like QuarkXPress and Pagemaker. Conversely, while you can do some editing of graphics, such as cropping and rotating, in XPress and PageMaker, you are usually better off performing those functions, at least the final edit, in the graphics applications used to create the graphics. There are some emerging trends in applications, such as customization of applications, which may dramatically change the way we choose and

▼ Figure 5.8 Font Resources
The font sets dialog box from ATM Deluxe, which is used on both Macs and Windows machines. Shown here is a list of font sets, which are virtual grouping of fonts. Font management utilities like ATM Deluxe allow much more control and flexibility in the management of our font files.

▼ Figure 5.9 PDF Distiller 3.0 Options
PDF files are created through Distiller. In order for PDF files to print properly, Distiller Job Options must be properly configured. Attention must be paid to the inclusion of the original font files and high resolution versions of your document's graphics.

work in our applications.

Cross-platform Acrobat PDF

It has become increasingly common for us to need to use our documents on other other platforms, operating systems, or applications than the ones with which we created that document. For instance, we may create a document on a Macintosh, using the Mac OS, in QuarkXpress 4.0, and we want to send this document to someone who is working on a PC in Windows 98, and all they have is Microsoft word. This need presents many cross-platform conversion problems involving incompatible document formats and the challenges inherent in translating font and graphic information.

The answer to this type of challenge is often found in the use of a document format called Adobe Acrobat PDF. PDF is short for Portable Document Format. PDF files are designed to be platform-, operating system-, and application-independent, that is, you need not have the same machine, operating system, or even the same application in order to view, print, and even edit a file.

PDF files are generally created by a program called Adobe Distiller. Typically, the original document file is converted in to a PostScript file by printing the document file to disk using a PostScript printer driver. This PostScript file is then processed through Distiller. Distiller converts the PostScript file into a PDF document. All that is needed to view and print a PDF document is an Acrobat Viewer, which is a free application. More sophisticated handling and even editing of a PDF file can be accomplished through the use of a program called Acrobat Exchange.

It is important to know that PDF was originally designed primarily as an on-screen viewing tool, so care should be taken during the creation of a PDF document if you intend to print a PDF file, and particularly if you intend to separate a PDF file for commercial printing. The Job Options in Distiller, Fig 5.9, need to be properly configured for the inclusion of the original font file and high resolution versions of the graphic files. If the original font files are not included with a PDF document, Acrobat will create simulated versions of your font characters, which often do not match the originals. Later versions of Acrobat, 4.0 and above, provide for more editability and better print control functions. I also use PDF files as a handy way to view and proof PostScript files. PDF is also internet friendly, which means that it can be sent across the internet without fear of corruption.

▼ Figure 5.10 System Resources

This dialog box from NOW Utilities shows a view of NOW's Startup Manager dialog box. This utility allows me to turn on only those system resources which I need for a particular job or activity. The check marks indicate those resources which I have activated for my scanning set.

Resources

Software resources are files which can be used by many different applications for the creation or editing of files. In most electronic publishing systems, important resources are available and distributed at the system level so that all applications may take advantage of them. Two of the most common and important resources are fonts and sounds. Fonts and sounds can be located in the system where all font-aware applications can access them. This central access to resources has not always been the rule. Prior to the development of the Mac OS and then Windows, fonts had to be supplied for each application. Details of font and font icons are covered in Chapter 11 "A Tale Of True Typesetting."

Utilities

Utilities are small applications which perform specific tasks. Examples of utilities include: virus protection, disk formatting, and font management. Two of the most common and useful examples of utility software are Adobe Type Manager, commonly referred to by its initials ATM, and ATM Deluxe (Fig 5.8), a full featured font management utility . Many utility applications like ATM and ATM Deluxe are also initialization files, commonly called inits. Inits automatically "boot"or start along with your computer's operating system, thereby launching at the same as and working directly with your operating system software. ATM and ATM Deluxe are available for and should be used on both Macintosh and Windows machines. Font management utilities such as ATM Deluxe allow much more control and flexibility over the management of critical resources such as our fonts files.

Minimizing your system

While there are many useful and interesting resources and utilities, it is a good idea to be very selective about what you load onto your computer. Be particularly watchful of resources which you place in your system file, as these files will be constantly accessed by your operating system and therefore take up RAM space and require both cpu and operating system attention to keep them active. Also be aware that some resources may conflict with others. For instance, a font management utility may interfere with a scanner plug-in module you may be using.

To minimize the conflicts and system overloads which may result from having too many resources open, I try to limit the resources I have loaded to only the ones I really need. I also divide the resources I use into groups and access them only as I need them. To manage my system, I use a resource management tool which allows me to create groups of system resources and access them as I need them. Figure 5.8 shows you a font management tool I use to access fonts as I need them. In Figure 5.10 you see an example of how I organize my system resources into task-specific groups such as scanning, presentation, and networking. Taking the time and energy to manage your system this way will dramatically improve your productivity and reduce your stress level and loss of hair commonly associated with system and application software problems.

One final word of advice. Before I update my system and applications software on my main boot drive, I always try out new versions on a copy of the system or application which I have placed on a separate disk. I boot my computer from the updated copy and use it while I work out the inevitable bugs prior to updating my primary drive. This is a good and inexpensive insurance policy to have.

PAULINE'S FILE PREP TIPS

File Prep Hint # 6

Know the versions of all the applications which you use to create files. Be sure to supply version numbers to your service bureau when you send your files out to be printed. Each version of an application has its own quirks, and knowing the version numbers of the creating applications can be a big help when setting up and troubleshooting files. It is a good idea to keep up-to-date on your applications versions. You don't have to buy the latest version as soon as it is available, but don't get more than one application version behind. You should, however, have the latest revision (r.) of whatever version you use. Revisions are generally brought out to fix problems which become apparent after a version is released.

File Prep Hint # 7

Remember that any software which you place on your computer complicates your computer. To help keep your system operating at its peak, limit the amount of software you put on your publishing system. Be especially brutal about removing software which installs files in your system folder. Those are the most intrusive and performance-robbing pieces of software. Yes, that means get rid of those cool screen savers, sounds, and games. Put those on your home computer. Use resource management utilities such as font and system file management tools to help you streamline your system resources.

DTP 201

File Fundamentals

BITS&BYTES

RESOLUTION

TYPESETTING

RIPPING

Graphics

Fonts &

6
Bits & Bytes

As the Byte Turns continues…

Will Danny and Pauline find a common language format with which to express themselves? Will Danny choose flowery formatting or settle for plain old ASCII??

Here is my "Wordstar" document with all my formatting!

Oh dear, what have I gotten myself into??

Wordstar… I haven't seen one of those files in a long time…
…I really need to give those salespeople a list of acceptable applications and make sure they use it...

BITS &·BYTES

Analog vs. Digital Clocks

Analog vs. Digital Clocks

Analog vs. Digital Switches

▼ *Figure 6.1 Analog vs. Digital*
Analog devices usually have a
continuously varying mechanism such as a sweep second
hand on a watch or rheostatic
dial. Digital devices, in contrast, usually have only two
settings, an "On" and an "Off"
position. With digital mechanisms small, changes in settings or values are accomplished by creating small differences between the "On" and
"Off" positions.

Two ways to view the world

Analog vs. digital devices & data

The key to understanding how a computer works is to appreciate how
a computer manipulates and stores information. A computer is a digital device; that is, it only understands information which is represented or recorded in a two-part code like "off and on" or "up and
down." A computer does not understand continuous uninterrupted
streams of information like light waves, sound waves, or a continuous
tone photograph. These are analog or continuous forms of information or data. For information to be comprehensible to a computer, it
must first be placed in a two-part code of information, or what is
commonly referred to as "digitized." Two good examples of pairs of
devices which clearly show the difference between analog and digital
devices are types of clocks and light switches (see Fig. 6.1). A clock
which has sweep second, minute, and hour hands is an analog device.
It continuously shows the passage of time. The record of the analog
watch can be broken into an infinite number of intermediate data
(hand) positions. In contrast, a wristwatch which relies on LCD (liq-
uid crystal display) technology is a digital device. It shows the passage
of time in discrete increments, usually seconds, and records only a
limited number of data positions. Both clocks perform the same
function, recording the passage of time, but one does so in an analog
fashion, the other digitally. Another common example of analog vs.
digital devices can be seen by comparing an on-off light switch with
a dimmer switch. The on-off switch is a digital device. It has only two
positions or data points which it can represent – on or off. By contrast, the dimmer switch is an analog device. It too can be in on and
off positions, but it can be in an infinite number of positions or
points in between. One of the advantages of recording and manipulating data digitally is that information can be recorded and manipulated with a limited number of discrete data points rather than the
infinite number of points required by analog devices.

Data which is in analog form, such as sound and light, must be digitized before it can be recognized, manipulated, and stored in a computer. Hence, we have data such as digital sound on CDs, digital
images such as PhotoCD, and digital video. Each of these forms of
data results from the transformation of original analog information
to digital data which can be used in a computer. A common analog to

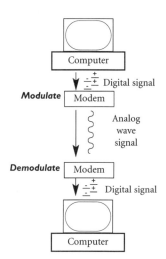

▼ Figure 6.2 Analog to Digital
When we work on digital systems, we are often required to communicate with or transfer information to nondigital, analog systems. A common example of this is when we send files over regular phone lines. The switching equipment used by phone companies is often analog and does not "understand" digital data. When we attempt to send data through these analog systems, we must convert our digital signals into analog signals. These analog signals are then reconverted back into digital signals at the other end of the connection. This conversion from digital to analog and back again is accomplished by modems. The word "modem" is compound shorthand for modulate/demodulate.

digital translation which many of us use is the modem. The word "modem" is short for modulate/demodulate. At a computer station which is sending information across phone lines, a modem's job is to translate, or modulate, the outgoing digital "off/on" information. The modem translates this digital information into an analog wave form which much of our present telephone switching equipment understands. At the receiving end of the phone line the modem's job is to digitize, or demodulate, the incoming signal (see Fig. 6.2). As more of our telephone switching systems become digital, the need for modems will be reduced. One day in the digital future we will look back at these quaint little devices and marvel at how we got along with this complex, slow signal translation, much like we look back at the telegraph today.

Basic computer language

When someone mentions computer language or programming, many of us recoil in fear because of our perspective that such a language is arcane and difficult. While it is true that the details of some programming may be arcane, the basics of computer language are rather simple. In fact, if you have mastered any other language, including English, then the fundamentals of computerese will be a snap. Don't believe me? Here's proof. How many characters are there in the English language? Twenty six (26), right? Right. Well, there are only two (2), that's right, two, in computerese. All the applications you work with – the text and graphic images you see on screen and print out, and the operating systems which allow you to operate your computer – are constructed out of sequences of just two characters: zero (0) and one (1). For instance, a simple black and white graphic of a black box surrounded by a white border (Fig. 6.3) is constructed out of dots or pixels which are assigned values of 0 for white pixels and 1 for black pixels. More complex graphics are built the same way, just with more complex sequences of 0s and 1s. Each 0 or 1 is known as a bit, designated with a lower case b. This assignment of 0s and 1s works fine for any solid areas including solid colors. These 0s and 1s can just as easily be assigned to represent Pantone spot colors as they can represent black and white areas. We will discuss how we generate continuous tone grayscale and color images a little later. By the way, our exclusive use of 0s and 1s is why we refer to our computers as being digital and our basic computer code as binary. Both "digital" and "binary" refer to the basic two-character format (0,1) which these computers and their applications understand.

▼ Figure 6.3 Digital Graphic Data

Graphics are captured, created, stored, and transmitted in the form of "0"s and "1"s. The above example shows how a simple black and white graphic would be constructed out of "0"s and "1"s. This type of graphic would be called a 1 bit graphic, because each pixel, or square, is composed of just one bit (0 or 1) of information. More complex graphics will contain multiple bits (8, 24, or 32) per pixel.

Graphic formats

Basic building blocks

The most fundamental building block of digital graphic images is a pixel. The simplest kind of pixel is a square which is assigned a single bit value of one (1) or zero (0). These are known as 1-bit pixels because they are only assigned values of either one or zero. The size of a pixel is determined by the resolution of the file of which it is a part. These 1-bit per pixel square building blocks can be assembled, like bricks, to create a wide variety of graphic line art images. Figure 6.3 shows how these simple 1-bit pixels can be assembled to create a black square with a white border. Note how the image is constructed from building blocks which are assigned values of either zero (0) or one (1), the only two values your computer understands. Later we will see how multibit per pixel images recreate continuous tone images. We will also see how pixel-based images can be converted into vector-based images.

Text formats

Straight text

Assigning bit values to text characters presents a challenge. There are 26 characters plus punctuation marks and other control characters in the English language, but there are only two computer characters, 0 and 1, which can be used to represent all of these characters. The solution to this dilemma has been to assign standardized sequences of 0s and 1s together in groups of 8. Each standard sequence of 8 bits is equivalent to a specific numeric or alphabetic character, punctuation mark, or control character such as a line break indicator. Each 8-bit sequence is known as a Byte and is designated with an upper case B. An example of this one Byte = one character system can be found by looking at the Byte equivalents of upper and lower case "a." Upper case "A" = 1000001 while lower case "a" = 1100001. Notice that a substitution of a 1 for a 0 in the second bit position of the Bytes is all that distinguishes "A" for "a" in the code list. So when we type "Shift A" on a computer keyboard, the bit sequence 1000001 is sent to RAM for immediate use and may be stored on a storage drive for later retrieval. This bit sequence is recognized by our application software as uppercase "A" and displayed and printed accordingly on our monitors and printers.

The complete list of sequences which have been assigned to all these characters is known as the ASCII character set. ASCII is an acronym for American Standard Code For Information Interchange (a complete list of the ASCII code sequences can be found in the appendix). There are several advantages to using a standard code such as ASCII. First, by having a tiny standard code for each character, we do not need to have a unique code every time we create a character. This keeps text file sizes very small. More importantly, having a standard code for text characters allows us to transport files easily from one computer or application to another and be confident that those files can be recognized. This ASCII code is the format in which raw text files are saved when you save a file as "Text" or "Text Only" or "Text Only With Line Breaks." This raw text file format retains all of the character information, such as numbers, letters, punctuation, and line returns, but discards any other formatting information such as typestyle, size, or paragraph format information. The ASCII text format is the lowest common denominator for text files and is what provides us with the basic text file transfer capabilities which we enjoy.

Formatted text

Each application such as Microsoft Word or QuarkXpress uses its own proprietary formatting code, which is added to the basic ASCII code sequences, for applying character and paragraph formatting to basic text. For instance, the following sequence represents additional code which QuarkXpress uses to assign formatting information:

[@Normal:<*p(7.2,0,0,16,0,3.6,g,"U.S.   English")$z14f"Helvetica-Bold">Peaceful Coexistence].

This code indicates that the following formatting will be applied to the words "Peaceful Coexistence:" 14pt B Helvetica Bold with 16pts of leading, a 7.2 pt. left indent, and a 3.6 pt. space after the paragraph. All of this formatting code is unique to QuarkXpress and cannot be interpreted by other applications without the use of a specific QuarkXpress filter. If this text were saved in straight ASCII format, all that would be saved would be the words "Peaceful Coexistence," but this copy could be imported and interpreted by most other applications without the need for a special filter. So for practical purposes, any time you want to transfer some copy from one computer or application to another and you are not sure if the receiving end will be able to "read" your formatted file, save your text in ASCII or "Text Only" format and you will be assured of transferability.

If you need to send formatted text, another option is to use RTF, or Rich Text Format. RTF is a commonly accepted text file format for formatted text. RTF files can be read by most word processors and many other applications. Ask the person who will be receiving your file if the application can interpret RTF files. Any time you send a formatted text, it is advisable to send along a proof of the formatted copy to show what the text looks like.

COMPUTERESE DEFINED:

The basics of bits, Bytes, & ASCII

bit (b)
The smallest unit of the digital or binary computer language, restricted to either a 0 or a 1

Byte (B)
A binary number which defines a computer character such as the number "1" = 8 bits

Kilobit (Kb)
One thousand (1,000) bits or 1000 0s or 1s

Megabit (Mb)
One million (1,000,000) bits = 125,000 bytes (1,000,000 bits ÷ 8 bits/bytes = 125,000 bytes)

KiloByte (KB)
One thousand (1,000) bytes or characters

MegaByte (MB)
One million (1,000,000) bytes or characters

ASCII
American Standard Code for Information Interchange. A code which translates binary numbers into number, letter, symbol, or control characters. ASCII or "text only" files is a format in which text files can be saved and nearly universally translated and read on a wide variety of computer platforms, operating systems, and applications.

Examples of ASCII code character translations:

A = 1000001   a = 1100001   1 = 0110001   ! = 0100001

Examples of ASCII code word translations:

English Language Words: Avoiding The Output Blues

ASCII Equivalent: 1000001 1110110 1101111 1101001 1100100 1101001 1101110 1100111 100000 1010100 1101000 1100101 100000 1001111 1110101 1110100 1110000 1110101 1110100 100000 1000010 1101100 1110101 1100101 1110011 Note that 100000 is a space. A complete list of ASCII characters can be found in the Appendix. Remember, even text files can change dramatically when transferred from one computer to another, so your hard copy proof serves as insurance for you.

PAULINE'S FILE PREP TIPS

File Prep Hint # 8

All text and graphic images in a digital file are constructed out of two values: zeros (0s) and ones (1s). The fundamental building block of graphic images is the pixel which, in its simplest form, is assigned a single bit value of either a zero (0) or one (1). More complex pixels can be assigned multiple bit per pixel values. The basic building block for text is a Byte, which contains eight (8) bits. Each Byte represents one character such as an "A" or a "b," Graphic images and text are composed of combinations of bits and Bytes. It is useful to think of your text and graphic images as combinations of bits and Bytes, as this will facilitate your understanding of how your text and graphic tools work when you are constructing and editing digital documents.

File Prep Hint # 9

When sending a text file to be output, be sure that your service bureau or printer can interpret or "read" your text file format. It is best to send an unformatted ASCII or "Text Only" file which can be universally recognized and interpreted. If you need to send formatted text, be sure to confirm the platform, application name, and version of the application used to create the text file (e.g., Windows WordPerfect, version 5.0). If you are unsure of compatibility, send the text file as an ASCII or text only file. Another option is to use RTF, or Rich Text Format, which is a commonly translatable form for formatted text. Even simple formatted text files can change when opened up on another computer, so if you send formatted text, it is a good idea to send a laser proof of the text to provide a visual example of what you intended.

7
Basic Computer Skills & Habits

As the Byte Turns continues…

Will Pauline help Danny clean up his system, improve his habits, and find true love in the process, or will she just tick Danny off???

I'm having all sorts of problems with my computer: I keep losing files, my HD crashed, my system bombs, I'm slow, and my wrist hurts!

WOW, it sounds like you have a lemon system.

I knew I didn't want to get a computer!

Does Danny have a lemon??

No. But it does sound like Danny needs to clean up his system folder, manage his files better, institute back-ups, and start working more from his keyboard.

BASIC COMPUTER SKILLS

Four basic skills

Point

This skill involves moving your mouse which in turn moves a cursor across your computer monitor/desktop. This movement of the cursor allows you to point at any icon or file you wish to manipulate.

Point and single-click

This skill is used for selecting any icon, file, or response button. After moving your cursor to a desired location by pointing, single-clicking on an icon or file allows you to select or activate that item. If the item you are pointing at happens to be a dialog box, clicking on the button will complete a response to that button. The most common example of this is the OK button found in many dialog boxes.

Point and double-click

This skill is used for opening or launching items such as disks, applications, and document files. In the case of type, double-clicking on text will usually select that text.

Point, click, hold, & drag

This skill is used for many purposes: moving items, accessing menus, resizing items, selecting areas, and drawing items are some of the most common.

Advanced skills

Back to the keyboard

Many of the skills and manipulations discussed above can be accomplished more quickly and easily through the use of keyboard commands. It may seem contradictory for me to send you back to the keyboard after the last chapter, when I made such a point about how easy it is to use a GUI with a mouse and menus. OK, call me mercurial, but that's exactly what I'm going to do. While using the mouse, menus and icons to navigate around and manipulate your computer is a terrific way to learn how to use your computer; it is also a relatively slow way to operate it. After you have are comfortable with your computer interface, begin to leave your mouse behind and learn keyboard shortcuts. Keyboard manipulation is at least two to four times faster than mouse manipulations in many circumstances. And you do not have to be a touch typist to be fast with keyboard manipulations. While it really helps to develop efficient and consistent hand positions (I've developed a special Tazmanian Whirlwind keyboard method), just using the keyboard will speed you up noticeably. Many applications have an organization or structure to their keyboard shortcuts. Take some time to figure out the keyboard shortcut structure and it will making learning them less tedious.

Keyboard position

While it is not possible in the space available here to teach you the entire Tazmanian Whirlwind keyboard method, I can at least get you started down the right path. I use a home position, similar to the idea of a home position used in touch typing for characters. Specific fingers are assigned to specific ShortCut keys. The ShortCut keys include the COMMAND, (ALT KEY key on Windows) OPTION, CONTROL, SHIFT, RETURN, ENTER, ARROW, and LOCATION KEYS (located above the ARROW keys).

Macintosh and Windows-based keyboards are very similar with the exception that Windows keyboards have no OPTION keys, and the

▼ *Figure 7.1 ShortCut Home Position*
The fastest way to control your computer is from the keyboard rather than with the mouse. As with touch typing, a standard home position with finger placement and movement helps increase the speed and accuracy of keyboard controls. Shown here is a Macintosh keyboard. A Windows keyboard is similar but it has no OPTION key.

ALT (alternate) key on a Windows keyboard generally performs the same function as the COMMAND or APPLE key on a Macintosh keyboard. Figure 7.1 shows the basic keyboard ShortCut home position with the fingers in their proper places. Using home keys allows you to work much more quickly and accurately without having to look down at the keyboard. The ShortCut home position can be used along with the typing home position by just shifting back and forth between the two home positions.

Think layers

Window layers

Many windows can be open at the same time but only one at a time can be active. A window can be activated–that is, brought to the front–by pointing and clicking at that window.

Page element layers

Each element (whether text or graphic) you place on a document page is essentially in its own layer. You need to think of your document page as a three-dimensional object because you will need to control the order of the items or layers on the page. Some applications (like many drawing and painting programs) allow you to actually create and manipulate distinct structural layers within a document file. Creating and using these layers can dramatically simplify both the creation and editing of graphic files.

Keep organized

System files

Your system folder contains the software necessary for operating your computer and many of the applications with which you will work. On a Macintosh the two primary system files are the System, whose actions are mostly transparent to you, and the Finder, which provides all of the interface controls which you use. The interface controls include: The desktop, windows, folders, various icons, and dialog boxes. Your system folder should be kept as clear as possible. The system folder also commonly contains a variety of system resources such as fonts, peripheral access files (commonly known as drivers), and printing-related resources. Do not add any files to your system folder

▼ *Figure 7.2 The System Folder*
The system folder holds all of the files which are essential to you allowing you to interact with and control your computer. The system folder should be modified only after careful deliberation.

unless you are sure of what you are doing. Every file you add to your system folder which is accessed by your system requires resources such as RAM and CPU power. The more system resources your computer supports, the slower your computer will operate and the more likely you are to have operating problems. As I mentioned in Chapter 5, "Software," I organize my system extension resources into job-specific groups, such, as scanning and telecommunications, and only load the resources I need for that particular job I am performing. This minimizes the utilization of CPU and RAM resources and reduces the number of system software conflicts which may occur.

▼ *Figure 7.3 Application Icons*
Each application has its own icon to represent it that tends to reflect the type of tool it is.

▼ *Figure 7.4 Document Icons*
Note how all the document icons have a dog ear in the upper right hand corner, indicating a document file.

▼ *Figure 7.5 Font Icons*
Shown here are icons for Type1 printer fonts. Note the abbreviation of the font names typical of Postscript names.

Application files

Each software application has its own distinct icon, which often has a graphic symbol representing the type of tool for which the application is used. Some applications like Claris Works are generalized applications which perform multiple functions such as word processing, database and spreadsheet, manipulation telecommunications, and drawing. Most applications used in professional electronic publishing are more narrowly focused with sophisticated tool sets devoted to a particular set of functions such as page layout (QuarkXpress), image editing, (Photoshop), or drawing (Freehand).

Document files

Document files are files which are created while working within applications. A simple example would be a page of text created in a word processor. Most document files show a "dog ear" on one corner of the icon. This dog ear is meant to simulate the corner of a page.

Font files

Font files are resources used to create type of various styles. The more fonts you have, the more varieties of ways you will have to display your text message. On most modern electronic publishing systems, fonts (like sounds) are system-wide resources; that is, they are not application-specific resources. They are available to all applications.

Utility files

Utility files are small applications which perform very specific tasks. Examples of utilities include: drive formatting, virus protection, disk copying, and font management software. Some utilities applications, such as Norton Utilities, may have several components to them, such as troubleshooting and disk optimization. The boundary between an

▼ **Figure 7.6 Utility Software**
Utility software is usually a single focus application intended to perform a very specific task. Shown here are icons for two utilities: Gamma, used for calibrating monitors, and HDT Prober, used for locating and mounting disks.

application and a utility becomes blurred with multifunction utilities such as these.

Safety habits

Saving

Save It or Lose It! Save! Save! Save! Any document which you create or any document to which you make additions or changes is not truly created or made in a physical sense until you save that document. The reason is that we work in RAM (Random Access Memory), which is an electronic environment only. If we turn off the computer, or the computer "crashes" and we have not saved creations or changes, our electronic creations will be lost. The act of saving a file copies the information for RAM onto a disk, usually a hard drive, which creates a magnetic copy of the information. This is not a bomb-proof version of the document, either, but at least it gives our information a physical presence. It is important that you develop good saving habits. Get in the habit of saving your file every few minutes; it is as simple as holding down the COMMAND key (ALT key in Windows) and typing the character "S." This "SAVING" action will save whatever creations or changes which you have in RAM to a physical location on your hard drive. This same action can be initiated from the FILE menu, but is more quickly handled through the use of the keyboard shortcut.

Backup and archiving

It is a smart idea to make extra copies of the files on your drives. Remember that the information on your drives is in magnetic form and is therefore susceptible to damage and loss. Backing up involves making a copy of an active file onto another disk. Archiving involves making a copy of an inactive file, one which you will not need to use in the near future, which is then removed from your active disk. Removing inactive files from your active disk helps keep your hard drive free for the use of active files. It is a good practice to have automatic backups made every day of your active files. Manual backups are always time consuming, often inconsistent, and prone to error. An alternating sequence of M,W,F and T,Th,Sat backups on two separate media provides for multiple copies of your active data. Archive data on a monthly or at least a quarterly basis. Archived files can be retrieved from their stored locations.

Viruses

Computer viruses are usually small self-replicating files which reproduce every time they are accessed. Many computer viruses "live" in the system files where they are constantly accessed and therefore encouraged to multiply. A multiplying computer virus rapidly consumes RAM and storage space and dominates your cpu resources, bringing the operation of your computer to a crawl. Viruses are the computer version of sickness. And just like with diseases, some viruses are more dangerous than others. Infection by a computer virus can be prevented by checking every foreign file (that is a file received via a disk or modem) with a virus-checking application/utility prior to launching the file.

Performance tips

Be a minimalist

Less is more, or at least faster and more trouble free. It is easy to load all sorts of sounds, screen savers, and games on your computer. Many of these files add additional resources to your system folder. Each additional system resource, while adding a capability, also adds a burden onto your computer by taking up RAM space, CPU time, and storage space. To help maintain a healthy and top performing computer, be ruthless about restricting the addition of unnecessary resources to your computer. If you have three rows of startup files which appear on you screen when you boot your computer, you are guilty of system abuse, and you will be punished! Resist the temptation to add those cool screen savers and nifty games. Keep your working computer pared down as much as possible. Be a minimalist!

Keep file sizes small

Graphic images often account for the lion's share space consumed by documents on your drives. The three variables which affect the file size of an graphic images are: 1) image dimension, 2) pixel depth, and 3) resolution. When capturing or creating graphic images, keep their file size as small as possible by minimizing these variables as much as possible. Image dimension can be minimized by proper cropping. Pixel depth is the least flexible variable, but some space can be saved by not converting your RGB files to CMYK images until absolutely necessary. File resolution, the most flexible variable, can often be lowered to dramatically reduce file sizes.

Never work off of floppies

Always copy work from removable media, including floppy disks, Syquests, opticals, Bernoullis, and the like, to your internal hard drive before launching an application or opening a file contained on the removable disk. Most removable disks are much slower (up to 300 percent in the case of floppies) than your internal hard drive, both in terms of read/write access to and throughput of data. Also, removable media tends to be less stable than fixed hard drives, and therefore more prone to file damage and loss. This warning about working off of removable media applies to using these media as scratch disks or virtual memory as well.

Archiving

Keep your hard drive performance near its peak by keeping at least 25 percent and preferably 50 percent of its total storage volume available. Archive on tape or optical drives. Floppy drives are not dependable enough media to act as good backup or archiving solutions.

▼ *Figure 7.7 Scratch Disk Volume*

To speed up the function of virtual memory-capable applications such as Photoshop, it is advisable to dedicate a specific hard drive volume for that use. This can be either a separate individual hard drive or a separate partition of a larger drive. In either case, I always label my dedicated volume as "Scratch Disk" so that no one is tempted to store any files there. Note that the 500 MB scratch disk volume is completely empty. Do not use removable media for scratch disks, as they are generally too slow for the job.

Virtual memory or scratch disk

Virtual memory is the use of storage memory, such as a hard drive, as RAM or active work space. In Photoshop this is called scratch disk space. Scratch disk space is used when an application does not have enough RAM memory to perform all the tasks required. The advantage of having the ability to use scratch disk space is that if an application runs out of RAM space, instead of just quitting, the application expands into the use of the scratch disk or virtual memory space. This is an obvious advantage for systems which have limited amounts of RAM space. Not all applications can take advantage of a scratch disk. RAM-hungry applications such as most pixel editing applications (like Photoshop), are commonly built with the ability to use a scratch disk.

Using a scratch disk, however, means that you will pay a performance penalty, and often a substantial one. Reading and writing data to and from a scratch disk, which is normally meant to store data only, is usually many times slower than working in RAM. When working in virtual memory, all of an application's functions slow down. The greater the percentage of virtual memory use, the slower your application will operate. Therefore, it is generally a good idea to limit the use of virtual memory and keep most of your application functions operating in RAM.

In the real world of digital imaging, few of us have enough RAM to satisfy our ever-growing needs. (The digital imager's lament: You can never have too much RAM or too much hard drive space.) While it is certainly prudent to have enough RAM to meet your everyday needs, there are always times when we end up using virtual memory. Applications, whether they are utilizing real or virtual RAM, require contiguous RAM space. That is another way to say that the memory space cannot be fragmented. To be sure that you always have enough contiguous hard drive space for Photoshop and similar applications to utilize for their scratch disk needs, it is best to dedicate specific hard drive volumes for use as virtual memory. I recommend a minimum of 500 MB by either assigning a separate hard drive for use as virtual memory or to partition a larger drive and dedicate one of the partitions as a scratch disk. I actually label my virtual memory partition as" Scratch Disk" so that I do not use this drive for data storage by mistake. Either way the object is to keep a large, clean, contiguous volume of storage space available for your virtual memory-capable applications to use. Do not use removable media such as Syquests or opticals for scratch disk space as they are too slow. Dedicating a volume to scratch disk use will speed up your applications and prevent dialog boxes such as the dreaded "Can't complete this; ran out of scratch disk space" from occurring.

Preference files

One other important time-saving habit to adopt has two parts. First, always take the time to set your application preferences before you begin creating images and documents. Setting your preferences customizes your application to behave the way you want it to. Doing so can dramatically improve your efficiency. Initially set your preferences without a document open. Doing so will set the default preferences the way you want them. These defaults will be automatically used with every document you create thereafter. Your default preferences can be altered to suit the needs of any specific document once you have opened up that document. After you set your default preferences for each application you use, make copies of these files and save them in a separate folder or directory. Later, if any of your preference files become corrupted, as they are wont to do from time to time, forcing you to throw the preference file away, you can just drag a copy of the copy back into the appropriate preference file folder or directory, thereby saving you the time and hassle of recreating the preference file. Each time you reset your default preference file for any application, be sure to replace the copy of the preference file with a new copy.

PAULINE'S FILE PREP TIPS

File Prep Hint # 10

A computer is a great tool, but it needs management and maintenance like any other system. Keep your system up-to-date and be a minimalist; remove unnecessary software from your system. Be sure to save regularly and perform "Save As" documents several times per day. Save copies of your preference files after you configure your computer, perform regular backups to protect your data, and archive regularly to remove inactive files to keep your active drive free for current use.

File Prep Hint # 11

Removable media like floppy disks, optical disks, and Syquest cartridges are too slow and undependable to be used for active work. Use them for storage only. So don't work off of floppies and do not use removable media such as scratch disk space.

File Prep Hint # 12

Don't be a mouser; work from your keyboard. It's faster and less stressful. Working from the keyboard is 100 – 400 percent faster than mousing around. Working more from the keyboard will also help reduce the incidence of carpal tunnel syndrome.

8
Resolving Resolution

As the Byte Turns continues…

*Will Danny and Pauline be able to resolve their differences,
or will their budding relationship be RIPed apart??*

My files printed fine on my 300 dpi laser printer. Why are you having problems outputting my files??

We should be able to??

Can't we print his file???

Just because a file prints at 300 dpi does not mean it will print at 2450 dpi. High resolution RIPing is much more demanding.

RESOLVING RESOLUTION

What is resolution?

The term "resolution" has its origin in the word "resolve," which means to distinguish or discern. To resolve a difference between two opinions, we take a close look at both opinions to distinguish how they are similar or different. When we look closely at an object, we often see that it is composed of smaller building blocks. The more closely we look, the more we magnify an object or issue, the more detail we can generally see or resolve. When we look at a house from a half mile away we see only the entire object, the house. As we move closer, we see that it is composed of walls, a roof, and windows. When we look closely at one of the walls, we see that it may be made up of a repeating pattern of small bricks separated by mortar between each brick. An even closer look at the mortar reveals that it is composed of grains of sand, and so forth. In each step we have a more enlarged or magnified view of the house, and we see more detail. By resolving the components of the house, we can understand the composition of the house and how it was constructed. A close look at the brick wall can help us see how it was constructed and have a good idea how to construct one like it.

A digital image, like the brick wall, is composed of building blocks. Some images, like the brick wall, are composed of a repeating pattern of all the same building blocks. Other images, like the house, are composed of several types of construction components. Similarly, some digital graphic images are simple and composed of one type of building block, while others are more complex and contain several varieties of building materials. Graphic images, like walls, can be made up of various sized building blocks. Some walls are composed of small bricks, others of larger cinder blocks, and some of even larger flagstones. With graphic images, the size of the building blocks determines the resolution of an image. The smaller the building block, the higher the resolution, and the finer the detail which can be shown. Some of the lowest resolution images are constructed out of pixels which are only 1/72 inch on each side. These images are said to have a resolution of 72 pixels per inch (ppi) and are simply referred to as 72 ppi images. Image resolutions from 300 ppi to 1200 ppi are common in electronic publishing. The highest resolution images may have as many as 2400 to 3600 ppi and be capable of producing very sharp images which resolve very fine detail.

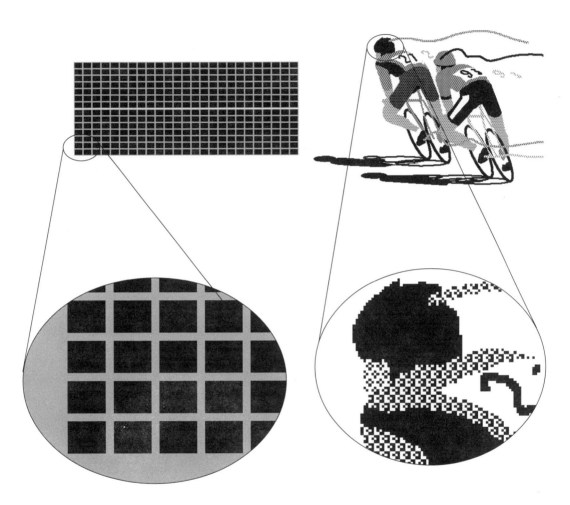

▼ Figure 8.1 Digital File Construction

Electronic graphic images are constructed out of either lines (vectors) or dots (bitmaps). Like a brick wall, digital bitmapped or raster graphic images are constructed out of smaller components. In the case of the wall, the construction materials are bricks. In the case of the graphic, the construction components are dots or pixels. The picture of the bicyclist above is a low resolution, 72 dpi image (paint file format) where each pixel is $1/72$ inch on a side. In this image, each pixel is either black or white. The greater the number of pixels an image has, the higher its resolution. Higher resolution images are generally higher quality, but they are also more demanding in terms of processing. The key to good file preparation is to reduce the file size of an image without adversely affecting the quality of the image.

Resolution vs. file size

Most people think that a 600 dpi laser printer is twice as good as a 300 dpi laser printer. In reality, it is four times better. The reason is that dpi, dots per inch, is not as important as dpi^2, dots per square inch. A 300 dpi laser printer has 90,000 dots per square inch, whereas a 600 dpi laser printer has 360,000 dots per square inch. This is a quadruple amount of information. A 1200 dpi imagesetter must process 1,440,000 dots per square inch (in^2). This accounts for why some documents may print on a laser printer, but not on a high resolution imagesetter. Therefore, keeping your documents, especially your graphics, as simple and therefore as small as possible is an important concept to keep in mind. See Figure. 8.2 for a review of the effects of resolution on file size.

Another word used to refer to the concept of resolution is the term "Res." You may hear the terms "Res 12" or "Res 14." Res is shorthand for pixels per mm. Res 12 is equivalent to 304.8 ppi. Conversion from Res to ppi is accomplished by multiplying the Res number, in this case 12, by 25.4. The term Res is most frequently used by people who work with high-end propriety publishing and scanning systems made by companies such as Scitex and Linotype-Hell.

Dots, spots, & pixels

There is much confusion surrounding the meaning and use of these three terms. All three terms are used when discussing resolution, and all three are used to discuss the building blocks of images. To sort these terms out, we need to think along the lines of two separate types of resolution, input (scan or capture or input) resolution and output (print) resolution. When we think of and discuss input resolution, we should use the term pixel (pixel/in or pixel/mm). A pixel is the size of the square area of an image which a scanner or digital camera captures. So a scan resolution of 600 pixels per inch means the scanner will capture an image in square increments of $1/600$ inch x $1/600$ inch. A pixel can contain one or more bits of information. The size of the captured pixels also determines the size which they will appear when viewed on a screen (pixels smaller than $1/72$ inch x $1/72$ inch need to be viewed at high magnification in order to be seen because most monitors are limited to 72 dpi resolution). An image which is scanned at 600 pixels per inch will appear on a screen composed of pixels which are $1/600$ inch square. Therefore, capture and view resolution are the same. However, when we are ready to print our 600 pixels-per-inch image, this image must be transformed into dots which can be produced by a printer. These dots are sometimes called "spots" or "laser spots" because the dot images are often produced by lasers. The pixels, which are captured by a digital camera or scanner, are not translated

RESOLUTION COMPARISON

RESOLUTION IS A SQUARE FUNCTION, NOT A LINEAR ONE. THEREFORE, AS THE LINE RESOLUTION DOUBLES, THE AMOUNT OF DATA INCREASES BY A FACTOR OF FOUR (4). FOR EXAMPLE:

- A 300 dpi laser printer prints 300 dpi x 300 dpi = 90,000 dpi^2
- A 600 dpi laser printer prints 600 dpi x 600 dpi = 360,000 dpi^2

This means that a 600 dpi laser creates four (4) times as much information as a 300 dpi laser.

- Calculate how much more information a 2400 dpi imagesetter must process than a 300 dpi laser:

     A 2400 dpi imagesetter produces _____ dpi^2

     This is _____ times as much information as the 300dpi laser.

- Calculate the file size of an 8x10 B&W image scanned at 600 dpi

     bits(b) _____, Mega bits (Mb) _____, Bytes(B) _____, Mega Bytes (MB) _____

300 dpi Laser Printer Resolution **300 dpi x 300 dpi** This square inch represents 300 dpi horizontal X 300 dpi vertical	**600 dpi Laser Printer Resolution** **600 dpi x 600 dpi** This square inch represents 600 dpi horizontal X 600 dpi vertical

1 in. with 300 horizontal dots

1 in. with 600 horizontal dots

▼ **Figure 8.2 Resolution Comparison**

Resolution is a square, not a linear, function. As the linear resolution doubles, the square resolution, and therefore the file size, quadruples. A 300 dpi image is actually a 300dpi x 300dpi image with 90,000 dots per square inch. A 600 dpi image is 600 dpi x 600 dpi or 360,000 dpi^2, or four times the resolution *and file size* of the 300 dpi image.

one-for-one in the printing process. (This transformation is the job of the RIP., see Chapter 10, "Ripping Up Your Files," for more details on this process.) A dot or a spot is the building block which is used by printers to reconstruct images which were captured/created on the computer. The size of those building blocks is measured in fractions of inches or mm. The smallest size dot/spot which a printer can produce determines its resolution. Hence, a printer which can produce a dot or spot which is $1/600$ inch x $1/600$ inch is a 600 dpi printer.

The confusion arises when we interchange input resolution with output resolution. Some of our earliest uses of resolution in desktop publishing, way back in 1984/85, were to describe the output capabilities of LaserWriter printers (300 dpi). These discussions were taking place prior to the advent of desktop scanning. When we began to use scanners to capture our images, we just transferred the output terms and units of dpi to input scanning resolution. But scanners don't capture spots or dots; they capture areas of images, which we should call pixels. These areas are then viewed on a screen as pixels. But when these pixels are printed, they are reproduced as dots or spots. So, in summary, we capture, create, and view pixels; we print dots.

Multibit contone images

Continuous tone (contone) images such as grayscale and color photographs, screens, and blends all require more than one bit per pixel to create them. All contone images contain one or more shades of gray. The human eye can distinguish several thousand shades of gray. In Postscript, we are limited to working with 256 shades of gray. Because a computer is a digital device and can work with only two values, in the case of graphics those are black and white, all continuous tone images whether they are grayscale or color are treated by the computer as grayscale images. Color images like RGB or CMYK images are stored as multiple grayscale channels, three in the case of RGB and four for CMYK. In order for a digital computer to create, manipulate, and store images with multiple levels of grayscale, it must use multiple bits per pixel to create images. Grayscale, with 256 shades of gray, requires eight (8) bits per pixel to record the 256 shades of gray. RGB and CMYK color images require three and four eight (8) bit grayscale channels, respectively (one for each color), for a total of twenty-four (24) and thirty-two (32) bits per pixel, respectively. Because contone images require multiple bits-per-pixel to create, file sizes increase by the factor of the pixel depth. For instance, an eight (8) bit grayscale image is eight times the size of a one (1) bit B&W rendering of the same image. Figure 8.3 shows some examples of how file size is affected by both resolution and pixel depth.

RESOLUTION GLOSSARY

Digital computer language

- Binary language has only two characters: 0 and 1
- 1 bit = Either a 0 or a 1
- 1 Byte = A series of 8 bits , 0s and/or 1s. For instance: 1000001 = 8 bits = 1 Byte
- 1 bit graphic = Black & White only
- Each black pixel (in a 1 bit graphic) = 1 bit
- Each white pixel (in a 1 bit graphic) = 1 bit

File size terminology

- bit = either a 1 or a 0
- Byte = 8 bits = 1 character: 1000001 = 1 Byte = the Character "A"
- Kb = Kilobits = 1000 bits
- KB = KiloBytes = 1000 bytes
- Mb = Mega bits = 1,000,000 bits
- MB = Mega Bytes = 1,000,000 Bytes

Scan or input resolution vs. file size

- 300 ppi scan captures 300 pixels vertical and horizontal
- 600 ppi scan captures 600 pixels vertical and horizontal
- 8x10 inch page scanned at 300 pixels (1 bit per pixel) = 7,200,000 bits = 7.2Mb = 900,000 Bytes -= .9MB
- 8x10 inch page scanned at 600 pixels (1 bit per pixel) = 28,800,000 bits = 28 = 28.8Mb = 3,600,000 Bytes 3.6MB

Output or Print Resolution

- Spots per inch also known as dots per inch (dpi) = smallest bulding block of print image

  300 spots per inch (dpi) = 300 dpi x 300 dpi (horizintally and vertically)

  600 spots per inch (dpi) = 600 dpi x 600 dpi (horizintally and vertically)

  2400 spots per inch (dpi) = 2400 dpi x 2400 dpi (horizintally and vertically)

- Halftone dots per inch also known as lines per inch or lpi = number of halftone dots printed in every inch
- Line art and text images are converted into small spots to create sharp edages
- Continuous tone images are converted into halftone dots to simulate grayscale values
- Halftone dots are constructed from patterns of spots (see Figure 8.4 for how this is accomplished)

▼ *Figure 8.3 Resolution Glossary*
Above is an overview of resolution terms and concepts. For clarity and to remove confusion, separate input/scanning resolution (pixels) from output/printing resolution (spots and dots). Line art and text are reproduced with small spots, while contone images are reproduced with patterns of larger halftone dots.

Halftone dots

One additional level of complexity which adds to our resolution confusion is the concept of the halftone dot. Since we cannot produce continuous tone images on a printing press, because we can only produce dots or spots, we are faced with the problem of reproducing these contones. We perform this feat by a process known as halftoning. Halftoning takes advantage of the resolving limitations of the human eye. The concept is basically this: If we place two small dots side by side on a page, up close we can distinguish or resolve those two dots. However, if we begin to move that page farther and farther away, at some distance we will no longer be able to distinguish or resolve those two dots and they will appear as one. We essentially trick the eye into seeing only one dot instead of two. Now, if we gradually vary the size of the dots across an area we will simulate a gradation. It is in this way that we create the impression of tone, using dots.

The technical problem with creating halftone dots is that most laser printers and imagesetters can produce only dots or spots of fixed sizes. The solution is to combine smaller laser spots or dots in order to create halftone dots of various sizes. Figure 8.3 demonstrates this process. A halftone dot is defined by and constructed from a grid of laser spots known as a halftone cell. Any of the cell sites can be filled in with laser spots or left blank. The greater the number of these cell sites which are filled in with laser spots, the larger the halftone dot will be and the darker the shade of gray which will be simulated.

Halftoning: where it occurs

A RIP is a Raster Image Processor. This is the portion of your computer-based publishing system which converts the images you generate on your computer into a form which can be reproduced on a piece of paper or film. To "rasterize" means to create dots, and that is what a RIP does. It generates dots. All elements on your page, text, line art graphics, and contone graphics must be converted by a RIP into a series of dots in order to be printed. In a Postscript publishing system, halftoning of contone images occurs at the RIP, not at the design or scanning station. All contone graphic images printed from a computer to a laser printer or imagesetter must be constructed out of a series of dots. In order for a continuous tone image to be rendered by these printers, the image must first be converted into a special series of dots known as halftone dots or cells. Halftone dots are composed of a series of smaller dots known as image dots. The number of image dots which make up halftone dots determines the number of shades of gray which can be rendered. The number of image dots which are

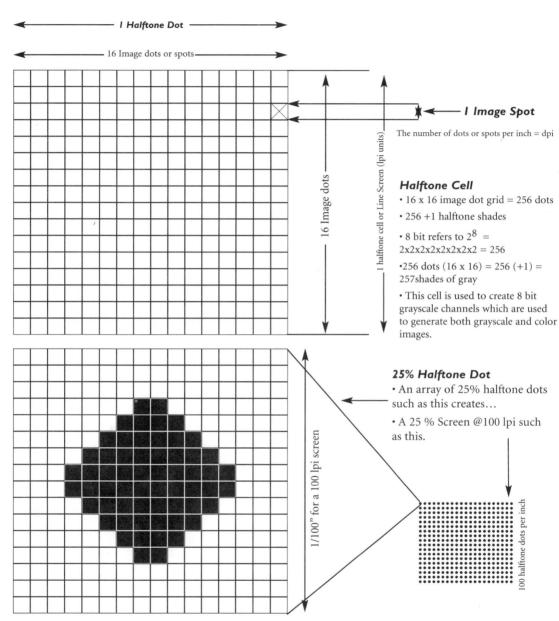

← **I Halftone Dot** →

← 16 Image dots or spots →

I Image Spot

The number of dots or spots per inch = dpi

16 Image dots

1 halftone cell or Line Screen (lpi units)

Halftone Cell
• 16 x 16 image dot grid = 256 dots
• 256 +1 halftone shades
• 8 bit refers to 2^8 = $2x2x2x2x2x2x2x2 = 256$
• 256 dots (16 x 16) = 256 (+1) = 257 shades of gray
• This cell is used to create 8 bit grayscale channels which are used to generate both grayscale and color images.

25% Halftone Dot
• An array of 25% halftone dots such as this creates...
• A 25 % Screen @100 lpi such as this.

1/100" for a 100 lpi screen

100 halftone dots per inch

▼ *Figure 8.4 Halftone Cells and Dots*

Traditional halftone dot patterns are created in set patterns determined by halftone cells. Laser printers and imagesetters use this cell pattern to determine spot placement on film or paper. Collections of image spots are used to create halftone dots. Halftone dots of various sizes simulate various grayscale percentages. Patterns of small and large halftone dots create the impression of light and dark grayscale, respectively. Patterns of variably-sized halftone dots are used to simulate the appearance of continuous tone grayscale.

available to construct a halftone cell of a particular size is determined by the dpi of the printer or imagesetter being used. The number of halftone dots-per-inch determines the resolution or sharpness of the rendered image. Here are some numbers to think about:

The number of halftone dots per inch is equivalent to the line screen of the printed image. That is: LPI = halftone dots-per-inch (hdpi)

shades of gray = DPI ÷ LPI (hdpi)

Example: (1600 dpi ÷ 100 lpi)= 16 dot cell : 16 x16 = 256 shades of gray

Example: (1200 dpi ÷ 100 lpi) 12 dot cell: 12x12 = 144 shades of gray

Problem: If you want to be able to reproduce 256 shades of gray @ 133 lpi, what minimum dpi will be required on your imagesetter?

DPI vs. LPI vs. shades of gray

The size of the halftone dot is limited by the line screen at which the image is printed. In fact, the side dimensions of the halftone cell are determined by the line screen of the printer. Therefore, LPI (lines-per-inch) is equivalent to HDPI (halftone dots-per-inch). Since halftone dots are created by a grid of laser dots or spots which fill in the halftone cell, the relationship of LPI to DPI is set by the grid dimensions of the halftone cell. If a halftone cell is composed of 256 cell sites, the dimensions of the cell will be 16 x 16 (16 x 16 = 256). Note that the number of cell sites in each halftone cell also determines the number of shades of gray which can be reproduced. If the halftone cell is composed of 144 cell sites, then the halftone cell will be composed of a 12 x 12 grid of potential laser spots. Remember that the laser spots are the smallest dots which can be created by the printer, and that these laser spots build the halftone dots.

Therefore, the dpi of the printer required to create any given halftone dot is determined by the line screen (which controls the physical size of the halftone dots) and the number of cell sites required in each cell (which will determine the number of shades of gray which can be reproduced). For example, if we want to print a photograph at 100 lpi

▼ Figure 8.5 Resolution and Interpolation

Pixels are the square building blocks of images. The size of a captured or created pixel is determined by the resolution of the capturing device (a scanner or digital camera). The optical or true resolution of an capture device determines the size of a pixel it can capture. Some devices can create smaller pixels than they can capture by a process known as interpolation. Interpolated pixels are one created from the pixels which are already formed. Interpolated images often have finer edges than non-interpolated images, but they cannot show any more detail, as the amount of detail in the image is determined by the true optical resolution of the capturing device. Interpolated edges also tend to be rougher than optical edges.

RESOLUTION AND INTERPOLATION

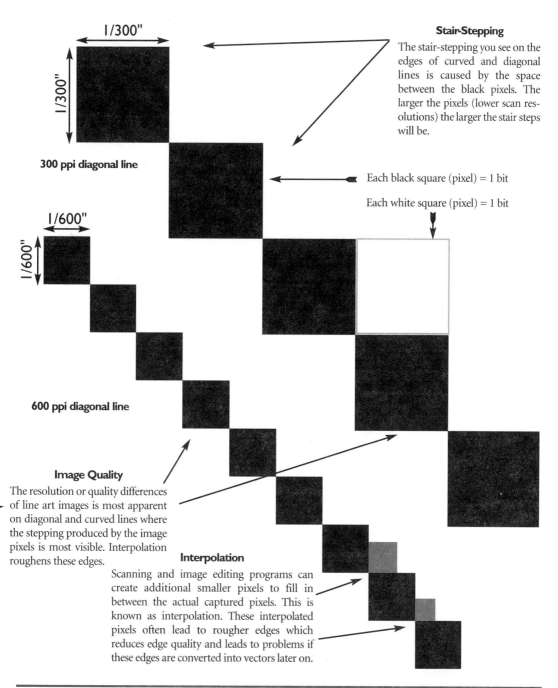

300 ppi diagonal line

1/300"

1/300"

1/600"

1/600"

600 ppi diagonal line

Stair-Stepping

The stair-stepping you see on the edges of curved and diagonal lines is caused by the space between the black pixels. The larger the pixels (lower scan resolutions) the larger the stair steps will be.

Each black square (pixel) = 1 bit

Each white square (pixel) = 1 bit

Image Quality

The resolution or quality differences of line art images is most apparent on diagonal and curved lines where the stepping produced by the image pixels is most visible. Interpolation roughens these edges.

Interpolation

Scanning and image editing programs can create additional smaller pixels to fill in between the actual captured pixels. This is known as interpolation. These interpolated pixels often lead to rougher edges which reduces edge quality and leads to problems if these edges are converted into vectors later on.

which will reproduce 144 shades of gray, we will need to create 100 halftone dots per inch with cell dimensions of 12 x 12 laser spots. This would require an imagesetter which can produce 1200 laser spots per inch (100 halftone dots per inch x 12 laser spots per halftone dot). If we want to reproduce this same photograph at 150 lpi, we will need an imagesetter which can produce 1800 dpi (150 lpi x 12 spots per halftone dot = 1800 dpi). Figure 8.4 shows you a graphical representation of these relationships.

Optical resolution vs. interpolation

Interpolation is fancy word which refers to the creation or generation of new pixels from already existing pixels. Interpolation can occur in a variety of circumstances including during the scanning and image editing processes. Most scanners can capture images at a variety of resolutions but they have only one hardware or optical resolution. The optical or hardware resolution of a scanner is the resolution, in pixles per inch, at which the scanner will capture an image. The scanners interpolated resolution will be any resolution which the scanner converts the image to after it captures the image. If a scanner has an optical resolution of 600ppi, it will capture pixels which are 1/600" on a side. If you choose a scan resolution of 1000ppi, the scanner will first capture the image at 600ppi and then rebuild the pixels at 1/1000" The interpolation process involves rebuilding the pixels at a new size (see Fig. 8.5). This same process of interpolation can occur when we resample or resize an image in an image editing application like Photoshop. If we resize a 200ppi image from 4" x 5" to 8" x 10" in Photoshop and keep the resolution at 200ppi, Photoshop will be forced to create a wide varity of pixels through interpolation, because the new 8" x 10" image will have four times as many pixels as the original image.

▼ *Figure 8.6 Optical vs. Interpolated Resolution*
On the left is a line art edge captured using the optical resolution of the scanner (600ppi). On the left is the same edge captured using an interpolated resolution (1000ppi). Note the greater "raggedness" of the lower quality, interpolated edge.

This interpolation process often leads to lower quality edges in line art images and fuzzier contone images (see Fig. 8.6). Interpolation of pixel-based images should be avoided whenever possible. Line art images which will be converted into vector should be scanned at 100% size using the optical resolution of the scanner. Scaling should be performed after the image is converted into vectors. Contone images, such as Photographs, which require scaling, should be scaled during the scanning process rather than in image editing applications such as Photoshop. Scanners will perform higher quality interpolation than image editing applications.

A final word about file sizes

There are three variables which affect the file size of an image: the dimension of the image (e.g., 5" x 7", 8" x 10" etc.), the image resolution (e.g., 300 dpi, 600 dpi etc.), and the pixel depth of the image (e.g., 1, 8, 24, or 32 bits/pixel). An increase in any of these variables will increase the file size of an image and therefore the requirements for processing that image. As an image's file size increases, so does its RAM requirements for opening the image, storage space for storing the image, CPU time for processing the image and, most importantly, the RIP time to print the image. In most cases, the size and pixel depth of an image are determined by the design of the document, and are therefore preset. The one variable which we can control to reduce the overhead which any image imposes is to keep its resolution as low as possible without adversely affecting the quality of the image. Chapter 12, "Taming Your Scanner," has a complete discussion of the resolution guideline for printing.

A final resolution

Given the various resolutions and kinds of image components which we need to separate, it is helpful to understand and use the correct terminology. For image capture and viewing, scanning and digital image capture, and monitor viewing, we should speak of resolution in terms or pixels/in or pixels/mm. For printing to a laser printer or imagesetter, we should use two terms: dpi and lpi. The building blocks of all images will be dots-per-inch(dpi)*. When describing the reproduction of continuous tone images, we will use the terms lines-per-inch (lpi) or halftone dots-per-inch (hdpi), knowing that halftone dots are constructed from grids of image dots or spots.

* Note: Some prefer the use of the word "spot" to "dot." Using the terms "spot" and "spot-per-inch" (spi) instead of "dot" and "dot-per-inch" (dpi) is desirable for a number of reasons. If we use spot instead of dot it makes the difference between spots and halftone dots less ambiguous. However, the terminology dpi is so ingrained in our industry that it might prove more difficult and confusing to try and substitute the word "spot" for "dot" in our lexicon. As an alternative, I suggest that we can accomplish our communication goals if we clearly distinguish between dots per inch (dpi) and halftone dots per inch (hdpi). We will also need to recognize that hdpi and lpi (another ingrained term) are equivalent terms.

PAULINE'S FILE PREP TIPS

File Prep Hint #13

Keep your resolution concepts and terminology straight. This will help reduce the confusion which surrounds us when we discuss resolution. We capture, create, and view pixels, but we print dots. Therefore, all input resolution, such as when we paint in Photoshop or capture images with scanners and digital cameras, should be discussed in terms of pixel per unit area, such as ppi (pixels per inch) or res (pixels per mm). By contrast, we print with dots, both single dots (more correctly called "spots") and compound dots, which are created through the combination of groups of the smaller spots, called halftone dots. Individual dots or spots are used to recreate single tone text and line art images. The larger halftone dots are used to recreate contone images.

File Prep Hint #14

Three variables affect file size of an image: image dimensions, pixel depth, and resolution. Increases in any of these variables will increase an image's file size and therefore increase the production demands of a number of variables. These include: storage space, CPU resources, RIP time, and transportation and storage resources. Image dimension and pixel depth are determined by the document design, so resolution is often the only variable which we can adjust to decrease a file's size. The goal is to decrease file size as small as possible without affecting the output quality of the image. Understanding the basic concepts of resolution helps us understand that resolution is a square and not a linear function. Therefore, whenever we double the linear resolution of a file, for example, from 300 ppi to 600 ppi, we quadruple the file size.

PAULINE'S FILE PREP TIPS

File Prep Hint #15

When discussing resolution with your printer, distinguish between input resolution (ppi) and output resolutions (dpi and lpi). Find out at what resolution your files will be output and create or adjust your file resolutions accordingly. Resolutions for pixel-based line art images should be between 600 ppi and 1200 ppi. Final resolutions of contone images should never exceed 2 X lpi (see Chapter 12, "Taming Your Scanner," for more advice on this topic).

9
Grappling With Graphics

As the Byte Turns continues…

Will Danny and Pauline see the big picture, or will they have one Tiff too many??

You told me to reduce my file size as much as possible. So I saved my graphics in PICT format because I noticed that the PICT format is very small.

Sounds good to me; the smaller the better.

I know small is better. I know Pauline will be happy.

Hey Pauline, guess what??

Oh no. PICT files should be used only for screen display. They are not made for printing!
This is a perfect example of a little knowledge being dangerous.

GRAPPLING WITH GRAPHICS

Types of graphic files

Bitmap/raster vs. outline/vector images

There are many different specific graphic file forms such as TIFF, RIFF, PCX, JPEG, PICT, GIF, EPS, etc., which are known as file formats. There are, however, only two basic types of digital building materials: pixels and lines. Images constructed out of pixels are called bitmapped or raster images, while those constructed out of lines are called outline or vector images. Bitmap refers to a map or pattern of bits or pixels. The origin of the word "raster" graphic is derived from a line of pixels on a television screen which is known as a raster. "Raster" and "bitmap" both refer to images composed of pixels. The word "outline" refers to graphic images which are composed of lines or outlines. The word "vector" is used for these images because these line images are made up of line segments geometrically referred to as "vectors" because, like all vectors, they have magnitude (length) and direction (orientation). There are two basic kinds of vector or outline paths. Open paths, such as straight lines, do not fully enclose an area. Closed paths, such as circles, do enclose areas. Closed paths can be filled with patterns, screens, and colors as well as being stroked because they have a boundary. Open paths can usually be stroked, but not filled.

These graphic image terms, bitmap/outline and raster/vector, exist because of two separate professional histories for each pair of terms. The graphically descriptive terms "bitmap" and "outline" were developed and used historically in the graphic design community, which has also historically been the Macintosh culture. The more technical terms "raster" and "vector" were developed in the physics and engineering community and were used predominantly by engineers and architects who worked with IBM-based computers or PCs or UNIX workstations, and worked in computer-aided design and manufacturing *(CAD/CAM)*.

Painting & drawing

Bitmapped images, which I think of as painted images, are created during the digital capture of images with scanners and digital cameras, or during the creation of graphics in painting and pixel-based image editing applications such as Adobe Photoshop or Fractal

▼ *Figure 9.1 Digital Graphic File Construction*
There are only two basic types of digital graphic files: bitmapped/raster images and outline/vector images. The file type you use depends upon the kind of image you are constructing. Like a brick wall, digital bitmapped or raster graphic images are constructed out of repeating patterns of smaller component building blocks. In the case of the wall, the materials are bricks. In the case of the graphic, the components are dots or pixels. Shown on the right is a bitmapped image of a biker. This is a low resolution, 72 dpi image where each pixel is 1/72" on a side and is either black or white. Shown on the left, the upper portion of the house is like an outline or vector image. Instead of being constructed out of building block components like bricks (or dots), both the house and vector images are made up of outline components which are linked. In the case of the house, the outline components are boards. In a vector graphic, such as the fox, outline components are lines instead of dots.

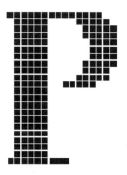

▼ Figure 9.2 Bitmap/Raster Graphic
Bitmap and raster both refer to graphics constructed out of dots. The preferred print file format is TIFF. Compare the file size of these two "Ps." This bitmapped graphic is larger (1MB) because the entire graphic form must be built out of dots.

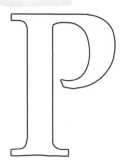

▼ Figure 9.3 Outline/Vector Graphic
The terms outline and vector both refer to graphics constructed out of lines. The preferred print file format is EPS. Compare the file sizes of this and the above "P." This graphic is smaller (100KB) because only the border between the black and white areas need to be recorded as lines.

Design Painter. Vector-based images, which I relate to illustration or drafting types of images, are created in drawing applications such as Adobe Illustrator, Macromedia Freehand, or Corel Draw. Images can be transformed from one type of format to another. For instance, bitmapped images can be converted into vector-based images using an application called Adobe Streamline, while vector-based images can be converted into pixels or rasterized in applications like Photoshop. Images with fine details, such as multitone images (photographs or bitonal images which exhibit fine details) are best saved as bitmapped.

Compound images

Complex images which contain both bitmapped and vector characteristics can also be created. A common example would be a contone photograph which contains a hard edged silhouette, where the edge of the silhouette is created through the addition of a clipping path in a pixel-based application such as Photoshop (see Figure 9.7). Other compound images can be created by placing pixel based images in a predominantly vector-based image constructed in a drawing application like Illustrator.

Graphic file formats

While there are only two basic file types, raster and vector, there are numerous file formats in which those two image types can be saved. File formats are usually use-specific; that is, you choose a file format based upon how you will use it. For instance, TIFF and EPS are the preferred file formats for images which will be processed through a Postscript RIP and printed. PICT and PCX file formats are used for images which will primarily be displayed on a monitor. There are specific file formats for nearly every conceivable use including multimedia, digital video, and the Internet. And new file formats are constantly being created. In this book we will concentrate on file formats which are used in print.

TIFF: Bitmap

The most common, one of the most flexible, and often the most desirable file format for bitmapped graphics which you intend to RIP and print is the TIFF (Tagged Information File Format). You will typically create and save TIFF files when you capture an image with a scanner or digital camera, or create or edit an image in a bitmap editing applications such as Photoshop, Painter, or Picture Publisher. Line art images which are captured as scanned images will almost always be

Graphic File Types

▼ Figure 9.4 1-bit B&W Bitmap

This 1 bit B&W image is the simplest form of a bitmap graphic. The butterfly image is constructed out of black and white pixels, each containing 1 bit of information. Fine detail images are best left as bitmaps rather than converted to outlines. This image can be edited by changing, adding, or removing pixels. The preferred print file format is TIFF.

▼ Figure 9.5 1 bit Outline Graphic

This is an outline graphic file constructed of lines instead of dots. The larger version on the left shows the finished product. The smaller version on the right shows the screen view of the outlines. Note the location of the control points which can be moved and edited to resize and reform the image. The perferred print file format is EPS.

Interior Bitmap Contone (TIFF)

Outline Clipping Path (EPS)

▼ Figure 9.6 8 bit Grayscale Bitmap Graphic

This image is a multibit bitmapped image. There are 8 bits for every pixel, instead of 1 bit/pixel, to record the grayscale information. Like the 1 bit B&W bitmap image above, this image is composed of dots or pixels. Each pixel is assigned a shade of gray which can be edited. This image should be saved as a TIFF for use in printing purposes.

**▼ Figure 9.7 Compound Image
Bitmap and Outline Graphic**

This graphic image is a compound image because it contains continuous tone bitmapped information from the original image, plus an outline around the edge where the silhouette was made. The outline, shown here as a black line, is invisible but it encases the entire contone. The outline forms a smooth boundary around the jagged bitmap portion of the image.

▼ Figure 9.8 EPS Preview Images
This dialog box in Photoshop shows some choices for creating low resolution screen views of your EPS files. Without a screen view, EPS images will not be viewable in a page layout file, but will still place and print okay. Choose the screen view which is appropriate for your image, keeping in mind that lower pixel depth previews will display and redraw more quickly.

saved intially as TIFFs because scanners create bitmapped images, and TIFF is usually the default format. Line art images which are too complex to be converted to EPS format through outlining (see EPS: Line art and EPS graphics below) should remain as TIFFs. The TIFF bitmap format is best used for line art when there is a great deal of detail to be reproduced. Outlining can sometimes ruin or alter the details of complex images. Grayscale and color contone images, which are always constructed from multibit pixels, are very often saved in TIFF format. When in doubt, save your contones as TIFFs.

EPS: Line art

The most common and desirable format for printing outline or vector based graphics is EPS (Encapsulated PostScript). You will use drawing applications such as Illustrator, Freehand, or Corel Draw for creating outline-based EPS files. When you export an image from a drawing application it should be saved in the EPS format, as this is the format which allows page layout applications like QuarkXPress and PageMaker to import them as placed images to use in layouts. When converting bitmapped line art images into vector-based outlines in applications like Adobe Streamline, those outline images should be saved in EPS format. In general, vector-based EPS files usually have the advantage of being smaller, simpler, and more scalable than their bitmapped TIFF cousins. This, however, does not hold true for contone EPS files, which are discussed below. Because EPS files are sealed or encapsulated, a page layout application cannot construct a low resolution screen preview from the high resolution EPS image. Therefore, when exported, all EPS files should be saved with a low resolution screen view image which can be placed as a viewable image in a page layout application. Pay close attention when you export an EPS file, for it is during the export process that the EPS generating application will give you a variety of screen preview choices. If you fail to save an EPS image with a screen preview, your page layout application will be able to place and print the image but you will not be able to preview the image in the page layout application. See Figure 9.8 for an example of an EPS screen preview creation dialog box.

EPS: Contone

In some circumstances, you will want to save images which are composed primarily of multibit pixels, such as photographs, in EPS format instead of the simpler TIFF format discussed above. If you perform image editing chores such as creating hard edge silhouettes of continuous tone images by adding vector-based clipping paths to

Figure 9.9 File Format, Size & Names

▼ **Figure 9.9 File Format, Size & Names**
This screen grab shows the same image saved in a variety of file formats, TIFF, EPS and JPEG. At the top of the list you see a folder containing a five-file DCS version of the image which contains four larger, high resolution files, one for each process color, and a smaller low resolution composite image. The EPS versions of the image are significantly larger than the TIFF versions. The JPEG(M) is compressed less with maximum quality, while the JPEG(L) is more compressed but with the lowest quality. Each image name contains four elements (Item, Pixel depth, Resolution, and File format). This naming scheme makes for unambiguous file names and easy recognition, especially for images with multiple versions.

contone images, you may end up creating a compound file, one which has dual characteristics; that is, it contains both pixels and vectors. A clipping path silhouetted image, for instance, has variable tone pixels (bitmapped) information surrounded by a clipping path (vector) outline which forms a smooth, sharp border. These type of compound images have traditionally been saved as compound EPS files out of applications like Photoshop. Unlike their simpler outline EPS cousins created in object-oriented applications like Streamline, Freehand, or Corel Draw (which are smaller and simpler than their bitmapped TIFF counterparts), compound EPS files are larger and more complicated, and therefore more difficult to RIP than either of its contone bitmapped or the outline components. Note: It is now possible to save these types of compound images as TIFFS (Photoshop 3.0+) with clipping paths rather than as EPS files. The primary advantage of the TIFF format here will be reduced image file size (see Chapter 12, "Taming Your Scanner," for more detailed information on outlining and silhouetting).

Contone images may also be saved as EPS files when you wish to include a Transfer Function which may contain image altering instructions, such as dot gain adjustment or screening instructions, which will be applied to the image when it is RIPed. In these cases the EPS format is required because these kind of Transfer Functions cannot be saved with a TIFF file. The EPS format forms a little storage packet or capsule (hence, the name EnCAPsulated Postscript) around the image which contains both the image data and the transfer function. Contone files saved in EPS format are nearly always larger than those saved in TIFF format because of the additional formatting information required to accomplish the encapsulation (see File format vs. file size on page 105, and Figure 9.9). Like the line art EPS images discussed above, contone images need to be saved with screen previews if you intend to place and view these EPSs in a page layout application (See Figure 9.8).

Five file EPS (DCS) format

There is a special version of the EPS format called a five-file EPS or, as it is also known, DCS (Desktop Color Separation) format. The DCS format was developed specifically for working with and printing color separated process color files. There are two versions of this format. DCS 1.0 and DCS 2.0. DCS 1.0 is used for contone images which have only the four standard process colors (C,M,Y,K). DCS 2.0 is used for images which contain spot colors in addition to the four process colors. DCS format literally creates five or more separate files. A standard DCS 1.0 file will have four separate high resolution

1 Bit B&W Image

A 1 bit line art image such as this contains only one layer of pixels with 1 bit of data per pixel. Each pixel is either Black (1) or White (0). These are the smallest and simplest types of bitmapped images. File size = 285KB at 300dpi

8 Bit Gray Scale Image

An 8 bit grayscale image such as this contains only one layer of pixels, but with 8 bits of data per pixel (8 b/p), and has the capacity to store and display 256 shades of gray. Contrast this to the 1 bit per pixel used to create the line art image above. This grayscale file size is eight times larger than the 1bit images discussed above. This 8 b/p file is also the basic building block for the RGB and CMYK color files discussed below. File size = 2.2MB at 300dpi

24 Bit RGB Color (Screen) Image

A 24 bit color image such as this contains three layers of pixels with 24 bits of data per pixel, or three 8 b/p grayscale files, one for each color (RGB). Each color can be shown in 256 shades. Therefore, the total number of colors possible is 256 R x 256 G x 256 B = 16.7 million colors. This RGB image file size is 24 times larger than the 1bit line art image. These images are used for displaying color images on monitors and printing to color film. File size = 6.6MB at 300dpi

32 Bit CMYK Color (Print) Image

A 32 bit grayscale image contains four layers of pixels with 32 bits per pixel or four 8 bit grayscale files, one for each color. A 32 bit CMYK image produces the same number of colors as the 24 bit RGB image above (16.7 million). The fourth black channel (K) is substituted for various portions of the three color channels (CMY). This K channel improves contrast and shadow detail and reduces ink coverage but does not add any colors. This CMYK image file is used for printing and is 33 percent larger than the equivalent RGB file, and 32 times larger than a similar 1bit image. File size = 8.8MB at 300dpi

▼ Figure 9.10 Pixel Depth Of Images

Electronic images can be divided into three basic categories: B&W, grayscale, and color. B&W images only require 1 bit per pixel for creation and display. Grayscale images require 8 bits per pixel to display 256 shades of gray. Color images require either 24 or 32 bits per pixel depending upon whether they are RGB or CMYK images. File size, storage space, and RIPing time increase as pixel depth increases. You will find a color version of this figure in the color plate section in the center of the book (see C-4).

Photoshop 3.0
Photoshop 2.0
Amiga IFF
BMP
CompuServe GIF
✓ EPS
Filmstrip
JPEG
MacPaint
PCX
PICT File
PICT Resource
Pixar
PixelPaint
Raw
Scitex CT
Targa
TIFF

▼ *Fig. 9.11: Graphic File Formats*
Shown here is a list of the graphic file formats in which an image can be saved. Although there are only two basic kinds of images, pixel and vector, there are numerous different file formats in which these two image types can be saved. The file formats have been devised to suit specific purposes. TIFF and EPS are formats in which images should be saved for print, while GIF and JPEG should be used for the internet. The top two formats Photoshop 2.0 and 3.0 are the native file formats for Photoshop which allow you to retain full editing functions such as layers and transparent backgrounds.

images, one for each of the process colors, plus a separate low resolution composite file which can be distributed as a separate file and imported for use in a page layout file. Figure 9.8 shows the EPS preview dialog box where you instruct Photoshop as to what kind of an EPS file you would like to create. Note the pull-down menu section for DCS file creation. This option will only appear when you are saving CMYK files, as the DCS format is designed specifically for use with color separated files. The advantage of the DCS format over the single file EPS is that with the single file EPS the entire image must be sent four times to a RIP to be imaged because the color separation information for all four colors are contained in the EPS which, because of its encapsulated nature, cannot be segmented on the fly during printing. After the creation of the five-file DCS, each high resolution color file can be sent separately, which reduces printing time by as much as 75 percent. The other advantage to the DCS format is that the fifth, low resolution file can be used separately for inclusion in a page layout file, thereby reducing the network and storage space overhead associated with working with the entire composite file. When a document using DCS images is RIPed, the low resolution composite image is merged back with the four high resolution separation files which are then sent to the RIP for processing. If you are ever sent a low resolution DCS composite file, do not rename this file, as its name will be used to remerge this low resolution image with its high resolution cousins at the printing location (see Figure 9.9 for a file view of a set of DCS files).

JPEG

JPEG format is a compressed file format used to reduce the storage file size of an image. Compressed file formats like JPEG should primarily be used for archiving, transportation, or telecommunication purposes. The use of JPEG images in print production should be avoided because decompression of files takes time. More details of JPEG are discussed later in this chapter under the section on compression.

Native formats

Most graphics applications have their own proprietary format(s) which may be used during file creation. For instance, you may want to work in Photoshop's proprietary format for performing extensive image editing chores (the Photoshop format is smaller and more flexible than TIFF or EPS). Application-specific file formats often allow you to work in layers, channels, and with transparent backgrounds. Examples of other application specific file formats include RIFF

(Raster Image File Format) for Painter files, and IVUE (Image View) format for LivePicture. After you are done constructing and editing your images, most applications allow you to save files in either TIFF or EPS as well as their own format. In general, you will want to send TIFFs and EPSs files to your printer or service bureau, rather than, or in addition to, the application-specific files. Send the application-specific files along if you think the printing company may need or want to edit your file.

PhotoCD (PCD)

The PhotoCD format is a special, very flexible, multiresolution, CIE color space compressed bitmapped file format developed by Kodak for saving scanned images. PCD format was originally a proprietary format which could only be created on a Kodak Photo Imaging Workstation (PIW). PCD format can now be created using PCD creation software such as BuildIt. Be careful to distinguish between digital photos on CD, which can be photos of any format which happen to be stored on a CD (compact disk), and PhotoCD which is a specific file format. More details about the PhotoCD format are contained near the end of Chapter 12, "Taming Your Scanner."

PICT, PCX, WMF, and others

PICT, PCX, BMP, and WMF file formats are commonly found on DTP systems. These file formats produce files which are often significantly smaller than TIFF and EPS files, so they are seductive. But resist the use of these files for Postscript printing. These files are made for screen viewing (PICT, PCX, and WMF) or for printing (BMP and PCX) on non-Postscript printers. If you have an image in a file format other than TIFF or EPS and you are having trouble converting it, try opening it in Photoshop first and saving it as a TIFF or EPS out of Photoshop. If Photoshop won't open the image, try one of the dedicated file conversion utilities like Debabelizer; these will nearly always work.

Right format for the right use

There is truly an alphabet soup of file formats in the world of electronic publishing, and there are more created every day. There are formats for multimedia, digital video, music, sound, and the Internet. For final images intended to be processed through a Postscript imagesetter, your choices should nearly always be TIFF or EPS. Ask you printing company which versions of the two formats they recommend and/or prefer before you send in your files.

File format vs. file size

When you convert an image from one file format into another, the file size will often change. Converting one bit TIFF files to EPS vector files will almost always significantly lower the file size of the image because you are often converting hundreds of thousands or millions of pixels to a few vector paths. Converting a multibit contone image into a contone EPS in Photoshop usually results in the opposite effect – the files size will grow significantly, because you are adding an EPS portion to the image rather than converting pixel data. Figure 9.9 contains some examples of an image which has been saved in various file formats. If you know what is happening to your image during a file format conversion, you will generally be able to predict a significant size change will occur as well. The compression of an image, such as saving in JPEG format, will dramatically reduce the disk storage size of the image, but when you open the image it will generally decompress back to a larger size. The amount of difference between the disk saved file and the open file will be determined by the amount or ratio of compression.

Cross platform file exchange

The two most common computer platforms used in Desktop publishing are Macintoshes and Intel-based machines operating under a Microsoft Windows operating system, so we will restrict our discussion to these two platforms. The good news is that Macintosh and Windows applications both support TIFF and EPS file formats. The bad news is that the two systems organize the data in these two formats slightly differently, so applications on one platform will not readily read file formats from the other. But there is more good news—applications on both platforms generally allow you to save TIFF and EPS in either format. So all you have to do is pay attention when you save your files. In Photoshop, for instance, when you save a TIFF file it will ask you if you want to save your image in Mac or PC format; choose the one you need (see Fig. 9.19.) If you are sending your file to a service bureau who uses a different platform than you do, you may want to save a separate set of images in their format and send those along with your files. So find out which platform your printing company or service bureau uses, and be sure to discuss all cross platform image transfers with your printer or service bureau before you send your files. If you are having troubles getting EPS files to transfer for one platform to another, try saving your drawing files in Illustrator 1.0 or 1.1 format, transport them to the other platform, and then create the EPS on the other platform.

File naming system

One of the least glamorous but potentially the most time and frustration-saving habit you can acquire, is to adopt a good file naming system and use it consistently. A good file naming system can save you hours of time when you are trying to find an image. This is particularly true if, like me, you tend to save several versions of a file. A complete graphic file name should include: item name, pixel depth, resolution, and file format. An example would be Trees CMYK 200.tiff. This type of attention to detail in file naming, while perhaps a bit cumbersome, will make your file management and finding chores much easier. In addition, it will make it easier for your printing company to identify your graphic images. I also use this file naming scheme to help me remember to change my non-print file format to printable ones. The most common example is reminders to change my PICT screen grabs to TIFFs before I send my image out for printing (see Figure 9.8 for some file naming examples).

Pixel depth

Various images require different amounts of information in order to create, view, and print those images. In electronic images, this information is referred to as pixel depth. Pixel depth is a measure of the number of bits of digital information per image pixel required to completely render that image for its final use. For instance, a black and white line art image only requires one (1) bit of information per pixel in order to completely create, display, and print that image. Only one bit per pixel (1 b/p) is required because any individual pixel only needs to represent either black or white, which can be done by assigning that pixel a value of either 0 for black or 1 for white. This is why black and white images are called 1-bit images.

Grayscale images, on the other hand, need to be able to store 256 tonal variations or shades in every pixel. This requires eight (8) bits of data, or 2^8, per pixel in order to completely represent one of the possible 256 shades of gray in each pixel. Since grayscale image pixels hold eight times (8x) as many bits per pixel as a one bit (1 bit) black and white image, 8 b/p grayscale images will have eight times larger file sizes as 1 b/p black and white of the same size and resolution.

Color images require even more information to represent them than grayscale images. Because your computer is digital, that is, it only understands two values, 0 and 1, your computer can't really capture, manipulate, and store true color data. All color data is actually stored as groups of grayscale information called channels. Your computer produces grayscale information to which color is applied when the information leaves the computer, most commonly to a monitor, color printer, or printing press. The grayscale channel information is converted into color by activating color phosphors on your monitor's screen. During the printing process, color inks and dyes are applied to grayscale channel information in order to produce final color images. Because your computer is truly only a black and white device, it is useful to think of your color images as collections of grayscale channels.

In electronic publishing we typically work with two kinds of color images: RGB (Red, Green, and Blue) and CMYK (Cyan, Magenta, Yellow, and Black) images. RGB images and files are used to display color images on monitors and print onto color film, while CMYK images and files are used for reproduction of color images in most printing applications (see Chapter 14, "Color Me Right," for a more complete discussion of these two color spaces). RGB images require the creation of three eight bit per pixel (8 b/p) grayscale channels, one for each color, R,G, and B. Since each pixel has eight bits of information for each of three colors, this requires that each pixel have a total of 24 bits of data for each pixel. This means that each RGB image contains three times (3x) as much data per pixel as a grayscale image, and twenty four times (24x) as much information per pixel as a 1 bit black and white image. This of course also means that RGB images will be eight times larger than grayscale and twenty four times larger than black and white images of the same dimensions and resolution. This also means that RGB images will require that much more RAM to open, disk space to store, and RIP time for processing. In RGB color images, each 8 b/p channel has the capacity to store a total of 256 shades of that color, so that there are 256 shades each of red, green, and blue. This means that when we multiply these three channels of 256 shades each together, we can have 256(R) X 256(G) X 256(B) = 16.7 million total possible color combinations.

CYMK images are treated very much like RGB images, with the difference being that there are four 8 b/p grayscale channels instead of only three. During the preparation of an RGB screen image file to a printable format, the RGB colors are converted into the closest CMYK equivalents available. Black, or K, is then substituted for various percentages of C, M, and Y in order to improve contrast and detail, as well as reduce total ink density. This black substitution is accomplished using one of two substitution processes, Under Color Removal (UCR) or Gray Component Replacement (GCR). UCR generally replaces CMY in neutral shadow regions, while UCR replaces neutral CMY values throughout a broader tonal range of the image. Because CMYK files have a fourth 8 b/p grayscale channel, these files are 33 percent larger than their RGB equivalents (see Figure 9.8 for an overview of pixel depth).

Working with graphics

Bitmapped TIFF graphics

As we have mentioned, TIFF is the preferred file format for bitmapped graphics which will be processed by a Postscript RIP and printed. The primary file preparation issue, besides image quality, with TIFF images is file size. Bitmapped images, and particularly multibit per pixel images, can become huge files. The three variables affected are image dimension (e.g., 5"x7"), pixel depth (e.g., 1, 8, 24, 32 bits/pixel), and resolution. Image dimension and pixel depth are generally determined by the document design and are therefore set. Resolution is therefore the one variable which can be altered to control the file size of an image. For multibit contone images, a good rule of thumb is generally not to exceed a resolution which is greater than two times (2X) the line screen at which the image will be printed. For instance, if an image will be printed at 150 lpi, then your image need not be greater than 300 dpi for a gray scale or color contone image. In most instances, even lower resolutions (1.25–1.5 X lpi) will actually suffice, but at least use the 2X lpi rule as an upper limit. One bit bitmapped line art images generally need to be created and saved at high resolutions (600 dpi+) due to their dependence on edge sharpness for image quality (see Chapter 12, "Taming Your Scanner," for a complete discussion of image resolution and line screen).

▼ *Figure 9.12 Photoshop TIFF Option*

When saving a TIFF, you have the option of saving it in Mac or IBM (Windows) format. If you work cross platform, choose the IBM platform. There is also an LSW compression option. This should be left unchecked for files used in printing.

Vector EPS graphics

As previously noted, the EPS is the preferred file format for outline/vector graphics which will be printed. Because of the outline rather than bitmap composition, EPS graphic images are inherently more difficult to rasterize or RIP. With bitmapped TIFFs we are converting pixels to other dots in the RIPing process, but with EPS graphics we must convert lines to dots, which is a more demanding task. There are three factors which control the ripability of an EPS graphic. They are path length, number of control points, and flatness ratio. Path length is measured from the start to the end of any closed path. A Postscript RIP must process an entire path, so the longer a path is, the more difficult it is to process. The number of control points along a path determines how complex the path is. The more control points there are, the greater a path's complexity and the more difficult it is to RIP.

▼ Figure 9.13 Simple Line Art
This simple 1 bit graphic is an excellent candidate for outlining. It is simple with large areas of black and white which will create only a few (4) short, simple paths. This outline form of this graphic was created in two steps:
1) Scanned at 600 dpi and saved as a TIFF with a file size = 250KB.
2) Outlined in Streamline and saved as an EPS EPS/outline file size = 50KB.
Note the dramatic 80 percent savings in file size.

▼ Figure 9.14 Intermediate Complexity Line Art
This graphic is more complex but still very convertible to paths. Many more paths (41) are created, but all the paths are relatively short and not very complex. This image was scanned at 600 dpi and saved as a 200KB TIFF. It was outlined and centerlined in Streamline, and saved as a 40KB EPS file which equals an 80 percent reduction in file size. Fine lines such as those that divide the sections of the butterfly's wings have been centerlined instead of outlined to preserve their delicacy.

▼ Figure 9.15 Complex Line art
This complex graphic creates a series of long complex paths when outlined. This image was originally scanned at 550 dpi and saved as a 200KB TIFF. It was outlined and centerlined in Streamline, and saved as a 60KB EPS file size which equals a 90 percent reduction in file size. The length, number, and complexity of the paths may offset any file size advantage in terms of RIP time. This image could cause RIPing problems. Care must be taken to split and simplify these paths, and increase flatness ratio of these lines prior to RIPing.

▼ Figure 9.16 High Detail Line Art
This highly complex graphic is an example of a poor outlining candidate. In addition to destroying the fine dot details, outlining this image makes a far too complex outline graphic. While the files size savings is moderate, Original Tiff = 242K, Outline = 100K, or 60 percent of the original size, the number and complexity of the paths definitely offsets any file size advantage in terms of RIP time. It took me 15 minutes just to outline this file and I never could get it through a RIP. This kind of file is much better left as a TIFF both for image quality and RIPing purposes.

▼ Figure 9.17 Complex Line Art
This is a complex line art graphic which has been saved as an EPS file. This graphic will benefit from the conversion from bitmap to outline format. The EPS format is smaller in file size than a TIFF file, and much easier to scale due to the line vs. bitmap construction of the image.

▼ Figure 9.18 Complex Paths
While converting this image into an outline image has advantages in file size and editability, this process also creates a fairly complex outline with long paths and many control points. After conversion, this image should be opened in a drawing application and have its long paths split and simplified, and flatness set to 2 or 3 to improve its RIPability.

Digital computers only "understand" straight lines. They do not understand curves, so all curved lines must be constructed out of progressive sequences of straight lines. Flatness ratio controls the number of line segments which will be used to construct a curved line. Flatness ratios generally vary from 1 to 10. A flatness ratio of 0 will require that a RIP create a large number of line segments to construct a curve, while a ratio of 10 will require very few lines. Both extremes are to be avoided.

Controlling path lengths, number of control points, and flatness ratios is important for all outline files. This includes EPS graphics created in drawing applications like Freehand, Illustrator, and CorelDraw; outlining applications such as Streamline; and clipping-type outline paths created in applications like Photoshop. Generally speaking, you will want to minimize all three variables as much as possible without adversely affecting the image quality. Path lengths should be split to reduce their length. The number of control points should be reduced by either manually removing them or through filters such as the simplification filter found in Freehand. The optimum flatness ratio depends upon the path characteristics, the printing resolution, and the RIP being used. However, a good rule of thumb is to assign flatness ratios of between two and five (2–5). Below is a list of some common EPS guidelines (see Chapter 15, "Application-Specific Tips," for more details. Also see Chapter 19, "Managing The Mess," for some specific EPS file prep procedures)

EPS file preparation guidelines:

❧ Simplify all path lengths prior to export of EPS from drawing applications.

❧ Split all paths prior to exporting EPS graphics from drawing applications.

❧ Set flatness ratio for paths between 2–5 for all exported EPS graphics.

❧ Simplify paths of outline graphics which have been created through an outline application.

❧ Set "Tolerance" preference to "Loose" prior to outlining a graphic in an outlining application such as Streamline.

❧ When creating paths from selections in Photoshop, and particularly if those selections have been defined through the use of the Magic Wand tool, be sure to set as high a tolerance as possible, usually greater than 1 when creating the path. This will reduce the number of control nodes which will be created when the path is drawn. I usually err on the side of simplicity and then fine tune the curves with the pen tool.

▼ Figure 9.19 Tight Fit Conversion
This image shows the results of setting the conversion preferences in Streamline to "TIGHT" during conversion to an outline from a bitmap As a result, these paths have many more control points than the image shown in Figure 9.20 below. Each extra control point demands more processing time at the RIP.

▼ Figure 9.20 Loose Fit Conversion
This image shows the results when setting the conversion preferences in Streamline to "LOOSE." These paths have far fewer points than the image shown in Figure 9.19 above. This image, with its fewer control points, will be much easier to RIP.

❥ When creating a clipping path from a path, always set the flatness to greater than 1, usually between 3 and 5 to reduce the number of individual vectors or straight lines which will be used to recreated curved lines.

Outlining graphics

Consider converting original TIFF files of scanned 1-bit line art graphics (logos for example) to outlined EPS files using an outlining application such as Streamline. Original images should be of high quality and scanned at high resolution to avoid jagged edges. Outlining can save 50–90 percent on file size. Outlining an image will allow you to scale, rotate, and skew images without any loss of resolution. Spot/Pantone color original images should generally be scanned as black & white images, converted to outline EPS files, and have the color built within a drawing program. This approach will net you smaller, more editable and color correct files. Don't use PICT files for printed material. These are mainly for on-screen, video, and multimedia creations.

While outlining is often a good idea for simple and intermediate complexity line art images, there are some potential problems to be aware of. Outlining may create paths which are very long and complex, which make them more difficult to RIP. There are several procedures you can follow to help eliminate or reduce these characteristics. It is generally a good idea to set the "FIT" preference to "LOOSE" in an outlining application like Streamline, as tighter settings tend to create paths which are too complex. Also consider running your outlined graphic through a drawing application like Freehand or CorelDraw so that you can simplify and split the paths, and set the best flatness ratios (see Figures 9.13 – 9.16 for examples of various line art images which lend themselves in various degrees to outlining). There are some images, such as that shown in Figure 9.16, which should never be converted to outlines, but should be left as bitmapped images (see Chapter 12, "Taming Your Scanner," for a complete discussion of evaluating a graphic image for outlining. Also, see Chapter 15, "Application-Specific Tips" for examples of applications such as Freehand and Streamline). All the above tips for reducing the complexity of vector based images through control of the number of control points and flatness ratios are important tools in our struggle to REDUCE & SIMPLIFY!

Blends

Always use blends, fills, and patterns judiciously. One problem which commonly occurs when creating blends is banding. Banding occurs most frequently in long blends containing a wide gray scale spectrum. Banding is caused by the Postscript limitation of 256 gray scale steps. When working with blends, choose the minimum number of steps necessary to create a smooth blend. Use a formula or a utility like Blender. Smooth, band-free blends, and especially large ones, are best created in bitmap-oriented applications like PhotoShop, rather than in object-oriented drawing programs like Freehand or CorelDraw. Unlike drawing applications, in bitmap-oriented applications, where you will create a blend between the foreground and background layers, you can redistribute pixels. The banding problem can be overcoming applications like Photoshop if you apply 3-4 units of Gaussian blur or dither the blend which redistributes pixels across blend borders. The Gaussian blur mainly affects midtones. This is an especially effective technique for blending large areas.

Imported or placed graphics

Graphic files are imported into page layout applications as low resolution versions unless they are imbedded. (This is why your Quark or Pagemaker documents are not as large as they they would be if they included the entire hi-res file.). The layout application links the low resolution placed image to the external high resolution graphic file for printing. Do not change a graphic file's name after importing the graphic into another application because the links are maintained through name recognition. The importing (page layout) application will not be able to find and link to the renamed file. If you make a change to the graphic which you have imported into a page layout application, and you are not using publish and subscribe capabilities, be sure to update your screen view in the page layout application. If you do not do so, you may be surprised at what you get when you print out the document.

Precropped, scaled, and rotated TIFF and EPS graphics print faster than those cropped, scaled, and rotated within a layout program. During the image creation process, plan to precrop, rotate, and scale the original or scanned image to the exact size you will ultimately need for printing. Doing so, particularly for graphic-intensive documents like catalogs, will save you hours of manipulation and RIPing time during the document construction and printing processes. If you are unsure of what the final crop and size will be, use your layout program as a design and iteration tool, but perform final graphic manipulations on the high resolution images in the original graphic applications prior to printing. Remember that images placed in page layout applications are only low resolution proxies for the high resolution images which are external to the layout document (see Chapter 13, "Document Construction," for a review of this concept). When a placed image is cropped, rotated, or resized in a page layout document, only the low resolution proxy is being manipulated. If you do not perform the final manipulations to the high resolution files, these changes will need to be processed "on-the-fly" during the RIPing process, which will dramatically increase processing times. This precropping, rotating, and resizing of images is particularly crucial with graphic-intensive documents such as catalogs where "on-the-fly" processing of hundreds of images can lead to unacceptably long RIPing times.

One other issue to be addressed is the imbedding of high resolution graphics in page layout documents. Some applications such as Pagemaker give you the option of including (imbedding) the high resolution version of a placed graphic image, as well as the low resolution proxy, which is always included. In most circumstances, it is better to *NOT* include the high resolution of a placed graphic. Imbedding the high resolution versions of placed graphics files will significantly increase the file size of the page layout document, making it more difficult to manage. Imbedding also makes editing and updating the graphic image much more difficult. It is better to keep the high resolution versions of your graphic images as separate files which will be sent along with the page layout document file.

Avoiding nesting graphics

Postscripts RIPs have a difficult time finding graphics files which have been placed one-inside-the-other. Avoid nesting graphics such as "PLACING" one EPS graphic into a drawing application document and then constructing additional graphic elements around it. Always "OPEN" a previously created EPS so that it is editable, then you can add additional graphic elements to the same file without creating a nested file. It is also dangerous to create EPS files out of a document which already contains EPS or TIFF files, such as a page layout document.

Type (fonts), which are just special kinds of graphic files set in an exported EPS file as editable text, may not be found by a RIP, or the entire file may not print at all! It is always best to limit the amount of type which you set in a graphic file which you know will be exported as an EPS file. Any type which is created in the outline graphic should be converted to paths prior to exporting it as an EPS file.

Some miscellaneous graphical do's and don'ts

Logo sheets with several (6 or more) logos on them will print fastest from the programs in which they were created; for example, Freehand or Illustrator. Imported logo graphics will generally print but will take longer and cost more money at the service bureau. Cut paths in drawn (object-oriented) graphics. Keep auto-trace paths as simple as possible.

Don't use "Hairline" widths for lines: always assign a specific value to a line's width. Hairline values are inconsistent from one application to another and many are too thin to print properly at high resolution. Don't assign line values below 0.25 pt., as they will often not print properly at high resolution.

Use graphics boxes instead of text boxes to create borders. Don't specify hairline rules or lines for files to be printed on an imagesetter, they may disappear. Specify a specific line weight, e.g., 0.5 or 0.25. Don't assign dot percentage on a small line. For files to be printed on an imagesetter, don't use an outlined Zapf Dingbats "n" to specify a check box (□); its outline stroke is too thin. Instead, use another font's box or try the Zapf Dingbat "o"(❏).

Feeling compressed

What is compression?

Compression is the reduction in the size of a file by reducing, through the use of shortcut data recording methods, the space required for storing the information contained in a file. Compressing a file is somewhat like squeezing a sponge. You can squeeze a sponge in your hand to 1/10th of its original size, but all the sponge information is still there, it's just in a more compact form. When you release your grip on the sponge, you decompress the sponge, and the sponge reassumes its original form. The sponge had a built-in memory of its original size and shape. This is similar to what happens with the compression of digital files. Some type of digital file compression retains all of the original information, like our sponge, and some do not.

Need for compression

As we have seen in this chapter and in Chapter 8, "Resolving Resolution," graphic files can take up huge volumes of digital space. Graphic file pages are hundreds to thousands of times the size of pages filled with text alone. A standard 8.5" x 11" page filled margin

▼ *Figure 9.21 Compression Scheme*

One technique used by nearly all compression schemes is to record and then remove redundant pixels when the file is compressed. The compression of a black line shows how this works. The black line above may require 2,500 black pixels stacked end to end, like the pixels in the expanded view, to construct it. This would require 2,500 bits of file space to record. We will use a redundant pixel record and remove compression technique to compress this 2,500 pixel line segment above. The first pixel is located and stored in the file. The compression software will note that the next 2,499 pixels are the same, but instead of recording each pixel, the software makes a notation like [+2499] which indicates that the next 2499 pixels are identical to the first black one. In this example, the compressed version of the file requires 56 bits of space for the notation (7 ASCII characters x 8 bits/pixel), plus one bit for the original black pixel, for a total of 57 bits of information. Compared to the 2,500 bits required to store the uncompressed version of the file, the compressed version achieves a 44/1 compression ratio with a reduction of 97 percent file size .

to margin with 12 point type requires a mere 5KB (kilobytes) of storage space. An 8.5"x 11," 300 dpi, 1 bit (bitonal, B&W) graphic takes up 1.05MB (Megabytes) of space, two hundred times (200x) the room required for the text only page. That same page at 600 dpi requires 4.2MB of space or eight hundred times (800x) the size of the text only page. And that same page created as a 32 bit/pixel CMYK image @ 600 dpi demands 135 MB of room, which is over twenty five thousand times (25,000x) the room required by the text only page!

As file sizes grow, so does the need for RAM space to work on those images, storage space to physically store and transport those images, and time to process those images. And sending these huge graphic images around our local area networks (LANs) and wide area telecommunications networks (WANs) becomes a daunting task indeed. The mushrooming image demands of digital video and multimedia are also driving the development of compression technologies. The practical storage and transportation of large graphic files has required the development and use of increasingly sophisticated compression schemes which provide continually improving decompressed image quality with increasing amounts of compression.

▼ Figure 9.22 Uncompressed Image

Shown here is an uncompressed 200dpi Photoshop image saved as a Tiff with a file size of 320K. Compare this with the image below, saved with JPEG compression with a file size of 64K.

Do you see any differences?

▼ Figure 9.23 JPEG Compressed Image

Shown here is the same 200 dpi Photoshop image shown in Figure 9.22 above, but this file has been saved with maximum JPEG compression out of Photoshop. The 64K file size represents a 5/1 compression ratio. Compare this with the image above which has been saved without JPEG compression. As you can see, even with maximum compression, the image quality is still very high. The differences between these two images is very subtle.

How compression works

There are many different varieties of compression schemes and some are quite ingenious and sophisticated, such as the nifty Huffman compression used in PhotoCD. One common routine used by most compression schemes is the removal of redundant information. Most images have large numbers of pixels which have the same, that is, redundant, values. When a file is compressed, instead of recording each identical pixel in a graphic format, shortcut notations can be made about the presence of these redundant pixels instead of actually storing the pixels. These shortcut notations require far less space to record than the actual pixel data. An example may help here. Redundant pixel compression of a long straight black line, like the one shown in Figure 9.17, will illustrate how this type of compression works.

The more redundant pixels an image has, the easier it is to achieve large high quality compression files. In general, bitonal or black and white images are easier to compress than contone images because, with only two tone values, they have greater numbers of identical or redundant pixels.

Types of compression

There are basically two compression technologies: lossless and lossy. With lossless compression technologies, an image does not loose any information during the compression/decompression process. Lossless compression generally does not provide greater than fifty percent (50%), that is, 2/1, compression. With lossy compression we can routinely expect to achieve from 90 to 98 percent (10/1 to 40/1) image compression. With this much compression we nearly always witness some loss of information as well. As a rule, the more an image is compressed beyond 50 percent, the more information we can expect to lose.

Lossy compression is required if we are to achieve significant amounts of file size and therefore processing, space, and transmission time reductions. Our 135MB CMYK file would only be reduced to 67.2MB with a 50 percent, 2/1 lossless compression. And while this will halve our storage space and transmission time demands, it is not enough. A 67MB file is still a monster. Conversely, a 40/1 compression of our 135MB file yields a 3.3MB file which is exceedingly more manageable in all aspects.

▼ Figure 9.24 JPEG Options
When using JPEG compression technology, you have the choice of saving your image in a variety of resolutions. Shown here is the JPEG Options dialog box from Photoshop. Here you choose "Image Quality." Maximum Image quality will provide you with the least amount of compression (2/1) while "Low" will provide the maximum amount of compression (40/1).

Compression formats

Compression file formats are proliferating like rabbits. Entire volumes are now being written and rewritten on compression file formats. We are also at a time when there is a great deal of confusion and disagreement about compression file format standards. Luckily, in the print arena, we have had a standard for some time, JPEG. JPEG is an acronym for Joint Photographic Experts Group. JPEG was developed by a group of industry experts (meeting clandestinely in the steamy, sulfurous atmosphere on Io, a moon of Jupiter) as a way of setting a high quality, predictable compression standard which all could use. There are both lossless and lossy versions of JPEG. But, as we have discussed, Lossy compression is required in order to achieve significant file size reduction. Other compression schemes like Quicktime are used for digital video and multimedia files. & MPEG.

Working with compressed files

If you need to compress image files to free up storage space or facilitate transmission over networks (local or wide area), be sure to be aware of whether the compression is lossless or lossy. If your compression is lossy, make sure you choose a compression ratio which does not degrade your image too much. Remember that some compression applications will allow you to selectively compress various portions of your image by varying amounts. Also, if you intend to send your compressed files to someone else, be sure that the receiving party has the ability to decompress your images. Many compression applications provide decompression utilities which you are free to send along with your compressed files. Using JPEG compression is generally a safe bet because most major applications like Photoshop, QuarkXpress, and PageMaker support direct access to JPEG compressed files.

Compare and contrast the images in Figures 9.22 and 9.23. The first image is a 200 dpi Photoshop image which has been saved as a Tiff file with no compression. The second file is the same image saved as a JPEG file out of Photoshop with maximum compression. The file size for the first, uncompressed image is 320K, while the JPEG compressed image is only 64K. This represents a 5/1 compression, which is only moderate compression, with a fivefold decrease in file size. As you can see, the differences between these two images is very subtle. Generally, JPEG compression ratios of 5/1 to 10/1 produce very good quality images which are difficult to distinguish from the original images. Other images with larger starting file sizes saved with maximum compression out of Photoshop may show greater ratios and more noticeable differences. There is one rule of thumb which you should try to follow: Avoid compressing a graphic file more than once. My general modus operandi is that while an image is in print production, I keep it in an uncompressed format like TIFF or EPS. When I am ready to archive an image or send it via modem or I am preparing it for viewing on the Internet, then I will compress it.

PAULINE'S FILE PREP TIPS

File Prep Hint #16

There are two basic types of electronic graphic images, bitmapped/raster images which are constructed out of pixels, and vector/outline images which are constructed out of lines. Choose the type of image which best suits your needs. Vector images are preferred for simple line art which needs to be rendered with sharp edges. Vector based images have the benefit of scalability without alteration of their resolution. The raster basis for an image is preferred when great detail is present such as in complex line art and contone images.

File Prep Hint #17

Match graphic file format with end use. TIFF and EPS are the preferred file formats for use in Postscript printing. Use TIFF format for high detail and continuous tone images. Use EPS format for low detail images and for scalability or for contone images which have additional information stored with them such as clipping paths and transfer function data. Do Not use PICT or PCX files for print pieces. These are screen format files. Stick to using EPS and TIFF file formats whenever possible for files to be printed.

PAULINE'S FILE PREP TIPS

File Prep Hint #18

Outline simple, low detail, one-bit line art TIFFs to create outline graphics in EPS format graphics. EPSs have smaller file sizes and are resolution-independent scalable images. Use EPS file format to reduce file size and improve editability (especially scaling and skewing) of line art files. Use dedicated outlining applications, such as Adobe Streamline, to accomplish this task; your control and results will be better than using the built-in outlining capabilities of your drawing application.

File Prep Hint #19

Create blends in bitmapped editing applications like Photoshop instead of in vector-based drawing or page layout applications. You will have more control over your blends and they will print faster and better. A pixel-based application like Photoshop allows you to add noise to your blends which helps reduce banding upon output.

File Prep Hint #20

Choose the proper pixel depth of your image depending upon how it will be used. Remember, increasing pixel depth increases file size. Use 1 bit for line art images, 8 bit for gray scale images, and 32 bit for process color images.

PAULINE'S FILE PREP TIPS

File Prep Hint #21

Vector-based (EPS) images are inherently more difficult to RIP than pixel-based (TIFF)images. Vector-based EPS files need to be specially prepared. Simplify (reduce the number of control points), split long or complex paths, and set "Flatness" ratio for paths between 2 and 5 prior to creation of an EPS file. Attention to these three variables will make your vector-based images much easier to RIP.

File Prep Hint #22

Exercise care when creating outline paths. When creating an outline in applications like Streamline, set "Fit Tolerance" preference to "Loose" prior to conversion to assure a simpler file with fewer nodes. This will make it easier for a Postscript RIP to process the paths created.

File Prep Hint #23

When converting paths from selections in Photoshop, be sure to choose a tolerance which results in a few number of path control points, usually ≥ 2. Also, when converting a path to a clipping path in Photoshop, select a flatness ratio ≥ 3; this will reduce the number of line segments used when the path is drawn during printing. This is similar to what we discussed in File Prep Hints 18 and 19, and will help simplify the vector-based portion of these primarily contone images for easier RIPing!

PAULINE'S FILE PREP TIPS

File Prep Hint #24

Do not assign "Hairline" widths for lines; they are inconsistent and usually too thin. Always assign a specific, unambiguous, thickness value to a line. Do not assign any line thickness values less than 0.25 points.

File Prep Hint #25

Do not assign patterns or grayscale values to thin lines (≤4pts), as these patterns or values will be rendered as halftone dots during RIPing and printing and will be displayed as discontinuous blotches on paper.

File Prep Hint #26

Find out in which file formats your printer or service bureau prefers to receive your files. While TIFF and EPS are certainly the universal formats, there are often several choices for saving a file within these two general formats. For instance, 1 bit line art images can be saved as TIFFs or converted to vector-based EPSs. Color contone images are perhaps the most variable. Find out if you should send in your file as a CMYK TIFF or a 5-file DCS. You should avoid creating single file CMYK EPS files as these are very time consuming to RIP.

PAULINE'S FILE PREP TIPS

File Prep Hint #27

If your printing company or service bureau performs scans for you or otherwise creates original graphics, be sure that when they send the file back to you that you know if it is a high or low resolution version of the graphic. If you intend to edit, correct, or otherwise perform pixel level alterations of the image, be sure you receive the high resolution version, as the low resolution version is useless for this purpose. A low resolution version will only be useful for placement purposes. In either case, and particularly if you receive a low resolution FPO (for placement only) image, do not change the name in any way. If the printing company has sent you a low resolution image, they have the high resolution image (which will be used during the the actual RIPing) stored on their drive. If you change the name your FPO image will not be recognized as a match for the high resolution print version when you return the image, and a low quality image will result during printing.

File Prep Hint #28

If you compress your file, generally choose the JPEG format, as it results in little image degradation. Be aware of the image degradation which will occur when you compress an image. Always save JPEG images which you may need later for print in the best or Maximum Quality mode. A 5/1 to 10/1 compression with JPEG is generally fine. PhotoCD is another useful compression format, although it is less "open" and more proprietary that JPEG.

10
RIPing Up Your Files

As the Byte Turns continues…

*Will Danny's plans to get together with Pauline have a chance,
or will Pauline RIP his plans to shreds?*

My file printed fine on my 300 dpi laser. What's wrong with you and your equipment???

*Well, ah,
I don't know???*

*We can't have
Danny upset !!*

*Can't we
make his file
print???*

What do you think I am, a Magician?!! To process these files at high resolution requires millions of more calculations than his 300 dpi laser!

THE POSTSCRIPT RIP

The generation of dots

What is a RIP anyway? The word RIP is not really a word at all but an acronym, or shortcut, for Raster Image Processor. Now this sounds like a complex, intimidating term but in reality the basic concept of the RIP is quite simple. Let's break the phrase down into its components. First of all, a Raster is just a fancy word for dot or line of dots. Image is self explanatory. Processor is a device which alters the characteristics of something or changes one thing into another. Now let's read the phrase backward. Processor Image Raster, or more simply – A RIP Processes Images Into Dots.

Every element on a page which is sent to a RIP is converted into dots. That is, all page geometry, text, line art, and contone graphics are converted into dots. This is the sole function of a RIP. While there are certain advantages to working with some graphic images which are constructed out of lines (EPS line art and printer fonts) and others out of dots (contone tiffs and screen fonts) while we manipulate them on the computer, all of these elements must ultimately be converted into dots when we want to print them.

▼ *Figure 10.1 Postscript Laser Printer*
Desktop laser printers such as this Apple LaserWriter have a Postscript RIP, or interpreter, built onto an internal board which is built into their cases. The print engine itself would not work without this built-in RIP.
Desktop laser printers have resolutions ranging from 300 dpi to as high as 1200 dpi. Laser printers generally produce lower resolution images than imagesetters and therefore produce far fewer dots which require far less data processing by the RIP.

Postscript printers and RIPs

Nearly all printers which are used in electronic publishing systems work in tandem with a RIP. Page information created on a computer is properly formatted and sent to the RIP. The RIP then rasterizes (makes dots out of) the information which the printer then images onto a piece of film or paper. The printer itself is merely the dot generation, or imaging, instrument. It is the RIP's job to translate all of the page information coming from the computer, which does all of the heavy work. While there are a wide variety of RIPs and associated printers, the vast majority of printers which are used with current open electronic publishing systems are Postscript printers. This means that these printers are matched with and connected to RIPs which "understand" or can interpret and process Postscript code into patterns of dots. Postscript RIPs are often called Postscript Interpreters because they interpret Postscript code into patterns of dots which the printer hardware can work with. Whether you are printing to a 300 dpi laser printer or a 5000 dpi imagesetter, a RIP is used to translate or interpret the information you create on your computer into a pattern of dots which the printer places on a sheet of film or paper.

▼ *Figure 10.2 Postscript Imagesetter*
Postscript imagesetters such as this Linotronic 3060 are high resolution cousins of laser printers. Imagesetters usually have RIPs which are separate from the actual imaging unit. The RIP may be a hardware version with its own RAM, CPU, and storage space, or software which operates on a separate computer station and utilizes the RAM, CPU, and storage capacity of the computer.
Imagesetters range in resolution from 1200 dpi to 6000 dpi. High resolutions require RIPs to generate from 16x to 200x the number of image dots generated by 300 dpi laser printers. This large number of dots means longer and more complex RIPing.

There are two kinds of RIPs: hardware RIPs and software RIPS. Hardware RIPs are really just very specialized computers that have a motherboard just like a desktop computer. Sometimes the RIP motherboard is housed in its own separate case, as is often the case with imagesetter RIPs, or the RIP may be built into the printer box itself as it usually is in most desktop printers. On a RIP motherboard the normal CPU chip is replaced by a Postscript processing chip. Hardware RIPs have their own RAM, storage capabilities, and communication ports just like any other desktop computer. And just like desktop computers, there are slow RIPs and fast RIPs, and fast RIPs cost more money. Built into the Postscript processing chip is a set of interpretation instructions which are designed to read Postscript instructions sent from an application and/or printer driver and convert that information into sequences of dots, which is the only kind of information that laser printers and imagesetters understand.

Dots per Square Inch
Based on an 8" x 10" Image

300 DPI	7,200,000	BASE
600 DPI	28,800,000	4 x
1200 DPI	115,200,000	16 x
2540 DPI	516,128,000	72 x

▼ *Figure 10.3 File Size vs. Resolution*
This chart shows the dramatic increase in the number of dots which need to be generated to fill a B&W 8" x 10" page as resolution increases. Note that as the linear resolution doubles, the number of dots quadruples. Seventy two times as many dots need to be generated to fill an 8"x10" page at 2540 dpi compared with the same page at 72 dpi. (See Chapter 8, "Resolving Resolution," for more detailed background information on resolution.)

Line Art Original

Pixel Version After Scan

RIPed & Printed Version

▼ *Figure 10.4 Line Art RIPing*
The above sequence shows how a line art image is captured and converted into dots at a RIP. An original line art image (top image) may be scanned and converted into pixels (middle image). This pixelized version is then converted into image spots or dots by the RIP/Printer combination (bottom image). The RIP determines the placement, and the resolution of the printer determines the size of the individual dots or spots. As shown above, the straight line of black pixels which compose a portion of the black background between the nose and the body of the fox are RIPed into a series of touching image spots. Text images are reproduced in a similar fashion.

Software RIPs perform the same function as hardware RIPs, that is, they convert Postscript information into dots, but instead of having a dedicated processor chip, a software RIP operates on a standard desktop computer. A software RIP uses the computer's CPU, RAM, and storage for its processing chores. The conversion or interpretation instructions are contained in the form of software instead of being hard-wired into a hardware chip. The advantage of software RIPs is that they are more flexible, easier, and less expensive to upgrade.

Resolution and RIPing

RIPs, be they hardware or software, that provide Postscript interpretation chores for high resolution imagesetters are required to generate vastly greater numbers of image dots per unit area than for a laser printer. Figure 10.3 shows the tremendous increase in dot generation required at increasingly higher resolutions. These greater processing (RIPing) requirements of high resolution printing often result in increased printing times for many files compared with lower resolution printing of the same file. Many files which print quickly on a 300 dpi laser may take much longer to print at 2540 dpi or, in some cases they may not print at all because there is seventy two times (72x) as much information to process. If a file will not print at 300 dpi, don't expect it to print at 2400 or 3600 dpi, it won't (see Chapter 8, "Resolving Resolution," for more detailed background information on resolution).

Text and line art images

Text and line art images are formed from combinations of continuous lines with well defined boundaries or edges, unlike contone images which are composed of areas which blend into one another with indistinct edges. As a result of this difference, RIPs handle text and line art images differently than they do contone images. Text and line art images are reproduced as sequences of touching spots. Refer to our discussion of halftone dots and image spots in Chapter 8, "Resolving Resolution," to remember that an image spot is the smallest dot which a printer can create. The crispness or sharpness of line art and text images depend upon the size and sharpness of the image spots which a printer produces. A 300 dpi laser printer creates image spots or dots which are $\frac{1}{300}$" across, while a 2400 dpi imagesetter generates image spots or dots which are $\frac{1}{2400}$" across. Consequently, text and line art images reproduced with a 2400 dpi imagesetter will be far sharper than those reproduced with the laser printer. Text and line art images are captured or created as pixels on your computer and then converted to sequences of image spots on your printer. The placement

Original Contone Image

Pixel Version
After Scan

RIPped & Printed
Halftoned Version

▼ *Figure 10.5 Contone RIPing*
In contrast to line art images which are recreated directly out of individual image spots lined up sequentially, contone images are reproduced through the generation of halftone dots which are constructed from collections of image spots grouped together to create the halftone dot. The above sequence shows the stages a contone image goes through during the print production process. The original contone image (top) is captured by scanning and converted into pixels (middle), The pixels are then converted into halftone dots by the RIP and printer (bottom). The size and placement of the halftone dots are controlled by the RIP.

of the image spots is determined by the RIP. Figure 10.4 shows the processing sequence a line art image goes through on its way to being printed. Note how the RIPing/Printing process converts the pixel-based version of the original line art images into spots.

Digital halftones

As described in Chapter 8, halftone dots are used to simulate continuous tone images. The job of the Postscript RIP is to convert the tonal information contained in pixels into halftone dots, which as we know are collections of smaller image dots. Depending upon the resolution of the image, that is, the number of pixels per inch used to create the image, what generally happens is that the tonal values from a group of pixels will be averaged together to create the information which is used to create a single halftone dot. The higher the resolution of the original image, the greater the number of pixels which will be averaged to create a halftone dot. In contrast to line art images which are recreated directly out of individual image spots lined up sequentially, contone images are reproduced through the generation of halftone dots which are constructed from collections of image spots grouped together to create the halftone dot (see Chapter 16, "Screening Your Images," for more information on the generation of halftone screens). Figure 10.5 shows the sequence a contone image goes through during scanning RIPing and printing. Note how the size of the halftone dots vary depending upon the grayscale percentage they are representing, while the spacing of the halftone dots remain the same regardless of the grayscale percentage presented.

> *Many files which RIP fine on a 300 dpi laser will take much longer to RIP at 2400 dpi or in some cases they may not print at all. If a file will not RIP at 300 dpi, don't expect it to RIP and print at 2400 dpi.*

Unlike line art images where precisely capturing edges is of utmost importance, with contone images one need only capture areas of tone rather than edges. The proper pixel size of the captured areas, that is, the input or scan resolution, will depend upon the line screen at which the final image will be reproduced. Because RIPs convert areas of tonal information into halftone dots, and higher image resolutions necessarily mean more RIP processing, one needs to be cognizant of the resolution at which contones images are created or captured (see Chapter 12, "Taming Your Scanner," for a complete discussion of scanning variables and rules).

Postscript Code

```
0 0 F 4
(l___Copperplate32bc) T F
/l_____CopperplateThirtyTwo
BC 0 T dfnt
0 18 18 f
246 48 135 96 m .55 0 14
149 .5 (Postscript Code)d
end
```

▼ *Figure 10.6 Postscript Code*
This is a small portion, text formatting information of the Postscript language description of the bordered text box shown above with the words **"Postscript Code"** set in Copperplate 32bc. The entire length of code for an 8.5" x 11" page with just this one bordered text box runs onto 22 pages.

The RIP as a funnel or filter

In order to be reproduced or printed on a postscript device, all elements within a document, text line art, and contone images must be rasterized or RIPed. All the fancy text and graphics which we can create on a computer must be renderable as dots (RIPed). Simple text and graphics are easier to RIP than more complex text and graphics. In fact, there are many types of text and graphic images which are very difficult or impossible to RIP. While the speed and capabilities of Postscript RIPs are always improving, the capabilities of creative software applications and the people who use them seem to be improving faster.

It is useful to think of a Postscript RIP as a funnel through which all document information must pass and be converted into dots. Like all funnels, the RIP funnel is a point of restriction, the publishing process slows down, and in some cases stops here. Whenever we are constructing a document which will be used for print, we should keep this Postscript funnel in mind and remember that whatever we are creating must fit through that funnel. It is a fact of Postscript life that there are many images we can create on a computer and view without problems on a monitor which may not fit through our Postscript RIP. Examples of these items include: very long and complex paths, nested EPS graphics and fonts, multiple font architectures, complex compound graphics with multiple clipping paths, overlapping gradations or multiple masks, and many out-of-gamut colors. We should always try to reduce the size of files and simplify files which we intend to print.

Postscript

Postscript is a page description language, developed by Adobe, which was specifically designed to enhance the creation and integrations of complex text and graphics for printing. Postscript is a shorthand language which is used to describe the page geometry as well as the size, shape, placement, and characteristics of text and graphic elements of electronic documents. Although it is unnecessary for you to learn to write Postscript code, it is very helpful to be at least familiar with how Postscript works. I highly recommend *"Postscript: A Visual Approach"* by Ross Smith as a good, understandable introduction to Postscript and how it works.

Postscript dictionaries

One key concept to understanding how a Postscript RIP works is understanding some of the basic parts of the RIP. While the entire RIPing process is multistepped and complex, there is one concept which I keep in mind when I think about trying to make my files "RIP Ready," and that is the concept of the Postscript dictionary. A Postscript RIP contains a series of dictionaries, each of which is devoted to processing a certain part of a document. There are font dictionaries, page geometry dictionaries, line art dictionaries, and bitmap art dictionaries. I think of these dictionaries as being storage and processing areas within the RIP. When a Postscript file is received by the RIP, it sends the font portion of the file to the font dictionary, the line art graphics to the line art dictionary, and so forth. The size of the dictionary depends upon how much RAM is assigned to that dictionary. If more information is sent to a dictionary than it can hold, you will receive a Postscript error, the dreaded: POSTSCRIPT ERROR: STATUSDICTFUL. This means that the dictionary is too full to receive any more information. This kind of error is common with long complex outline files such as clipping paths and line art that has been converted to vectors using Streamline. A Postscript RIP must be able to process the entire length of a line art file in order to continue. If the line art dictionary becomes full prior to completing the processing of an entire line or line segment, a Postscript error will be generated and the RIPing will come to an end, that is, the RIP will "bomb." Dictionary overflow errors can be prevented with line art by decreasing the length of and complexity of line art files. This is why we split paths, increase flatness ratios, and simplify path lengths of line art files (see Chapter 9, "Grappling With Graphics," and Chapter 15, "Application-Specific Tips" for a more complete discussion of line art files and how to treat them). This same attention to reducing size and decreasing complexity with all aspects of a document will help reduce the probability of Postscript errors, particularly when printing to a high resolution device.

PAULINE'S FILE PREP TIPS

File Prep Hint #29

Remove unnecessary elements from your document pages. Don't just cover them up. All elements within active margins will be processed by a RIP which processes a page from the bottom up, and it has no idea what is on top. The concept of out of sight *but* not out of RIP applies here. To help find extraneous items, I set my view on "Fit Spread In Window" so that I can see my entire page as well as the pasteboard. Then I scroll through the document and check for items on the pasteboard. Another trick is to select all the items on a page. This will activate the handles of any extra items which are underneath foreground items.

File Prep Hint #30

Create complex graphics (especially line art EPS graphics created in drawing applications) in separate layers. Doing so will allow you to create the graphics more efficiently and will let your printer troubleshoot and edit them more easily.

File Prep Hint #31

Make sure you can RIP and print every graphic you create on your low resolution desktop laser printer before you send it out to be RIPed by someone else on a higher resolution RIP. If it won't RIP and print at low resolution on your laser printer, it certainly won't RIP and print on a more demanding higher resolution RIP. However, be aware that just because an image RIPs and

Pauline's File Prep Tips

prints on your system does not guarantee that it will be able to be RIPed and printed on another system.

File Prep Hint #32

Avoid including the high resolution version of graphic images in your page layout documents. Including the high resolution images makes the page layout document much larger and more unwieldy. It also makes troubleshooting, editing, and updating the file while it is imbedded impossible. Send along the high resolution images as separate files.

File Prep Hint #33

Nesting is for the birds! Be conscious of not nesting text and graphic elements in your documents, as nested elements are difficult for RIPs to locate and process. Avoid placing previously created EPS graphics inside of a drawing document when you intend to later export that document as an EPS file. Type set in a drawing document to be exported as an EPS should be outlined/converted to a graphic prior to creation of the EPS. Saving entire document pages as EPS files will generally create nested elements, and should be avoided when possible.

11

A Tale Of True Typesetting

As the Byte Turns continues…

*What type of setting will Pauline find when she visits
Danny to teach him about her style … sheets?*

*You charged me a bundle
for editing my copy in that
catalog you printed for me
last month. Why was
it so much??*

*Apparently, it took us a long
time!!!*

*I wonder why it
took so long ??*

*Why did Danny's
last catalog job
take so long and
cost so much?*

*We had to reformat and proof
400 pages of text with five different levels of heads and subheads
by hand. If Danny had used
style sheets, we could have
accomplished the reformatting in
minutes instead of hours.*

A TALE OF TRUE TYPESETTING

What is a font?

The terms "typeface" and "font" are often used interchangeably and while they are related, they are not the same. The classical definitions of "font" and "typeface," which come from the days of hot and cold type, are still useful. "Type" is defined with three basic terms: typeface or typeface family, style, and size. For instance, the body copy of this paragraph is set in 12 point Minion Regular (or Roman). The typeface is Minion, the style is plain or Roman or Regular, and its size is 12 points. Varieties of this font are:

Minion Regular (Plain or Roman) 18 pts
Minion Italic 18 pts
Minion Bold 18 pts
Minion SemiBold Italic18 pts

All four lines of type are set in the same typeface, StoneSerifMedium, and all are the same point size,18 points. But their styles differ from Roman, to Italic, to Bold, to BoldItalic. Therefore, each line is set in a different font. If we just changed the point size, would we have a different font? *Yes*

Type control

In addition to adjusting the point size of type, we routinely adjust the space between lines of type (leading), the general space between multiple words and characters (tracking), and the specific space between two characters (kerning). We also control the placement of type on a page by controlling the indent of lines and the spacing between paragraphs.

Finding your fonts

Location

On a Mac, fonts are by default placed in a fonts folder inside your System folder. Fonts placed in a System fonts folder are automatically made available to any application which is launched. I prefer to keep all of my fonts outside of my System folder and access them indirectly through a font utility such as Suitcase. This indirect access allows

Typeface
style } *Font*
size

TYPE CHARACTERISTICS
Font: StoneSerif-ITC (Roman/Plain) 60pts

▼ *Figure 11.2 Contents of Screen Fonts Suitcase*

Opening a screen fonts suitcase will reveal the screen fonts inside. Note how the screen fonts have full names followed by specific point sizes. Also note how the names of their printer fonts partners (which are abbreviated and indicate no specific point sizes) do not exactly match the screen font names.

▼ *Figure 11.1 Two Locations of Fonts on a Macintosh*

On a Macintosh, fonts are located in either the fonts folder in the System folder or in a separate folder outside of the System folder. Generally, it is best to keep most of your fonts outside of the System folder so that they can be readily activated and deactivated.

▼ *Figure 11.3 Type 1 Screen Fonts*
Screen font files are named using full names and have point sizes beside them.

Screen Fonts – Helvetica

▼ *Figure 11.4 Screen Font Suitcase*
Screen fonts can be stored in a suitcase to make transporting easier and access quicker. Helpful hint: You can put a space before the suitcase name to keep it at the top of your list for easy access.

▼ *Figure 11.5a Type 1 Printer Fonts*
Printer fonts are named using abbreviated names and have no point sizes beside them. You need to send both screen and printer fonts with your document.

Chicago

▼ *Figure 11.5b Truetype Font*
A Truetype font file contains both screen and printer font information and is recognized by the triple *A* on the icon.

me to quickly and easily control which fonts are accessible or "open" and which are not.

Font file structure

The two most common types of font architectures are Postscript Type 1 fonts and Truetype fonts. Type 1 fonts are constructed of two files, a screen font, and a printer font. Screen font files are low resolution, fixed size, bitmapped font files used for displaying font characters on your screen or monitor. Printer fonts are high resolution, scalable, outline, or Postscript font files accessed when characters are printed. TrueType fonts consist of a single file which contains both the screen and printer font information. While TrueType fonts are easier to manage because they are a single file, Postscript Type 1 fonts are preferred for printing on high resolution lasers, imagesetters, and platemakers because the RIPs which process font files during the printing process are Postscript-based and therefore more compatible with the Postscript information contained in the Type 1 files.

Font naming

The font naming schemes which have evolved on computers are among the most diabolical naming systems ever conceived. On the Mac, the screen and printer fonts use different naming formats. Adobe Type 1 Screen fonts are named using full names and have point sizes beside them, e.g., Helvetica 12. Printer fonts have abbreviated Postscript names with no point sizes next to the name, e.g., Helve is the printer font match for the screen font Helvetica 12. Screen fonts are designated with point sizes because they are bitmapped and therefore a specific size. Printer fonts are not designated with point sizes because they are Postscript outline files and therefore inherently scalable. TrueType fonts are single font files which have both screen and printer font data in one file and have a naming scheme which utilizes characteristics of both screen and printer fonts. A Truetype font has a full name, like screen fonts, but has no point sizes like the printer fonts, e.g., Helvetica.

Fondling your fonts

Here are some tips for managing your fonts

❧ Keep the number of fonts used in a document to a minimum. This is both good technical advice and a good design habit to have. On the

▼ **Figure 11.6 Macintosh Screen & Printer Font Organization**

In Windows 3.1, users of Postscript fonts need to look in the psfonts folder (directory) for the .pfb and .pfm files. There are matched sets just like there are with Mac screen and printer fonts. The .pfb files are located directly in the psfont folder. Note the .pfm folder (subdirectory).

▼ **Figure 11.7 Contents Of Screen Font Suitcase**

The screen font suitcase should contain one pair of screen fonts, usually 10 and 12 point, for each printer font needed. Having the screen fonts located in a suitcase allows them to be accessed and transported more easily. The screen font suitcase and their associated printer fonts should always be loaded in the same folder, and preferably separate from the system font folder.

▼ **Figure 11.8 Finding Postscript Fonts In Windows 3.1**

In Windows 3.1, users of Postscript fonts need to look in the psfonts folder (directory) for the .pfb and .pfm files. There are matched sets as with Mac screen and printer fonts. The .pfb files are located in the directory "psfont folder." The .pfm folder (sub directory) is a separate folder inside the psfonts folder.

▼ **Figure 11.9 Finding Postscript Fonts Pairs In Windows 3.1**

In Windows 3.1, the .pfm file matches for the .pfb font files are located in the .pfm folder (subdirectory) in the psfonts folder (directory). Both files must be sent along with your documents.

The·space·control·for·this·type·is·done·incorrectly...¶
··········Note·that·the·inderts·for·these·lines↵
··········are·controlled·by·multiple·spaces·instead¶
··········of·by·tabs...And·note·the·double·spaces·at¶
··········the·end·each·sentence...¶
¶ ↖
¶
¶
Also·not·the·use·of·multiple·returns¶
···This·should·also·be·avoided¶
···Also·note·the·use·of·hard·returns¶
···where·there·should·be·soft·returns...¶

▼ Figure 11.10 Improper Type Formatting
This is an example of all the wrong ways to control type. Errors include: multiple spaces to move type horizontally, hard returns used for line breaks instead of soft returns, double spaces placed at the end of sentences, and multiple hard returns used after a paragraph to control space between paragraphs. See Figure 11.11 to see the proper methods for these type controls.

The·space·control·for·this·type·is·done·correctly.↵
➤   Note·that·the·inderts·for·these·lines↵
➤   are·controlled·by·tabs·instead↵
➤   of·by·multiple·spaces.·Also·note·the·single·spaces·↵
➤   instead·of·two·at·the·end·of·each·sentence.¶
↖

Also·not·the·use·of·one·return↵
➤   between·the·twp·paragraphs,↵
➤   and·the·use·of·soft·returns·to↵
➤   control·line·breaks·

▼ Figure 11.11 Proper Type Formatting
Here we see correct methods for the control of type. These include use of tabs to control horizontal placement of text, soft returns to place line breaks, single spaces used at the end of sentences, and the placement of only one hard return between paragraphs.

technical side, the greater the number of fonts you have in a document, the longer the processing time will be. In terms of design, it is easy to complicate and clutter a document's message with too many different fonts.

❧ Be sure to send both screen and printer fonts for Mac Files, and Font Metric (.pfm) and Outline font files (.pfb) for Windows files for all the fonts in a document.

❧ Screen fonts can and should be stored in a screen font suitcase for ease of transportation and rapid access. Keep an empty suitcase handy in your fonts folder on your hard drive to copy to your output disks. This will make organizing screen fonts easier when you are sending out fonts.

❧ Both screen and printer fonts should be placed in the same folder both on your hard drive and when traveling on a disk so that they will automatically be linked to each other for screen display and printing.

❧ Due to naming convention inconsistencies on the Mac and name abbreviations in Windows, there is often some confusion about which members of a typeface family need to be sent along with a document file. Send the entire font family (Roman, Italic, Bold, and BoldItalic faces) if there is any question about which members of a typeface family need to be sent with your document file.

❧ As mentioned in the Chapter 13, "Document Construction," don't mix TrueType and Type 1 PostScript fonts in the same document. Using more than one font architecture in the same document will, at the very least, slow down the printing process and can lead to the failure of RIPing.

❧ Avoid using bitmapped city name fonts such as New York and Chicago. City named fonts are meant to be used for monitor display by the Mac and for non-Postscript printing. Also avoid using pseudo-condensed laser printer specific fonts such as Helvetica Narrow.

❧ Prior to printing or creating PostScript files, check for and remove miscellaneous fonts as these extra fonts will just make a large file even bigger.

❧ Set as much type as possible in the parent printing program (usually Quark or PageMaker) rather than in graphics applications such as Illustrator, Freehand, or Corel Draw.

❧ Speed up printing on your own system, download non-resident fonts to your printer prior to multiple printing sessions.

❧ Note font type or manufacturer used in your documents when you send them out to be printed: e.g., Adobe, Bitstream, Font Haus, etc.

▼ Figure 11.12 Tab Settings Dialog Box

Tabs, instead of spaces, should be used to control the horizontal spacing. Using tabs provides you with flexibility, precision, and editability. The use of tabs is particularly important when you need to align variable spaced type. Tabs can also be assigned as a portion of style sheet formatting.

▼ Figure 11.13 Paragraph Formatting Dialog Box

This is a paragraph formatting dialog box in QuarkXPress, similar to controls in other applications such as PageMaker. Think of typesetting in terms of paragraphs, defined by the presence of a hard return, when planning the placement and spacing of your type. Paragraph controls should be used for controlling the vertical placement of type. Paragraph formatting of type provides for greater accuracy, speed, and editability than manual formatting.

➥ Don't buy cheap fonts. Also avoid using Truetype fonts if you are printing to high resolution imagesetters. There are some items you should not skimp on and fonts are one of them. Avoid the too-good-to-be-true font offers: 75 fonts for $50.00. These cheap fonts are often poorly constructed and do not always print well on high resolution printers. Stick with high quality Adobe Type 1 fonts to help minimize font problems during output.

➥ Use font management utilities like Suitcase and MasterJuggler on the Mac and FontMinder on Windows machines to help you identify, organize, and manage your fonts.

Typesetting vs. typewriting

Different techniques and capabilities

Perhaps the most marvelous book ever written on typesetting is called *The Mac Is Not A Typewriter* by Robin Williams (marvelous for its clarity, brevity, and insight as well as for its completeness). Robin's book is a "must read" for anyone who sets type on a computer of any sort. Her basic thesis is that typesetting and typewriting are two related but ultimately very different endeavors. Basically, typewriting is a very crude and imprecise way of placing text on a page. Typesetting, in contrast, provides us with the tools to elegantly and precisely control the look and placement of type on a page. Typesetting is an art as well as a set of skills. I encourage everyone to own and read and reread *The Mac Is Not A Typewriter* every once in a while. Until you do, here are some basic typesetting guidelines which will help you create more professional looking type and allow you more control over its formatting and reformatting.

Some typesetting guidelines

➥ Don't use multiple em spaces to control text placement horizontally. Use tabs instead. On a computer which uses Postscript typefaces, each character has its own character width. This approach contrasts with typewriter characters which are monospaced, that is, all characters occupy the same width area on the page. Trying to align variable spaced type with the space key is a losing battle. In addition, type placement which is controlled with tabs is infinitely more editable than space bar-controlled type. Don't place two spaces at the end of a line; postscript type automatically recognizes periods and places additional space at the ends of lines. As a general rule, if you need more than one space, set it with a tab.

▼ Figure 11.14 Style Sheet Dialog
This is the basic style sheet dialog box in QuarkXPress. Similar ones can be found in other applications such as PageMaker. Note all of the type formatting controls available in one location. Any characteristics which are set in a style sheet can be applied as a template to automatically format any new or previously created text.

▼ Figure 11.15 Style Sheets
This is a list of some of the style sheets used in this book. There are several style sheets used on this page. They are shown by the arrows. The use of style sheets helps improve the speed and consistency of your typesetting and dramatically improves the editability of the text after it has been initially set. *All of* the subhead text in this entire book was formatted with the style sheet labeled "Sub Head 2," with just a few clicks of the mouse.

❥ Don't use multiple paragraph returns to control text placement vertically; use paragraph format settings instead: "Space Before" and "Space After." The rationale here is similar to our discussion of tabs above. The accuracy, flexibility, and editability of paragraphs is severely limited through the use of multiple paragraph returns. You should never have more than one paragraph return. If you need more than one paragraph return, adjust the paragraph formatting.

❥ Don't use automatic leading; set absolute leading values. This practice will eliminate uneven line spacing (leading) problems which can result from applying superscript, subscript, or superior formatting to individual characters in a line of type.

❥ The proper control of horizontal and vertical placement of text, especially through the use of style sheets, makes for easier, faster, and more consistent and accurate text formatting and editing of text.

❥ Use style sheets to format recurring text.

❥ Use the correct typesetter versions of '…' and "…" instead of '…' and "…".

Typesetting with style

We introduced the concept of style sheets in the chapter on document construction. Style sheets allow you to assign a comprehensive set of formatting instructions and to create a template of these instructions which can be applied to any new or previously created text. It is preferable to use style sheets for consistency of repetitively formatted type, such as heads, subheads and body copy . Examples of the use of style sheets appear on this page. Figure 11.15 shows a list of all the style sheets used in this book and indicates the location of the the style sheet formatted text on this page. You will note that I use style sheets to format all of my copy. This helps improve the speed and consistency of my typesetting and makes any text formatting changes quick and easy. Any time I want to edit the formatting of any text, all I have to do is edit one style sheet instead of manually selecting and reformatting dozens or even hundreds of individual sections of text.

Setting type in drawing applications

In general, you should avoid setting much type in outline graphics applications such as Illustrator, Freehand, and CorelDraw, particularly if you intend to export the graphic as an EPS for inclusion in a page layout application. Most type elements which will be part of an exported EPS file should be converted to graphic outlines to facilitate the RIPing of the file. See the discussion and file prep hints in Chapter

10, "RIPing Up Your Files" and specific instructions on type conversion in Chapter 15, "Application-Specific Tips" under the section on drawing programs. Also see Chapter 19, "Managing the Mess," for some suggestions on when and how to create a finished exportable EPS file.

PAULINE'S FILE PREP TIPS

File Prep Hint #34

Use thumbnail sketches to plan your document prior to beginning construction of a document. Using thumbnails will help you construct your document in the most efficient manner. Your thumbnails should include characteristics such as page size and orientation, facing vs. non-facing design, margins, number of columns, text flow, list and placement of master page elements, style sheets, and notes about document specific preferences you need to set.

File Prep Hint #35

Use master pages for repetitive page elements and style sheets for repetitive text formatting. Using master pages and style sheets enhances the consistency and speed of document creation and dramatically improves the accuracy and speed of editing.

File Prep Hint #36

Use Postscript Type 1 rather than Truetype fonts. If you use Truetype fonts, use them exclusively; don't mix Truetype with Type 1 in the same document.

PAULINE'S FILE PREP TIPS

File Prep Hint #37

Choose typeface styles from the font menu rather than from keyboard shortcuts or font style palettes. This will prevent the on-screen creation of fonts which do not exist.

File Prep Hint #38

Be careful about adding too many fonts to your documents. This is both good design and good technical advice. Each font increases the complexity of your document.

File Prep Hint #39

Avoid reversing small and serif typefaces, as the character shapes are difficult to create and maintain when they are printed.

File Prep Hint #40

Do not baseline-shift large blocks of text; move the entire text box or area. Baseline-shift should be used to adjust individual characters or words.

File Prep Hint #41

When making custom adjustments to character spacing, work at high magnification on-screen so you can see small changes in space adjustments. Track first to make coarse adjustments, then kern individual characters to fine-tune the look. Avoid massive kerning adjustments to body type.

Pauline's File Prep Tips

File Prep Hint #42

Assign leading absolute values rather than using auto leading. Auto leading may create inconsistent leading when individual characters are baseline-shifted, such as when using superscripts and subscripts.

File Prep Hint #43

Your computer is not a typewriter, it is a sophisticated typesetting tool. Don't use multiple spaces and returns to control the horizontal and vertical placement of type. Use paragraph formatting and tabs to position type. Read Robin William's book, *The Mac Is Not A Typewriter*. I think this is the single best introduction to typesetting ever written.

File Prep Hint #44

Snap body copy type to baseline grids when working with multicolumn text pages. This will keep the baselines of your body copy consistent from one column to another.

DTP 301

Project
Construction

FoxRun

APPLICATIONS

STYLE SHEETS

MASTER PAGES

COLORS

12
Taming Your Scanner

As the Byte Turns continues…

*Can Danny capture Pauline's imagination, or
will Pauline just give him a one-pass scan?*

*I have a 1200 dpi scanner!
Now I can scan all my
images at high resolution
and get great results!!*

*Yeah, go for it! That'll
make all your images
print great !!!!*

*Oh dear, what have
I gotten myself into??*

Shouldn't he ???

*You told him to go ahead and
scan at WHAT resolution !!!*

Visualization in scanning for print

History

Traditionally, those of us who created images which were to be reproduced for printing relied upon professional photographers and scanner operators to capture and reproduce our images. Typically, we would leave a blank area on our composite page where the photographed or scanned and imageset image would be placed. Even with the advent of desktop scanners, most of us choose to use our scanners primarily for FPO (for position only) work and leave the final image capture and manipulation to the professionals. There are, however, many reasons, including creative control, experimentation, and cost and time savings, for wanting to take control of the capture and production of our final art images. So over time as the resolution, tonal range, and quality and capabilities of available scanning and image manipulation software improved, we have become bolder, more adventurous scanner operators. We have become more interested and more willing to take on the challenges of capturing, manipulating, and preparing our own graphic images for output. The dawn and growth of direct digital image capture through the use of digital cameras has emboldened us even more. Most of us started with simple B&W line art images and progressively tested our mettle on more complicated and demanding images such as detailed line art, grayscale, and then color images. I remember my first introduction to scanning, circa 1985, way back in the dawn of the desktop publishing age. I bought one of the first "desktop" scanners called a Thunderscan. It was a small plastic unit which fit on my dot matrix Imagewriter printer. The scanning unit took advantage of the transport mechanism of the printer to move the image during scanning. It took 20 minutes to capture a 3"x 5" image at 200 dpi. I waited patiently for the image to be captured and transported through the serial port to my hard drive. I was thrilled when the first image popped up on my 9" B&W screen. Today, barely 10 years later, we work with desktop scanners which can capture 11"x17" 10 bit color images at 2400 dpi or more at amazing speeds.

How scanners work

It is always helpful to know how an instrument works if you want to learn how to control it more effectively. In concept, color scanners are relatively simple devices. All scanners have in common at least four

▼ Figure 12.1 Types of Images
There are three basic categories of images: line art (top), grayscale contones (middle), and color contones (bottom). Each type of image has its own scanning challenges. Line art images usually involve capturing edge detail. With grayscale and color images ,the challenges revolve around reproducing tonal ranges accurately and completely. Color contone images have the added requirement of reproducing color values as well as tonal ranges accurately. There are some images which contain characteristics and challenges of all three types of images. Note: A color version of this image can be found in the Color Plate section in the center of this book.

basic components: a light source, an image holder or carrier, a filter system, and a light capturing and converting device. The basic scanning process proceeds like this: light, usually produced from a bulb-based light source, is either passed through or reflected off of a secured image. This light is then filtered through red, green, and blue filters which separate an image into three different channels (R,G, &B) of light. These three channels of light are then collected by a light capturing mechanism, either a photomultiplier tube (PMT) or a charge couple device (CCD), which not only captures the light but converts the light into electricity, a form of energy your computer understands. In this way, your image is captured and converted into a sequence of on and off electrical signals stored as bits on your computer. It is important to realize that all images, even continuous tone (contone) color images, are captured and stored as black and white or grayscale images. Your computer, being a digital device, understands only two data values, on and off, 0 and 1, black and white. Color images are stored and manipulated as black and white or grayscale images on your computer. The three RGB color channels you capture with your computer are really three grayscale channels to which color is added when those images are sent to output devices. Examples include the red, green, and blue phosphors on your monitor or the colored inks on a printing press.

Goals for scanning

Your scanner can be used as a tool for either recreating and reproducing an image or for altering an image. In scanning for reproduction, our goal is to match the final version of the image as closely as possible to the original. A scanner can also be used as a tool to alter images, such as changing contone images into line art or color into grayscale or B&W. In this chapter we will concentrate on scanning to reproduce originals. Once you master scanning for reproduction, you can then more confidently and predictably use your scanner as an instrument of change.

Types of images

There are three basic types of images: line art, grayscale contones, and color contones. A fourth category could include complex images which have the characteristics of two or three of the basic types. Examples of line art include images, such as logos, which are constructed from line-based drawings. Pure line art images do not contain continuous tone information; that is, they are composed of lines

Scanning: Digitizing

Viewing: Pixels on screen

RIPing: Halftone dots for printing

▼ *Figure 12.2 The Changed Image*
The process of scanning, viewing, and printing an image changes it significantly. Here you see how an original continuous tone image is transformed into 0s and 1s during the scanning process, then into grayscale pixels for screen view, and finally into a pattern of halftone dots for printing.

or areas which can be rendered as either black or white. Colored line art can be captured by your scanner as areas of black and white. Grayscale and color contones are similar to each other in that both are composed of areas of continuous tones. Grayscale images are captured by your scanner as one grayscale channel. Color images are captured as three grayscale channels, one for each color (R,G,B). An example of a complex image would be an image which contains a combination of line art and continuous tone images such as a piece of cloth with a logo label on it.

Parts of an image

When your goal is to reproduce an image, you often have a range of image characteristics which need to be reproduced. These include image size, image area, shapes, tones, contrast, color, detail, and edges. Different images may have different characteristics. For instance, line art images usually have edges which need to be captured. With contone images, edge capture is not nearly as important as tone reproduction. Not all scanners do an equally good job of capturing all of these characteristics, and few scanners can maximize the capture of all these characteristics at one time. Your job as a scanner operator is to evaluate the characteristics of your images, determine what are the most crucial components of your images, and adjust your scanner to concentrate on those characteristics.

Scanning goals & challenges

Reproducing images and particularly continuous tone color images for print is one of the most technically demanding challenges we face in electronic publishing. Scanning for reproduction involves trying to match the tones, contrast, color, and detail of an original image. Scanned images are often too dark or light or have altered contrast and color balance when compared to the original. These changes can be related to five basic challenges which we face when we try to reproduce an original image through scanning and printing. They are: changes in the image, loss of data, media changes and dot gain, gamut conversion, and impure image inks.

Challenge # 1: changes in image

During the process of scanning, viewing, and printing, an image is transformed quite dramatically. For instance, a continuous tone grayscale or color photograph is digitized into a sequence of 0s and 1s

TONE REPRODUCTION

▼ *Figure 12.3 The Tone Pyramid*

Over 90 percent of the tonal information is lost from an image during its transformation from its original screen to printed piece. Our eyes can recognize approximately 5000 tonal gradations. High quality positive photo film captures 20 percent of the original, while in Postscript we are limited to 256 shades of gray.

during scanning, converted into pixels for viewing on a monitor, and finally rasterized into a pattern of dots known as halftone screen dots for reproduction during the printing process. Halftoning, rendering a contone image as a pattern of dots, is required in order to reproduce contone images on a printing press because a printing press cannot print continuous tone information. They can print only solid areas and dots.

This halftoning process is the most dramatic of the three transformations because at this point your image no longer contains any true contone information. Halftone screen dots are "sleight of the eye" impostors for the areas of continuous tones which make up the original photograph. The technique of using halftone dots to reproduce original continuous tones is nearly as old as the printing process itself. The halftone concept takes advantage of the human eye's limited capacity to resolve small dots at a distance. Halftone dots are so small and so closely spaced that at normal reading distances the human eye does not see individual dots but rather a blur of the dot patterns which our mind interprets as grayscale or continuous tone information. The larger or more closely spaced the dots are, the darker the image appears and the darker the shade of gray the eye "sees" (Figure 12.2).

It is important to realize and remember that it is the job of the Postscript RIP (Raster Image Processor) and not of the scanner to perform this miracle of translation from grayscale pixels to halftone dots. These dots are then placed on various kinds of paper or film by a laser printer, image setter, printing press, or other printing device. In fact, an image may go through several generations of printing reproduction, film, and plates. Clearly, any image is significantly transformed during this process of scanning, viewing, RIPing, and printing. It helps to understand and visualize what happens to an image as it goes through these various stages and processes if you want to be able to predict what any given image will look like when it emerges at the end of this process.

One of the consequences of this scan, view, and print process is that nearly all contone images appear flatter or in lower contrast than their originals after they have been scanned. This contrast must be replaced if you want to come close to reproducing the original image.

Challenge #2: loss of data

The human eye can distinguish about 5000 tonal shades. High quality film can capture about 20 percent or 1000 of those original 5000 tonal shades. In Postscript we are limited to working with 256 tonal values, a mere five percent of the original 5000 shades. On a printing press we can reproduce between 80 and 120 tonal gradations (~2%) of the original scene. Our challenge is to capture the best possible 256 shades for use in Postscript and then distribute that information to the most important parts of the image. Images which are too light or dark are often the result of not properly reproducing the best 256 shades of gray (Figure 12.3).

Challenge #3: calibration & dynamic range

Calibration

▼ *Figure 24 Calibration*
On the left is an image scanned on an uncalibrated scanner. On the right is the same image scanned on the same scanner with the same settings, but this time after linearization. Notice how overall image brightness, contrast, and shadow details are improved through calibration.

Every image capture device (including scanners) no matter what their cost or capabilities, needs to be calibrated to assure consistent results. Nearly all scanners tend to capture images darker than they actually are. Each device is different and is affected over time by variables such as temperature and bulb age. Calibration helps to standardize the capture response of the scanner and is accomplished by scanning a target with known grayscale values. The values which the scanner "sees" are then compared with the actual values of the target. The scanner is then adjusted or corrected so that it captures the target values correctly. To assure accurate and consistent scanning of your images, calibration should be performed prior to each scan session. See the sections on how to calibrate your scanner beginning on page 158.

Dynamic range

▼ *Figure 25 Dynamic Range (Dmax)*
On the left is an image scanned with a scanner which had a dynamic range of 2.5. On the right is the same image scanned with a scanner (PowerLook III) with a Dmax or maximum density of 3.4. Note the much improved shadow details captured by the PowerLook III. Look specifically at the hair, and you will see how much farther along the hair you can see.

The measure of a scanner's ability to capture a range of grayscale values is known as its dynamic range. Dynamic range varies on a scale from 0 to 4.0 with each integer step being a ten-fold increase in grayscale recognition capacity, and with 4.0 being the most capable. A scanner's dynamic range is most noticeable in the shadow regions of an image. Scanners with good dynamic range can see a lot of shadow details, while those with poor dynamic range can see little. A scanner's dynamic range is largely determined by the quality of the CCD used in the scanner, which is not an adjustable feature. However, a properly calibrated scanner allows us to take full advantage of its dynamic range. Increased dynamic range is one of the capabilities you pay for when you purchase more expensive scanners. Your scanner should have a dynamic range of at least 3.0 to be an effective tool for capturing good shadow details.

▼ Figure 12.4 Dot Gain
During the printing process the
size of halftone dots tends to
increase as ink spreads out,
causing photographs to darken.
Dot gain tends to be greatest in
the midtone region, where the
percentage of dot gain may be
20 percent or more.

Challenge #4: media changes & dot gain

Another challenge involves knowing what happens to an image when
it is reproduced on different types of media. The appearance of any
image will change if it is rendered on different kinds of media. For
example, a photographic image reproduced on a tee shirt looks very
different from that same image reproduced on paper. In print-oriented electronic publishing, an image may be displayed on several types
of media. An original contone may start out as an image on photographic paper, be viewed as pixels on a glass monitor, printed on film,
reproduced onto a metal, fabric, or paper plate, and then finally printed on paper stock. An image will look different on each of these media
and the appearance of the final printed image will vary depending upon
what kind of paper is used.

Dot gain

The inks which we use in the printing process react differently on different media. An image printed on coated stock will be much sharper
and brighter than an image printed on uncoated stock. Inks applied
to uncoated paper are absorbed more and tend to spread out more
than inks applied to coated paper. This spreading out of ink is known
as "dot gain." Dot gain can vary from as little as five percent on hard
glossy stock to as much as 30 percent on porous news print (see
Figure 12.4). Dot gain tends to be greatest in the midtones of an
image and decrease toward the highlight and shadow portions of an
image. The more an ink spreads out, the larger the area it covers,
resulting in darker and duller images, especially in the midtone
region. Dot gain must be compensated for before an image is printed
on film. Here again, knowing the process through which an image is
transformed, the various media on which that image will be rendered,
and particularly the final media on which the image will rest, will help
you predict how that image will ultimately look.

Challenge #5: gamut conversion

Some of the colors we capture in the original RGB scan are not reproducible with CMYK ink and will be lost during the conversion from
RGB color space to CMYK color space. To print a colored image
which has been scanned into RGB color space, we must first convert
that image into CMYK color space. The range of colors which are
reproducible in RGB color space, the RGB capture and viewing
gamut, is generally much larger than the CMYK printing gamut. This
means that some of the original RGB colors are not reproducible with
CMYK ink and will be lost during the conversion from RGB color

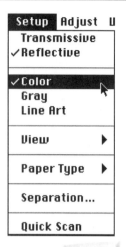

▼ *Figure 12.5 Scan Mode Choices*

A scan mode setup dialog box should provide at least three scan mode choices: line art, grayscale, and color. If your scanner has the ability to capture images from film (slides and negatives), then you will select either transmissive (film) or reflective (paper) mode as well as an image type. Line art mode, which captures 1 bit per pixel, should be used when scanning B&W line art and for color line art as well if you can assign the color values (spot or CMYK) during the post scan process. Grayscale mode should be used for capturing grayscale contones and detailed line art. The color mode should be used when capturing color contone images. The halftone option, which creates a halftone version of your image during the scanning process, should be avoided in most cases.

space to CMYK color space. This color space transformation is known as a gamut conversion. To predict how our images will print, it is therefore very helpful to know the gamuts of our various printing devices to which we will be printing. We must be aware of which colors will be transformed and which will not. In addition, we *cannot* depend upon our color monitor to provide us with a faithful view of what the printed piece will look like because it is an RGB device (see Chapter 14, "Color Me Right," for a full discussion of color, color spaces, gamuts, and color calibration).

Challenge #6: impure image inks

The process inks (CMYK) we use to reproduce contone images are not pure. Magenta and yellow both contaminate Cyan and each other. Because our inks are not pure, we must not only contend with the challenge of translating an image from one color space (RGB) into another (CMYK), but also adjust the color of our images to compensate for impure image inks. Most Cyan (C) inks are actually about 60 percent C and 40 percent M & Y. Our Magenta inks are 55 percent M and 40 percent Y, and Yellow, the purest of all, usually about 90 percent Y and 10 percent M. The reasons for using impure inks is that pure ink colors, while attainable, would be very expensive. Obviously, Magenta and Yellow are found in all the inks. The overabundance of these two inks, and particularly of Magenta, because it is more visually dominant than Yellow, must be compensated for when we print an image. Failure to compensate for the overabundance of Magenta will typically result in images which appear to have a overall red cast to them. We must adjust for the overabundance of these two inks to avoid unwanted red color casts.

So, any scanned images and particularly contone images go through significant reconstitution on their way from scanner to monitor to various printers. No final image will ever exactly match the original. Our challenge is to get our final image as close as possible to the original.

Visualization

It is these format and media changes which demand the most attention. My basic conceptual approach to scanning images for print is to apply a technique I learned in photography years ago. As photographers we were taught to "see like the camera sees." Similarly, I try to view my images as a scanner would see them and as a laser printer or imagesetter or printing press will reproduce them. I find it very helpful to visualize the process which occurs when an image is dig-

▼ *Figure 12.6 Bitmap Image*
This graphic image of the character "P" is constructed out of dots and should be saved as a TIFF.

▼ *Figure 12.8 Compound Image*
This silhouetted image contains two parts. Part one is a contone TIFF of the two people. Part two is an invisible EPS outline called a clipping path. The clipping path defines a sharp border around the silhouette, which cleanly removes the background of the photo. Note: The addition of the clipping path increases the file size from 160K to 288K.

▼ *Figure 12.7 An Outline Image*
This graphic image of the character "P" is constructed out of lines and should be saved as an EPS.

▼ *Figure 12.9: Three Scanning Modes*
Here is the same image shown in three different modes: line art, continuous tone (contone) grayscale, and contone color. When scanned, the line art image will be a 1 bit B&W image, the grayscale image will have 8 bits per pixel, and the color image will have either 24 bits per pixel or 32 bits per pixel, depending upon whether it is saved in an RGB or a CMYK format. Note: A color version of this image can be found in the Color Plate in the center of this book.

itized during scanning and then the conversion of these digital images to dots during printing. Whenever I look at an image which I am about to scan, I try to visualize what that image will look like in digital form and then how that digitized image will be transformed again when it is halftoned and printed. Of course, the more you understand about the scanning and halftoning process, the easier this visualization process is. This process of visualization has been very important in helping me understand why I need to capture and manipulate my images.

Scanning approach

The original image

Start out with a good quality original. While there are a number of image enhancement tools available in most image editing applications, creating good quality images from poor originals is, at best, very time consuming, costly, and often impossible. The old adage "garbage in, garbage out" applies here.

Original line art images such as logos need to be clean, high contrast, sharp, and of reasonable size (larger than 2" x 2"). The more complex the original image, the larger, sharper, and higher contrast it should be. It is very difficult to capture detail from small, low contrast, and fuzzy line art images. In general, contone images such as grayscale and color continuous tone photographs should be in focus, have good contrast, and have a wide range of tonal values.

Image analysis and scan modes

Assuming I have been able to acquire a high quality original, the next step is to determine how I want to capture the image at hand. Most scanners provide us with at least three or four scanning modes or options. The most common ones are line art (which will produce a 1 bit bitmapped file), grayscale (which will produce an 8 bit bitmapped file), and color (which will generally produce a 24 bit RGB or 32 bit CMYK bitmapped file). Many scanners offer a halftoning option. This option should generally be ignored when working with Postscript printers. When you print a contone image scanned in halftone mode, the result is a horribly moiréd (patterned) image. The descreen option is used for scanning previously screened (printed) images. Some scanners provide on-the-fly RGB to CMYK conversion, but the original capture will be done in RGB. One important point to make is that all scanned images start off their life as bitmapped as opposed to

```
File  Edit  Setup
  New Overview
  New Prescan
  Test Scan 1
  Test Scan 2
  Save Scan...
```

▼ *Figure 12.10 The Prescan*
Nearly every scanning session
should begin with a prescan. A
prescan is a quick scan which
captures your entire image at
low resolution, usually 72 dpi.
This low resolution image is
then used to evaluate and set
scanning parameters for performing a final high resolution
scan. These parameters
include cropping, scaling, resolution, tone compression,
gray map adjustment, color
cast correction, sharpening,
file format choice, and saving
location. The object of the low
resolution prescan is to allow
the scanner to perform as
much adjustment of the image
as possible during the scanning process. Employing a
prescan technique saves time
and improves image quality.
The widely used process of
capturing a raw scanned image
which is then adjusted in
Photoshop should be avoided.

outline images. Some images can be converted to outlines, but they
must be captured as bitmaps first. Scanners capture images dot by
dot, so they naturally produce dot-based bitmapped images.

While any of these scan modes can be used creatively on any type of
image (using line art mode to capture and convert a multibit contone
image into a one bit line art file), we will restrict this discussion to
scanning for reproduction of originals. For line art such as logos
which will be reproduced in B&W, spot colors, tints, or gradations, I
will typically scan in one of two modes, line art or grayscale. I use line
art scanning mode for the simplest and cleanest images. I employ
grayscale mode when I have line art images which have many fine
lines and/or fine line detail. Contone images I scan in either grayscale
or color depending upon the nature of the original. For color images
which I wish to convert to grayscale, I generally scan the original in
color mode and then convert the image to grayscale. Regardless of
which mode I decide on, I always visualize how each mode would
affect the image to help me decide which mode and process will serve
my needs best.

Before I scan any image, I try to make four determinations: 1) What
kind of image do I have, – line art, grayscale contone, color contone,
or a compound image? 2) What scan mode should I work in? 3) What,
if any, editing or manipulations will I have to perform on this image?
and 4) Into what file format will I ultimately save my image? Knowing
these four items largely determines how I will scan my image.

For line art images, I analyze how sharp the edges of an image are as
this will affect the final resolution that I choose. For line art with
sharp edges, I will generally scan at high resolution, while images with
fuzzy boundaries will permit lower resolution scanning. Simple line
art images will generally dictate line art scan mode, while complex or
detailed images may require grayscale scan mode. Grayscale contones
should be scanned in grayscale mode, and color contones require
color mode. If you have the option of saving your images in RGB or
CMYK format, you should initially choose RGB; this will be a smaller and more versatile file format. But remember that your images will
need to be converted into CMYK format prior to printing.

There are basically three kinds of images found in digital imaging: 1)
bitmapped or raster images, 2) outline or vector, and 3) compound
images which are combinations of the first two. Bitmapped images
are constructed out of dots. Outline images are constructed out of
lines. Compound images such as silhouettes are often bitmapped
images surrounded by smooth outlines known as clipping paths. All
scanned images start out as bitmaps; this is how they are captured by
a scanner, as dots. The two basic print-specific graphic file formats are

TIFF for bitmapped images and EPS for outline images. Most compound images are saved as compound EPS images out of Photoshop which contains both contone and outline line art components. Recently, it has become possible to also save TIFF files with integrated clipping paths out of Photoshop 3.0.

Scanning process

Prescanning

Standard scanning procedures for most desktop publishers have been to scan in an image and then perform all of the editing and corrections in an application like Photoshop. This process is both time consuming and robs the image of quality. Every time you alter an image in Photoshop using curves or levels, you remove information from that image. Perform five or six alterations and you have significantly reduced the quality of that image because so much data will have been lost (see Figure 12.10 to see the effects of performing tone compression on an image after it has been scanned). A far more efficient and higher quality approach to scanning is to perform nearly all of the image correction functions during the scanning process by performing a quick low resolution (72 dpi) prescan of an image prior to performing a high resolution final scan. With this prescan method, the low resolution image is analyzed to determine appropriate corrections which will be performed during the final high resolution scan. This process is faster than performing the same functions in Photoshop and results in less loss of data from the image. The use of pre-scan image analysis for final scan setup has long been used by professional scanner operators for the efficient creation of high quality scans.

Calibrating your scanner

Calibrating your scanner is the first key step to the creation of scanned continuous tone images like photographs with good quality. Without calibration you will rarely experience consistent results from your scanner. The fundamental calibration procedure for grayscale and color images is linearization. Following is a 9 step linearization procedure. This is performed on one channel for grayscale images, and on three channels for color contone images.

RGB
255
222
191
159
127
102
76
51
25
0

ogies, Inc.

▼ Figure 12.11 Calibration Target

Scanner calibration requires the use of a multiswatch grayscale target with known values, such as this ten-step target. Note that the RGB values are conveniently listed on the right side.

9-step linearization procedure for grayscale images:

Clean your scanner bed and place your 10-step calibration target (see the back of this book for ordering information) and your first images squarely side by side on the scanner bed (see Fig 12.11).

Simple step-by-step linearization calibration for grayscale images:

1) Set the Preview size of your scanner to its maximum area. Then Prescan the target in 8-bit mode (grayscale mode).

2) Select the 10 step grayscale portion of the calibration target, including the pure white and pure black end swatches.

3) Select an editable histogram tool in your scanning software. A histogram will show you the frequency and distribution of grayscale values in an image. An editable histogram will allow you to adjust highlight, shadow, and midtone values (see Fig. 12.12).

4) Adjustment: Move the highlight and shadow pointers so that they are at the beginning and the end of the data peaks. This can be confirmed by measuring the grayscale values of the pure white (255) and pure black (0) swatches.

5) Zoom in a bit on the middle portion of the grayscale target so that you have a good view of the middle swatches. Use swatch # 5 (127) to start (counting down from the white swatch).

6) Now with a built-in intensitometer, measure the grayscale value of the #5 target swatch. Swatch # 5 will probably register a grayscale value lower (darker) than its actual value of 127 (see Fig. 12.13).

7) To make a quick overall correction of your scanner's response to grayscale values, adjust the midpoint of the gamma curve value for your scanner until the scanner measures the #5 target swatch at about 127. The default gamma value in many scanners is in the range of = 1.0 – 1.5. Adjust the gamma curve midtone value up until the #5 grayscale swatch = 127 (see Fig. 12.13). Perform this change incrementally, 0.1 per change, and watch how the intensitometer readings gradually increase. You may have to jiggle the intensitometer slightly (move the cursor) after each adjustment to make sure the software registers the change in grayscale value. A typical adjusted midpoint in the gamma curves may be 1.7 –2.0. Note how the curve arches up and the entire image lightens when you make this adjustment. Don't worry if the intensitometer doesn't read exactly 127, or if the value varies slightly (by one or two points) as you move the intensitometer around the swatch. Remember that a one unit movement only represents a 0.4 percent change!

Gamma Curve   Editable
               Histogram

▼ **Figure 12.13 Intensitometer**
An intensitometer is used to measure grayscale values on targets and images. Note the starting (113) and ending (127) values before and after gamma curve adjustment calibration.

▼ *Figure 12.12 Gamma Curve Linearization*

Seen here is an editable histogram and gamma curve. The top curve box shows the default settings. The bottom dialog box shows the calibrated settings. Compare the top and bottom boxes for: 1) positions of the highlight and shadow pointers; 2) shapes and positions of the gamma curves, 3) the position of the midpoint and the midpoint numbers (1.5 and 1.75). The calibrated settings are obtained by setting the shadow pointer (far left) and highlight pointer (far right) so that the first (white) and last (black) grayscale swatches measure "255" and "0," respectively. Then adjust the position of the midtone number so that the fourth grayscale swatch measures "127" when measured with the scanner's intensitometer. The midtone gamma curve number will generally be between 1.9 and 2.0 after the adjustment.

8) Save the corrected scanner settings as default settings, so that they will automatically be applied to each image scanned. The gamma curve should not be touched again while adjusting individual images. To do so would destroy the calibration you have just performed.

9) For best results, this linearization calibration should be performed at the beginning of each scan session.

Color contone calibration: neutralization

Calibration for scanning color contone images will proceed like the nine step grayscale linearization calibration detailed above, but will be done on all three color (RGB) channels instead of just on the one grayscale channel as in grayscale contone image scanning. When linearization is performed on all three channels in an RGB image, this type of three-channel calibration is know as neutralization. Once neutralized your scanner will measure equal RGB values on any grayscale swatch on the calibration target.

Note: Protect your targets. When not in use, keep your targets in moisture-proof light-tight containers. Constant exposure to light and humidity will progressively degrade the target, and it will no longer be consistent with its published data sheet values.

Note: This simple linearization adjustment provides you with an easy way to make noticeable improvements in the overall quality and consistency of your scanned images without

▼ *Figure12.14 Simple Line Art Image*
A simple image like this is well suited for outlining. The file size decreases from 240K to 60K when it is converted from a TIFF to an EPS.

▼ *Figure 12.15 Intermediate Complexity Line Art Image*
This is the type of image that should be scanned at high resolution in 1 bit line art mode, then converted to an outline image.

▼ *Figure 12.16 More Complex Line Art Image*
This is the type of image which should be scanned as a grayscale (8 bit mode) and then converted to a 1 bit bitmapped image.

drowning you in technical details, long procedures, or costly purchases. Remember, once you have set the gamma curve midpoint, do not adjust it when you are scanning individual images, or you will destroy the calibration setup. Any tool, such as the gamma curve tool which is used for calibration, should not be used for any other purpose.

Line art scanning

Line art images, even colored line art, should generally be captured as B&W or grayscale images. If the original line art image is colored and built from known spot or process color builds, the color can be applied in postscan process. There are two big advantages to this method. The first is that you are able to capture and manipulate much smaller 1 bit black and white files as opposed to having to manage 24 bit RGB color files which are 24 times larger than the black and white versions. Second, by assigning the exact color values after the image is captured, you need not worry about having to capture the color accurately; you can very accurately assign the color during postscan editing.

Remember that your digital computer really captures, stores, and manipulates B&W images because it only "comprehends" two values, 0 and 1. Therefore, your scanner only sees areas as black or white anyway. On your electronic publishing system primary output from your computer is black and white or grayscale; color is added at your monitor, at your color printer, or on a printing press. Scan characteristics which should be set during the analysis of the prescan of a line art image include: cropping, scaling, rotating, thresholding, and resolution

Postscan image editing may include pixel editing of the bitmapped image (addition or removal), conversion to outline format in an application like Streamline (for simple line art), editing the outline, and finally, addition of color as spot color, process color builds, or tints. Color assignments for the line art file will usually be performed by opening and editing the converted line art file in a vector-based drawing application like Illustrator, Freehand, or CorelDraw.

Simple line art images should be converted to outlines and saved in EPS format using an outlining application such as Adobe's Streamline. Outlining reduces file size, makes editing easier, and permits resolution-independent scaling. Complex line art can be better captured in grayscale mode and then converted to a B&W image after resolution enhancement, sharpening, and thresholding. Complex line art should generally remain as a bitmapped image. Converting com-

▼ Figure 12.17 Tone Compression

Tone compression, or setting the highlight and shadow points of an image, is one of the most important basic scan parameters you choose. The highlight area or dot, known as the diffuse highlight dot, should be set on the lightest area of your image which shows detail. Your diffuse highlight point should not be set on an area which shows no detail such as a gleam off of a bumper. Such an area, known as a specular highlight, will be reproduced as a pure white area with no printed dots inside and should be avoided. The shadow area or dot should be set on that area which is the darkest image area to show detail. Note that the shadow dot is not completely black and therefore should not be captured and reproduced as pure black.

plex or detailed line art to outlines may ruin the look of the image and create very complex files which are difficult to RIP and print. Outlined images can be colored and edited in drawing applications such as Illustrator, Freehand, or CorelDraw.

Complex line art

Complex line art images which contain much detail, such as reproductions of wood carvings, are often difficult to capture effectively in 1 bit line art scanning mode. Closely spaced lines and dots often merge together, while fine lines and small dots may be lost altogether. A good procedure to use with complex line art is to scan the original image in 8 bit/grayscale mode. This allows the scanner to act as a more sensitive instrument and gives your scanner a broader range of choices for capturing an image. In grayscale mode, the scanner has 8 bits instead of 1 bit of information for each area which it samples. Once captured, this 8 bit image can be manipulated with resolution enhancement, unsharp masking, and thresholding in an image editing application such as Photoshop to develop the detail of the image effectively.

Contones: grayscale and color

Contone images require the same attention to scan geometry, cropping, scaling, and rotating as line art images do. In addition, with contones we must worry about tone, contrast, and color reproduction. The grayscale and color modes will generally scan original grayscale and color contones. Grayscale and color images have many similar requirements. Grayscale and color contones both demand accurate tonal reproduction. Color images have the added requirements of color correction. For contone scan settings include scan geometry, cropping, scaling, rotating, tonal compression (setting highlight, midtone, and shadow points), gray map adjustments, color correction, and sharpening as keys to producing high quality final images. Again, we should perform a low resolution prescan of the image to be scanned and then set the final scan parameters.

Scan geometry

Determine the exact size, shape, and orientation which the image needs to be before you perform the final scan. Cropping, scaling, and rotating an image during the scan process will allow you to capture the exact area, size, position, and file size of the image you need. This will save you considerable amount of time during the page layout and

▼ Figure12.18 Scan Geometry

Configure the scan geometry to select the exact cropping and enlargement you will need for the final image. This will save you editing time later and reduce file size as well. Here a 3.5" x 5" area will be scanned and enlarged 200 percent to a 7" x 10." The enlargement you choose will also affect the resolution you choose and the resulting file size.

RIPing/printing processes. These production time savers can be significant with contones because of the large file sizes associated with these 8, 24 and 32 bit images.

Tone compression and gray map adjustment

The problem of lost and altered data which we discussed earlier in Challenge # 2 can be largely addressed through obtaining the proper tone compression and gray map adjustment of an image. Tone compression involves taking all of the tonal values contained in an image (256 for grayscale and 256/color for RGB images) and distributing them properly between the highlight, midtone, and shadow points. More detailed controls on some scanners even allow for control of the quarter and three-quarter tone points. Setting the highlight involves finding the lightest point on your image which still has detail and setting a dot value for that point. Setting the shadow point involves a similar process for the darkest point of detail. Adjusting where the midtone dot occurs controls where the 50 percent gray point should fall on your image. Improper adjustment of highlight, midtone, and shadow points on an image can result in images which are too light or too dark.

▼ Figure12.19 Incorrect Tone Compression

The dark image (top) shows the result of initial incorrect tonal compression. The first diagram shows the distribution of tonal values in this image. The tonal values are grouped near the shadow end of the histogram. The tonal grouping at the shadow end is due to location of highlight point on the very bright florescent lights. Most of the tonal values in the image are much darker than the pixels in the lights. The lights represent a specular highlight. The second histogram shows how the tonal compression would be adjusted in Photoshop using "Levels." The highlight point is adjusted down to a diffuse highlight position. The second image shows the visual results of the third adjusted tone compression. The third histogram shows the consequences (lost data) of making the tonal corrections as post-scan adjustments. Each blank level indicates a missing tonal value. Primary tone compression should be performed during the scan.

▼ Figure 12:20 Curves Adjustments

The "Curves" dialog box above shows the tones adjustments made in Figure 12.19 performed in Curves. Curve adjustments of midtone grayscale values to adjust overall image brightness and contrast, are generally superior to Levels adjustments because, as shown here, the entire tonal curve is adjusted with gradual changes along the entire gray map occurring rather than only adjusting the tonal values at the highlight, midtone, and shadow points as in Levels. Contrast the Curves histogram shown here with the last Levels - generated histogram shown in Figure 12.19.

Setting these points should happen during the prescan phase with the use of an on-screen intensitometer/densitometer. An on-screen intensitometer/densitometer, a tool provided with your scanning software, allows you to measure the grayscale and color values of any pixel on the screen. You choose your highlight, midtone, and shadow points on your low resolution prescanned image and set the dot values you want for each of those points. During the final high resolution scan, these points will be set as the high, medium, and low points of your images and all the rest of the image tonal data will be distributed between them.

Brightness and contrast

After the highlight and shadow portions of an image are set using an editable histogram, overall brightness and contrast should be controlled through the use of a curve control (see Fig. 12.20). Overall image brightness is adjusted by moving the midpoint of a curve up or down. Image contrast is controlled by altering the slope of the curve in various sections of the curve. Grayscale is concentrated wherever a curve is lowered (flattened). Performing these brightenss and contrast adjsutments during the scanning process, rather than after the scan is completed, will result in higher quality images.

Because of the limited tonal information you have to work with in Postscript, you may want to distribute your tonal information into one area of your image or another depending upon the requirements of your image. If the highlight and midtone areas of your image are more important, such as in an image of a light skinned person or a fruit basket, you may want to distribute tonal data there. Alternatively, for a dark-skinned individual or an image of furniture which contains dark wood grain, you may want to concentrate tonal data more toward the shadow region. This type of data redistribution is known as "gray map adjustment," accomplished through the use of a gamma curve type of adjustment as in Photoshop. Your scanning application should provide you with a similar type of adjustment tool.

Global Color Cast Correction

With color contone images you want to make sure that your colors are properly balanced so that your final image has the same appearance as your original. Having an unwanted color cast or abundance of one color is a common problem with color images. Color cast may come from several sources: incorrect initial exposure, lighting, scanner color, and color bias imposed by the use of impure image inks. Not all color cast is bad. For instance, an image of a sunset should

▼ Figure 12:21 Color Cast Removal

Color cast adjustments are accomplished through the adjustments of color values at the highlight, midtone, and shadow points through the use of dialog boxes like this one in Optronics ColorRight scanning software. When working with print-bound images, it is useful to work with CMYK percentages as well as RGB. Always use a densitometer to measure the impact of the color values of an area, never depend upon the "look" of your image on screen.

RGB and/or CMYK values are adjusted so that neutral areas of an image, such as the white highlight areas in this piña colada, obtain a 5% highlight the RGB values would all equal 5%. The CMYK values might be C=6%, M=4%, Y=4%. Note: A color version of this image can be found in the Color Plate section in the center of this book.

▼ Figure 12.22 Obtaining Neutral Densities

These images show how adjustments in the RGB or CMY percentages of highlight dots change the appearance of an image. We want this highlight dot to print as a white area without cast. The top image has a CMY color mix of 19/2/5 and prints too blue. The second image which shows a color mix of 3/2/3 is closer to a cast-less white, but the dot percentages are too low and cannot be reproduced on most presses. The result is that large areas of the white will be reproduced without any dot detail and will appear "blown out." The final image, shows a CMY color mix of 5/3/3, has enough dot density to be printed and therefore show detail and the right mix of CM&Y to compensate for the impure image inks. The highlight range of 5/3/3 to 6/4/4 works well for most printing presses. Try CMYK color mix of 55/40/40/20 to obtain a neutral midtone gray and a CMYK color mix of 95/85/85/75 for a neutral shadow dot. Ask your printer which percentage values work best on their presses for obtaining neutral highlight, midtone, and shadow values. Note: A color version of this image can be found in the Color Plate section in the center of this book.

have an overall red color cast, and its removal would destroy the appearance of the image. Neutralization of your image capture device, through neutralization calibration, discussed earlier in this chapter, will remove any color cast which might be imposed by the scanner ot digital camera.

Global color cast removal involves neutralizing any color cast from the highlight, midtone, and shadow areas of your image, making them neutral gray. Remove the color cast by measuring, on your prescanned image, each neutral area with your on-screen densitometer to determine their color values. Then adjust the color at those three points so as to neutralize them. Each scanning application has its own tools for making these adjustments. Some use gamma curve adjustments, others use slider type adjustment tools such as those shown in Figure 12.21, while others allow you to set numbers. The results of these adjustments, however, should be the same: your highlight, midtone, and shadow areas should all be neutral grays. Don't measure a single point or pixel, but rather measure an average of an area of at least five square pixels to perform your color measurements.

Neutralization can be performed initially in RGB mode for the scanning process. Neutralization of a neutral area of an RGB image, such as a white highlight, is accomplished by making all three (RGB) values the same. For instance, a five percent (5%) highlight area would register at five percent (5%) values for the red, green, and blue channels of the image. A neutral midtone in RGB would have all three values equal to fifty percent (50%). For print images, it is also a good idea to think in terms of CMYK values in addition to RGB values.

▼ *Figure 12.23 Sharpening*
All scanners reduce the contrast of images when they capture and digitize them. In order to reproduce the look of the original image, contrast must be added back in. With digital images, this is accomplished by increasing the difference in tonal values between adjacent pixels, thereby giving the image more contrast. This process is known as "sharpening," sometimes referred to as "unsharp masking." Above are four examples of sharpening applied to a strawberry image. Too little sharpening results in a flat, unclear image. Too much removes too much tonal gradation and begins to create edges and posterize the image. A 50 percent sharpening is a good place to start. If your scanning application allows you to preview the effects of sharpening, try several amounts and pick the one you like best.

Here are some values to get you started. A neutral white point should have dot values of 6% Cyan, 4% Magenta, and 4% Yellow; neutral mid-tones should be 60% Cyan, 45% Magenta, and 45% Yellow; neutral shadows should print with 95% Cyan, 80% Magenta, and 80% Yellow (black will also be substituted into the midtone and shadow regions).

This abundance of Cyan ink values in all three areas will compensate for the contamination of Magenta and Yellow in the printing inks used in the printing process. Adjustment of the color values at the highlight, midtone, and shadow points will assure a good color balance throughout the image. (If you are sending your images out to be printed, you may want to consult your printer concerning the neutral ink values they recommend for their specific inks and presses.) As mentioned in Challenge # 3, Gamut Conversion, you are always viewing your image in RGB mode, but you print in CMYK mode. So make all your color measurements with your densitometer. Don't base any color move or make any changes based upon how your image looks on screen.

▼ *Figure 12.24 Image Sharpness*
On the left is a portion of an image which has been scanned properly but not sharpened. On the right is the same scanned image, with sharpening applied. Note how the high contrast portions of the right image, such as the eyes, eyebrows, and hat fabric are sharper and appear to be in better focus. This sharpening can be applied either during the scan or in the postscan as it was here in Photoshop. Note the Threshold value is set at 5 to protect the facial skin areas from too much sharpening.

Sharpening

All scanners reduce the contrast of an image when they digitize them. This is one of the image changes we discussed in Challenge #1, Changes in an Image. This contrast reduction is an unavoidable artifact of the digitizing process. This problem can be easily corrected, however, through the use of sharpening tools. Sharpening tools come in various forms and names. Sometimes sharpening is called "unsharp masking," sometimes "edge sharpening," and sometimes just "sharpening." The result of sharpening is to increase the difference in grayscale value between two adjacent pixels. Increasing contrast between pixels will result in an overall increase in contrast and therefore sharpness across your entire image. A word of warning here, however: Oversharpening an image removes too much tonal variation and your edges may begin to look too abrupt and develop white halos along some edges.

The sharpening tools built into many low-end scanning applications are not very sophisticated, with most providing you only with a simple linear scale with one composite variable. Many do not distinguish edge areas from non-edge areas, as do more robust unsharp masking tools. Experiment with your scanning application and compare the results against those you can produce in Photoshop. If you perform unsharp masking in Photoshop, I suggest starting with an amount of 50 percent, a radius of 1.5 – 2, and a threshold of 3 – 4. It's easy to add more sharpening, but you can't easily remove it once it's applied.

▼ *Figure 12.25 Resolution Guidelines*

These three Scan Geometry dialog boxes show how Resizing (Magnification), Original image size (Width and Height), Quality Factor (Minimum quality), and Printing or output resolution (Screen frequency– lpi) affect the Scan or input resolution (Resolution) and Image File Size (Disk req'd). The first dialog box shows a scan set up for a 3" x 5" image with no scaling, a quality factor of 1.25, and an lpi of 150. The file size becomes 1.8MB. The second box shows the effect of increasing the quality to 2.0. The file size increases to 4.5 MB. In the third scan setup we have scaled the image 200% which results in a quadrupling of the file size to 18.2 MB.

After you have worked with your scanner and your software for a while, you will develop a sense for how much sharpening is required.

Dot gain

As we discussed under Challenge # 5, Changing Media, images print differently when they are reproduced on various types of media. Dot gain is one of the variables which changes from media to media. Dot gain is a description of how much inks spread out when they are applied to paper. Dot gain percentages vary from 10 percent on glossy stock to 30 percent on some porous newspapers. Images printed without dot gain compensation will print darker than they should, so dot gain must be compensated for in the printing process. One good rule of thumb to follow is to increase dot gain compensation in the midtones because dot gain tends to be greater in the midtones than it is in the highlight and shadow regions. Increasing midtone dot gain will lighten up the midtone region, giving your image better overall contrast. Ask your printer how much dot gain to expect on their presses and where dot gain should be controlled. The printer may have you control it, or may want to control it in the production process.

RIPing considerations

Two important variables which control the "RIPablility" of a file are a file's size and its complexity. File size is determined by image dimension, pixel depth, and resolution. As linear resolution doubles, file size quadruples. As file size increases, so does the time required to RIP that image. Image dimension and pixel depth are usually fixed by the design requirements of the document; therefore, we need to minimize a scan file's resolution without adversely affecting the quality of the image. Following are some guidelines for helping you decide your input scan resolution (see Chapter 8 "Resolving Resolution," and Chapter 9, "Grappling With Graphics," for more detailed information on these file size and complexity characteristics).

Resolution guidelines

Setting the proper resolution of your scanned images is crucial to obtaining high quality and RIPable results. The key is to scan at the lowest resolution possible without degrading the quality of the image, and higher resolution is not always better. Here are some guidelines.

Line art scanning resolutions

Original line art with crisp, sharp edges should generally be scanned at high resolution in order to capture the precise, crisp edges of the lines accurately. My definition of high resolution starts at 800 dpi and goes up. An image captured at anything less than 800 dpi will show visible stairstepping on curves and diagonals. Line art which has rough edges and low detail can often be effectively scanned at resolutions as low as 300 dpi with good results. Scanning rough-edged line art at high resolution will generate large file sizes without necessarily producing any better results than 300 dpi scans.

Contone scanning resolutions

Unlike line art, where edge capture is the key concern, with contone images we are concerned with capturing areas of grayscale which will be recreated as halftone dots. For this reason, continuous tone images can generally be scanned at a relatively low resolution of 200 to 300 dpi. Your choice of input/scan resolution is dependent on the line screen at which the image will ultimately be printed and the amount of scaling which will occur. Input scan resolution = lpi x (1.25 to 2.0) x scaling factor. The LPI or lines per inch is set by your printer. The range of 1.25 to 2.0 is known as the quality factor which you will set depending upon the type of image you are scanning. The scaling factor is determined by how much you intend to enlarge or reduce your image. For example, the scan resolution for a 5" x 7" image to be printed at 150 lpi with no scaling would be: 150 lpi x 1.25 x 1 = 188 dpi. A quality factor of 2.0 would yield a scan resolution of 300 dpi. Using a quality factor near 1.25 will work well for images which are of a completely continuous tone in nature. A higher quality factor should be used for images which have areas of high contrast, such as product shots which have dark type on lighter backgrounds or where detail needs to be captured from dark shadow areas. Keeping input resolution (particularly of multibit contone images) as low as possible is a key tool in our battle to REDUCE & SIMPLIFY!

If we need to scale that 5" x 7" image up 2x to an 8" x 10" for printing, the scan resolution will also double from 188 dpi to 376 dpi. [150 lpi x 1.25 x 2 = 376dpi]. With experience you will learn which quality factors work best with your images, equipment, and software setup.

Postscan manipulation of line art images

After you have scanned your image, you will need to decide what, if any, corrections and/or editing need to be performed. With 1 bit line

▼ Figure 12.26 File Saving Option

Most scanner interfaces will provide you with several file options for saving a scanned image. For images which you intend to take to press, you should save all of your images as TIFFs. You may decide to convert some of your line art TIFFs to line art EPSs after you scan them, but they should initially be saved as TIFFs. As shown here, some scanners give you the choice of saving a color image in RGB or CMYK format. A scanner always captures color images in RGB format, then converts them to CMYK format. Initially, save your image in RGB format if you intend to use the image for anything other than printing. CMYK is a much more restricted color space than RGB. Saving an image in RGB format preserves a wider range of color information, and allows for more flexible use of the file for media such as a monitor display, transparency film, or for presentations which can reproduce a wider range of colors than offset printing.

art images you basically need to choose whether you will leave your line work as a bitmap file or convert it to an outline file. Conversion to an outline image, through the use of an outlining application like Adobe Streamline, has several advantages. Outline images are constructed out of lines; these contrast with bitmap images, which are composed of dots. Outline images, compared with their bitmapped counterparts, tend to be smaller in size by as much as 90 percent, easier to edit and add or build colors, and more suited for rotating and scaling. Bitmapped images tend to be more appropriate for more complex images and those which contain fine detail. Images with the highest complexity, such as very fine and closely spaced lines, I choose to scan as an 8 bit grayscale image and convert to a 1 bit image after resolution enhancement and sharpening. I use threshold adjustments during the grayscale to bitmap conversion to control detail rendering.

Pre/Postscan manipulation of contone images

As mentioned earlier, contone images will be scanned and captured as either 8 bit grayscale or 24 or 32 bit color images depending upon the nature of the original and the scanner used. As with the line art images, after you have scanned your contone image, you will need to decide what, if any, corrections and/or editing need to be performed. Contone images will generally remain as bitmap files unless you are silhouetting or performing extensive image editing. Although it is always preferable to perform your basic image correction manipulations during the scanning process, you may occasionally need to perform these functions on images which have already been scanned.

There are four major manipulations you will generally perform on contone images which you intend to reproduce: tonal compression, tone curve adjustment (also known as gray map adjustments), color cast correction, and sharpening. These adjustments can be made either during the scanning process or in postscan manipulations in image editing applications like Photoshop. The most efficient procedure is to perform these adjustments during scanning. Tonal compression is necessary to distribute all of the limited grayscale information across the entire 256 shades of gray available to an image in Postscript.

Tone curve adjustment is important to setting the general distribution of tones and contrast in an image. Most scanned images are too dark, particularly in the midtones, resulting in images which look muddy, flat, and undetailed in shadow. Many people use contrast and brightness controls to adjust how light or dark their images look, but this is generally a bad approach. Brightness and contrast controls affect all portions of an image equally, that is, in a linear fashion, which causes large shifts in tonal values across the entire image. This approach generally results in loss of detail at one end of the tonal range or the other. Nonlinear correction using tools like the CURVES dialog box in Photoshop are preferable. It is also possible to perform these manipulations in a LEVELs type of tool, but with only three points available for adjustment, highlight, midtone, and shadow, the transitions are not as smooth as those made in CURVES, where all the points along the gray map are gradually adjusted. Figures 12.19 and 12.20 show a comparison of the use of CURVES and LEVELS to manipulate the gray map of an image. You should note that the LEVELS-adjusted image shows a more abrupt change in the image map around the midtone point than the CURVES-adjusted image which shows a more gradual transition. In either case, when CURVES or LEVELS are used to adjust an image in a postscan environment, there is a significant loss of image data (see Figure 12.19 for a comparison of the histogram of an image both before and after a post-scan manipulation of an image has been performed in Photoshop). This is one obvious reason for performing these manipulations during the scan.

Color cast correction is used to remove any image-wide color cast. The presence of significant color cast can be easily seen as an overall tint of a particular color. A quantitative measurement of color cast can be gained by measuring the color values of an image area which should be neutral gray with the on-screen densitometer. This measurement can be performed after a prescan in your scanning software or on a final scan in Photoshop. The quality and quantity of needed shift can be judged by either the RGB or CYMK values which compose the neutral gray area. Once you have determined the shift which needs to be made, these adjustments can be made in either the Color Balance or Hue/Saturation controls found under the Adjust submenu of the main Image menu in Photoshop.

The final adjustment is image sharpening or unsharp masking. Sharpening is necessary to counteract the general softening which usually occurs when an image is processed through digital scanning. A wide range of sharpening capabilities exist depending upon the application used. Some applications allow you to apply different amounts of unsharp masking to various tonal levels, while others provide only overall unsharp masking. In Photoshop there are three possible adjustments: Radius, Amount, and Threshold. The Radius affects the width of the zone over which the unsharp masking will be applied. Amount determines the percent of shift which will be applied to adjacent pixels, and Threshold determines the difference in tonal values which must exist between adjacent pixels before unsharp mask will be applied to those pixels. Setting any of these values too high will result in too much increase in contrast and the development of halos on edges of items in the image. Here are some starting values for you: Radius = 1.5, Amount = 50 (the default), and Threshold = 4. Others have recommended high values for Amount up to 200, but I prefer to start lower and build; you can always add more. After I apply my final unsharp mask, I usually have one more look at my tone histogram in levels to see if any of my pixels have been pushed too far toward black or white. I may make final tiny adjustments in my highlight and shadow points if my histogram shows some open ends.

Image and file formats

Among all file formats which exist including PICT, PCX, Paint, BMP, EPS, WMF, Gif, Riff, TIFF, and others, two formats – TIFF and EPS – are the preferable file formats to be used for files to be printed. Nearly all scanners save their images, or at least provide you with an option of saving in a TIFF format. TIFF is one of the most flexible bitmapped file formats, and it is designed to be used for printing. File formats such as PICT are not designed for printing. Most of your contone images should be saved in TIFF format as should your complex or detailed line art files. The EPS file format should be used primarily for line art files which have been converted from original scanned TIFFs to outline files through an application like Streamline. EPS is also the preferred file format for compound images such as silhouetted contones, which contain both contone bitmaps, and outline segments, which define the edge of the silhouette. If you are thinking of saving your images in some file format other than TIFF or EPS, call your printer or service bureau and ask for their guidance. If you will need to transfer your files from Mac to PC or vise versa, there are a number of options, but two standards will work for most files. To translate bitmapped files on either platform, convert your file to a TIFF first and then open the TIFF in Photoshop and save it as a TIFF in the platform you want. For outline files, the most compatible format is to save the EPS in Illustrator 1.1 format, which has consistently been the most compatible cross-platform format for EPS files.

The two print specific graphic file formats are TIFF for bitmapped images and EPS for outline images. All scanned images start out as bitmaps; they are captured by a scanner as dots. Line art images converted to outline should be saved in EPS format. Images which remain as bitmaps should be saved as TIFFs for printing.

Color
Plates

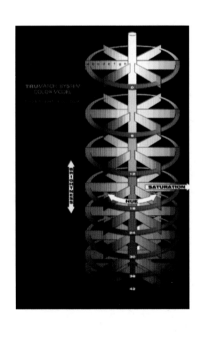

DOCUMENT
Low Resolution Screen Images vs

Low Resolution Screen Font File
- Low resolution (72ppi)
- Bitmapped file and image
- Used to display text on screen
- Not included in page layout document
- Must be sent along with document on disk
- Linked to external scalable outline printer font file

Screen Font Name
Palatino

Quark, PageMaker Document

PAGE LAYOUT DOCUMENT

HEADLINE TYPE

Chicken

Link to High Resolution Graphic File

Imported PICT or Tiff Preview
- Low Resolution (72ppi)
- Included in page layout document
- Linked to external high resolution EPS graphic

72 ppi Screen Image = 18 K

Low Resolution Screen Image
- Low resolution (36 or 72ppi)
- ~18 K @ 72ppi
- Low Res bitmapped PICT or TIFF
- Used to display graphic images on screen
- Included in page layout document.
- Linked to external high resolution graphic

▼ **Figure 8.11 Document Construction**
Page layout documents are shells into which proxies for type and graphics are placed. Low resolution versions of graphic images are stored in the page layout document itself. High resolution versions, used for printing, are stored externally to the page layout document. Font information is entirely external. All the external files need to be sent to your printer along with the page layout document itself.

CONSTRUCTION
High Resolution Printing Images

Link to High Resolution Printer Font File

Printer Font Name
PalatRom

High Resolution Printer Font File
- High resolution Postscript/Outline file
- Scalable
- Not included in page layout document pages
- Linked to external low resolution screen font file
- Not seen on screen, but used to print document
- Must be sent along with document on disk

Chicken

Graphic Type

Editable Type

Chicken

Type to graphics,
Split paths,
Flatness = 3

Export as EPS
graphic

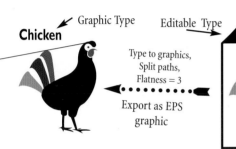

Original Parent/Native Documents
- Original Photoshop or drawing file
- High resolution pixel and/or vector image
- May contain layers, channels and/or editable type
- <u>NOT</u> included in page layout file
- Should be sent as separate unlinked graphic file along with page layout document and linked graphics on disk

Exported EPS Graphic
- Encapsulated Postscript
- Vector /Outline: Resolution independent
- For importing into page layout file
- <u>NOT</u> included in page layout document.
- Must be sent along with document on disk
- Linked to low resolution preview

Drawing Document
- Freehand
- Illustrator
- Corel Draw

Flatten layers and
remove alpha channels
Export as TIFF or EPS
Graphic

**200 ppi 4.34MB
RGB Photoshop Image**

**High Resolution TIFF or EPS
CMYK Printing Image**
- High resolution (200 ppi – 300 ppi)
- 370 KB @ 200 ppi (No layers or channels)
- High resolution bitmapped TIFF or EPS
- Used for printing graphic images
- <u>NOT</u> Included in page layout document
- Sent along with document on disk
- Linked to low resolution graphic file

**200 ppi 370KB
CMYK Print Image**

1 Bit Black & White Image

1 bit line art images such as these contain only one layer of pixels with 1 bit of data per pixel. Each pixel is either Black (1) or White (0). These are the smallest and simplest types of bitmapped images. File size = 285KB at 300ppi.

8 Bit Gray Scale Image

8 bit grayscale images contain only one layer of 8 bit pixels which has the capacity to store and display 256 shades of gray. Contrast this to the 1 bit per pixel used to create the line art image above. This grayscale file size is eight times (8x) larger than the 1bit images discussed above. This 8 b/p file is also the basic building block for the RGB and CMYK images shown below. File size = 2.2MB at 300ppi.

24 Bit RGB Color (Screen) Image

24 bit color images contain three layers of 8 bit grayscale pixels, one for each color (RGB). Each color can be shown in 256 shades. Therefore, the total number of colors possible is 256 Red x 256 Green x 256 Blue = 16.7 million colors. This RGB image file size is twenty-four times larger than the 1bit line art image. File size = 6.6MB at 300ppi.

32 Bit CMYK Color (Print) Image

A 32 bit grayscale image contains four layers of 8 bit grayscale pixels, one for each color. Note: A 32 bit CMYK image produces the same number of colors as the 24 bit RGB image above (16.7 million). The fourth black channel (K) is substituted for various portions of the three color channels (CMY). This K channel improves contrast and shadow detail and reduces ink coverage but does not add any colors. This CMYK image file is used for printing and is 33% larger than the equivalent RGB file, and 32 times larger than a similar 1 bit image. File size = 8.8MB at 300dpi.

Figure 9.10 Pixel Depth Of Images

▼ Digital images are divided into three basic categories: Black & White (1 bit), Grayscale (8 bit), and Color (24 or 32 bits per pixel depending upon whether they are RGB or CMYK images). File size, storage space, and printing time increase as pixel depth increases.

Basic Color Theory

Blue

Magenta

Red

Cyan

Yellow

Green

Center Point

White, (RGB)

Black, (CMYK)

Yellow

Green

Red

Cyan

Magenta

Blue

**Additive RGB Color Space:
Used on Monitors and Scanners**

Red, green, and blue light combine or add to create colors. Contrast this process with the subtractive process below which is used in printing.

R, G

R,G,B

Yellow Surface or Dot

R , B

R,G,B

Magenta Surface or Dot

G, B

R,G,B

Cyan Surface or Dot

▼ *Figure 14.1 Subtractive CMYK Color Space Used In Printing*

Transmitted (RGB) light is selectively absorbed by various combinations of the three process colors (C,M, & Y). The color(s) we see on a printed piece comes from the light which is transmitted and reflected rather than absorbed by the process colors.

▼ **Figure 14.3 RGB/HSV Color Picker**
To the left is the HSV color picker. By manipulating the sliders in this dialog box, you can create all of the colors which this monitor can display.
• The Hue, or basic color, is represented by the colors on the <u>outside</u> edge of the color circle. We are working in RGB color space so the values are recorded in percent of RGB.
• The Saturation is represented by all of the colors <u>inside</u> of the rim of the color circle. As you can see, the colors nearer the center of the circle are lighter, that is, less saturated, than the colors nearer the rim.

Progressive amounts of white are added to any Hue (rim color) at positions tending away from the rim toward the center. The center is pure white or 100% Red + 100% Blue + 100% Green.
• Value is a measure of the percentage of grayscale which a color contains. Value ranges from 0% to 100% and is controlled (added or subtracted) by sliding the large vertical slider up and down. In its current position, the value of this color is 0% grayscale. If the slider were moved all the way to the bottom of its track, 100% gray would be added to the color and it would be pure black.

▼ **Figure 14.4 Color Assignment Palette**
In most applications colors can be stored in and applied through a palette such as this QuarkXPress color palette. The three Pantone colors are spot colors. RGB colors are monitor colors and should not be used for printing. CMYK colors are used for building and printing process colors. The Registration color is assigned to page elements such as crop, registration, and fold marks which should occur on every separation.

▼ **Figure 14.5 Color Models**
This shows a list of the more common color matching systems which are used in graphics applications. The Pantone System is the most widely used. The system labeled Pantone contains the spot color guide colors. The Pantone Process system contains the process color guide colors. And the Pantone ProSim contains the closest simulated process color matches for the spot colors. The Focoltone, TruMatch, Toyo, and DIC systems offer process color matching guides similar to the Pantone Process system.

▼ **Figure 14.7: Color Choice Guides**

Three basic types of color Swatch book choice guides appear here. From left to right they are: 1) Pantone spot color guide, 2) Pantone CMYK process color guide, and 3) Pantone process simulation (ProSim) color guide. The spot color guide shows a range of spot colors 250CV to 255CV. ("CV" means printed on coated stock and "U" means uncoated stock.) They are the same color but appear different because of the printing substrate. CVP designates process simulation of a spot color, while the S prefix indicates a color chosen from the Process color swatch chart. The process guide shows the closest regular Pantone process colors to these spot colors. As you can see, the match is not good, especially in the lighter, more saturated colors. The ProSim guide is a special collection of process colors built specifically to simulate, as close as possible, the Pantone spot colors. Look closely and you will see that the ProSim guide has color values designated by single and even half percent values rather than the standard 10% and 15% value changes. Even this specific, focused attempt to match the spot colors with process colors fails with the more saturated colors. *Note: All spot colors shown on this page are printed with process colors and are therefore not accurate. The above charts are meant to show the differences between the spot and process values for the same colors.

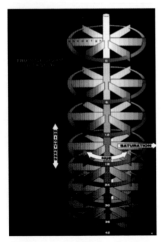

▼ Figure 14.2 Color Space Model

This is a three-dimensional model of HSV (Hue, Saturation & Value) color space created by TruMatch Corp. Hue is represented by the outside rim of the cylinder. Saturation, color purity or intensity, varies across any cross section of the cylinder with maximum saturation on the outside rim and minimum at the center. Value, which is a measure of grayscale value or brightness, varies along the vertical axis of the model cylinder, with 100% gray at one end and 0% gray at the other. The color picker diagram on the facing page is a cross section view through the cylinder. The slider to the right of the pie changes the value or view position along the vertical axis.

▼ Figure 14.6 Color Gamut Comparison

The entire color picker circle shows the gamut of the RGB colors which can be seen on the monitor. The roughly triangular Red area inside of the color picker circle is the limited range of those colors which can be reproduced by CMYK. The black dot in the lower half of the color circle shows the position of the Pantone spot color 251 CV, which is well out of gamut and will not be reproducible in CMYK.

▼ Figure 14.8 Color Gamuts

Color gamut describes the range of color that a particular device can capture or reproduce. This diagram is a two-dimensional slice through three-dimensional color space. Note how much larger the visual gamut of the human eye is (green CIE area) than either the red RGB (monitor) or orange CMYK (printer) gamuts.

▼ Figure14.9 Color Gamuts

This diagram shows the color gamuts for three different color spaces: HyperColor, RGB, and CMYK. The gamuts for RGB color space and the human eye are much more extensive than the CMYK printing gamut. HyperColor is a version of HiFi color which utilizes double hits of CMYK to increase the process color gamut.

▼ Figure 14.11 Q 60 IT8 Chart

This industry standard chart is used as a scanning target. During a calibration this target is used to create correction curves to adjust the scanner. Similar calibration curves can be constructed for monitors and printers.

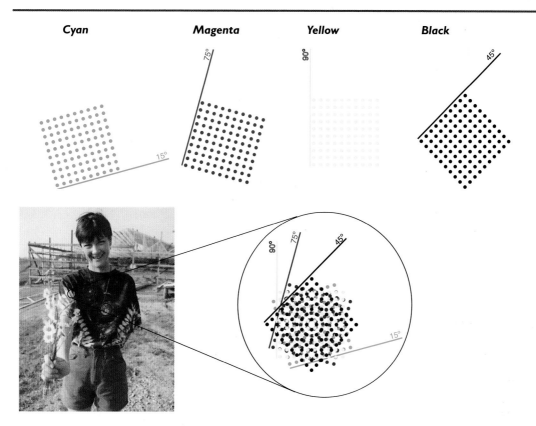

Cyan	Magenta	Yellow	Black

▼ *Figure 16.2 Color Contone Images: Overlapping Four Color Process Halftone Screens*
Complex color contones such as this photograph are reproduced using a complex pattern of four overlapping screens of halftone dots. There is one screen pattern for each process color. Each color is printed at a different angle to avoid the generation of moiré patterns. Colors are separated as much as possible across the available 90°. The three strongest colors – Black, Cyan, and Magenta – are each separated by 30°. The fourth and weakest color, Yellow, is separated from two of the other colors, in this case Cyan and Magenta, by only 15°. When all four color screens are combined, a continuous tone color image simulation is produced. Note the rosette pattern which results when the four screens are in perfect registration.

▼ *Figure 16.3 Moiré Pattern Generation*
When two or more overlapping screens are printed out of registration, repeating geometric patterns known as a moiré pattern can result. Printing each screened color at a different and optimum angle helps reduce the occurrence of moiré patterns. It is the repeating pattern of halftone dots which makes conventional screening technology prone to the development of moiré patterns. The use of frequency modulation screening technology, where image dots are more randomly placed, can mitigate this problem of moiré pattern development.

▼ Figure 17.1 Knockout
This figure shows a knockout. The Cyan area under the black T is removed or knocked out from behind the T.
If the T is considered the foreground object, then a choke trap would have the Cyan background move in, or choke in, around the T. A spread trap would enlarge or spread the T out into the Cyan background.
An overprint would print the black T directly on top of the background without removing any of the Cyan. Overprinting is the safest way to trap because there are few alignment problems. However, overprinting will result in color alterations of the overprinted object unless it is very dark (>95 grayscale value).

▼ Figure 17.2 Trap Example
Different applications use different methods for applying trap, but they all spread, choke, knockout, and overprint in one way or another. The Freehand trap dialog box shows the foreground T being spread by 1 pt. If the reversed button were activated, then the background would choke.

▼ Figure 18.3 Spot Color Separation
This edit color dialog box in QuarkXPress demonstrates how to designate a spot color to separate as a spot color. Here the spot color 3395 is assigned from the Pantone spot color swatch chart mode. Note that the Process Separation check box near the upper lefthand corner is <u>not</u> checked. If this box is checked, Quark XPress will separate all items assigned to this color on the four process color plates.

▼ Figure 18.1 Color Palette
This is a color palette from QuarkXPress showing the four process colors; a Pantone process color, a custom process color build, using the four process colors, one Pantone spot color, and a varnish. There will be six individual separations printed on their own individual pieces of film from this list of ten (10) colors. Note that the RGB colors have been removed from the color palette because they should not be used in the printing process. Also notice that the varnish is listed and will be applied and separated, like a spot color. The process colors will be combined together during the printing process. The registration color (generally a composite black) should be applied only to items such as crop, trim, registration, and fold marks which need to be placed on each film separation.

7/C Chicken built with 7 Spot Colors

7/C Chicken built with 4 Process Colors

Pantone 213 Plate

Pantone 2726 Plate

Pantone 389 Plate

Pantone Black Plate

Pantone 252 Plate

Pantone 3395 Plate

Pantone 486 Plate

▼ Figure 18.4a Spot Color Palette

Each of the assigned spot colors seen in this palette will be printed on its own plate. Each differently colored portion of the image is separated and has a specific spot color applied to it from a different press cylinder. Note that all the extraneous colors have been removed from this palette. While multicolor spot color printing like this allows you to use vivid custom colors, it is far more expensive than using combinations of process colors to produce the many color variations.

▼ Figure 18.4b Process Color Palette

All seven of the colors used here are created from various combinations of CMYK. Since only four sets of separations, film, plates, and cylinders are required to print this image, it is much less expensive to print than its spot color "equivalent." Note that all the extraneous colors have been removed from this palette to avoid confusion.

▼ Figure 18.4a & b Spot vs Process Separations

This seven-color chicken is built and separated first with seven spot and then with four process colors. Note how the spot colors requires the use of seven separations and therefore sheets of film and press cylinders, while the process build requires only four of each.

▼ Figure 18.5 Printing Ink Setup (SWOP)

Prior to converting an RGB image into a CMYK image in Photoshop, you should pay close attention to: 1) the ink color set chosen and 2) the dot gain percentage. Contact your printer to obtain both pieces of information. The dot gain percentage, 20% here, should be for the dot gain at 50%. The values set here will affect the appearance of the Separation Setup dialog box shown below.

▼ Figure 18.7 Printing Ink Setup (4/C Laser)

Here the Printing Ink Setup is being set for a four–color laser copier. Note the increase in dot gain to 33% from the 20% standard for the SWOP coated shown in Figure 18.5. See Figure 18.8 below to view what effect the change in Printing Ink Setup has on the associated separation curves.

▼ Figure 18.6 Separation Setup

The values set in the Photoshop Printing Inks setup dialog box shown in Figure 18.5 affect the curves shown here. Your choice of UCR or GCR will also affect the separation curves. Note how the Black generation begins at the three quarter tone for the UCR curve and at the quarter tone for the UCR curve. Also note the lower overall placement of the UCR curves due to the differences in beginning of the Black generation. Compare and contrast these curves with those used for a Canon four-color laser copier. Each type of printing device has its own set of curves. Note how the SWOP curves automatically compensate for the reduced amount of Cyan ink (top curve), while the laser curve compensates for weaknesses in both Cyan and Yellow toners. Obtain values for Black Ink Limit and Total Ink limit from your printer.

▼ Figure 18.8: Separation Setup

The curves above show the Separation Setup curves which will be applied to an image which will be color separated for printing on a four-color laser copier which uses thermoplastic toners instead of the transparent inks used on a printing press. Note the difference in the starting positions and the effects of the Black generation curves in the UCR and GCR variations. Remember to obtain values for Black Ink Limit and Total Ink limit from your printer. All of these curves will be applied to an RGB file when it is converted to a CMYK image in Photoshop, so be sure to make and set the correct choices and values in both the Printing Ink Setup and Separation Setup dialog boxes prior to performing any RGB to CMYK conversions.

▼ *Figure 12.27 Master PhotoCD*
This is the disk produced from the Master PhotoCD station which handles 35mm film images exclusively. It can hold up to 100 scans in Image Pacs with five (5) different resolution files for each image.

▼ *Figure 12.28 Pro Photo CD*
This is the disk produced from the Pro PhotoCD station which handles 35mm film images exclusively. It can hold up to 100 scans in Image Pacs with six (6) different resolution files for each image.

PhotoCD images

There are many circumstances in which you will be working with images you have not personally scanned but someone else has. If an image you are using has been scanned on a drum scanner by a highly trained professional scanner operator, the chances are good that your image will be at least reasonably well prepared for printing. Good scanner operators know about tone compression, gray map adjustments, print-specific color correction, and sharpening. With other images you may not be so lucky. One source of outside scans will probably be PhotoCD.

What is PhotoCD?

PhotoCD is an *inexpensive* and *flexible* way to capture, store, and distribute digital images which originally have been captured on photographic film. PhotoCD is not just one product, but rather a collection of related imaging technologies and products. This collection currently includes two special film scanners with related scanning stations and associated software, a color proofing system, a CD writer, a unique image compression scheme for storing the PhotoCD images, some third party production software products, and several software products offered by Kodak. The two primary PhotoCD products from which you are most likely to acquire images are Master and Pro PhotoCD.

❥ *Master PhotoCD* is the original PhotoCD consumer product. This product is produced from 35mm slides and provides an image pack which contains five (5) images at five different resolutions for each slide. Each Master PhotoCD disk holds about 100 images.

❥ *Pro PhotoCD* is the professional version, which offers the ability to scan 4"x 5" film as well as 35mm and many film sizes in between. Pro PhotoCD offers the same five resolutions as those offered by the Master PhotoCD, but also provides a sixth high resolution format which is attractive to professional photographers who want to work with higher quality images. Each Pro PhotoCD disk holds between 25 and 100 images depending upon which resolutions are stored.

▼ *Figure 12.29 PhotoCD Station*
This is the Master PhotoCD
station. The 35 mm PCD 2000
scanner is behind the operator.
The Spark20 cpu (bottom),
the PCD Writer (middle), and
a CD reader (top) are to the
left of the scanner.

▼ *Figure 12.30 PhotoCD*
Image Pacs
These are the Image Pac files
which were produced on the
Photo Imaging Workstation
(PIW). Image Pacs contain the
compressed image informa-
tion for all of the Pro
PhotoCD images. There is one
Image Pac for each scanned
image stored on the disk.

Multiple resolutions: why and how?

The core of the uniqueness and flexibility of PhotoCD technology is
in how images are sampled and stored. Current PhotoCD disks have
either five (Master) or six (Pro) different files for each scanned image,
each with a different resolution. Each resolution is useful for reproduction of different sized images. If you need to reproduce an image
as an 8"x 10" one day and as a 3"x 5" the next, each size should use a
different resolution. The 8"x 10" reproduction requires 5.6 times
more information, or resolution, than the 3"x 5" image does. If you
use the highest resolution to reproduce all of your images, you waste
too much time in processing, hence the need for the various image
resolutions which PhotoCD provides. Each resolution contains a specific number of pixels of information, has a specific file size, and is
useful for the reproduction of different sizes or kinds of images.

These are the six possible resolutions currently available and their
characteristics:

Level	Resolution	Size(RGB)	Screen Use & Print size at 133 lpi
base/16	128 x 192	72K	Thumbnails & Screen
base/4	256 x 384	288K	CD Catalog and 1.3" x 1.9"
base	512 x 768	1.13MB	TV and 2.5" x 3.8"
4base	1536 x 1024	4.5MB	HDTV and 5.0" x 7.5"
16base	3072 x 2048	18MB	Full resolution and 10" x 15"
*64base	4096 x 6144	72MB	20" x 30"
256base	8192 x 12,288	288MB	40" x 60" (Future)
1024base	16,384 x 24,576	1152MB	80" x 120" (Future)

*Pro Photo CD only

Note that the various levels of PhotoCD are designated as a base that
is multiplied or divided by a 4, 16, or 64. The original images (35mm
to 4"x 5") are scanned at the highest resolution (3072 x 2048 for
Master and 4096 x 6144 for Pro PhotoCD) and then sampled down,
either two or three times, to the base level. This base level is then used
to construct, through either sampling up or down, the other resolutions which PhotoCD offers.

PhotoCD utilizes a unique lossless compression scheme called
Huffman compression, which uses a series of interpolations, comparisons, and residuals to create the base image and then recreate the
other resolutions without any loss of data. This same Huffman compression scheme is also used as the basis for lossy JPEG compression.

▼ Figure 12.31 PhotoCD Folders

The Photo folder contains five folders, one for each set of different resolution files. Each folder contains a specific resolution file for each scanned image. This disk indicates that it has eight images recorded on it. The file data is contained in the Image Pac as above.

PhotoCD file format

The PhotoCD file format is a special one called YCC. The YCC format is a generic color format easily transformed for a variety of uses including video, TV, and even print. The origin of YCC is in television. The Y is a luminance or brightness channel; the two Cs contain the color information, channels, one for hue and one for saturation. If you are familiar with the HSV (Hue Saturation and Value) model for describing color, then the YCC format will be an easy transition. The YCC format is similar to an RGB file, but is organized into an HSV file format so that V (Brightness or Value) can be adjusted separately from the chrominance (Hue and Saturation) channels.

Challenges of PhotoCD print production

The PhotoCD technology was originally developed for on-screen viewing and was not intended to be used for commercial print purposes. The YCC format is an excellent general format for viewing images on a wide variety of screens. After all, the YCC format was adopted from a TV format. This original orientation toward screen viewing created two problems related to using PhotoCD images for high quality offset-press print reproduction. One problem has been solved, while the other remains.

The first problem involves file formats. In order to use PhotoCD images for print, they must be converted into CMYK format. Initially, this was a problem because the YCC images had to first be converted to RGB images prior to the final conversion to CMYK. This double conversion resulted in too much loss of image quality and significant calibration problems as well. As with most conditions in the world, if there is a void, nature moves to fill that void. And so it was that several third party companies, most notably Parup with its PhotoImpress product, developed applications which would allow for the direct conversion of YCC images into their CMYK equivalents with minimal loss of image quality.

The second issue is the quality of the original scan. One good yardstick of scanner quality is the dynamic range of the scanner. Dynamic range is a logarithmic scale which measures the range of tonal values which a scanner can "see" and capture. The dynamic range scale starts at zero (0) and goes to (4), with four being the best tonal range capture. The best drum (PMT) scanners have dynamic ranges between 3.5 and 4.0. High quality flatbed (CCD) scanners generally sport dynamic ranges of 2.8 to 3.5. Both PhotoCD scanners have dynamic ranges of 2.8, which is equivalent to many high quality CCD scanners but well below the best drum scanners. The high dynamic range of drum scanners is mostly required for capturing fine detail in shadow areas. So, for the highest quality scanning requirements such as high quality ads and high line screen color reproductions, PhotoCD images fall a bit short. However, all is not doom and gloom, because 75 percent to 80 percent of all color scan jobs do not require the highest tonal range reproductions. There are a growing number of service bureaus who are making very successful livings providing scanning services for commercial printers and their clients. The technology exists to increase the dynamic range of the PhotoCD scanners. I think that in the near future we will see PhotoCD scanners with dynamic ranges well above 3.0.

Access to PhotoCD is provided through an increasing number of applications including Photoshop 3.0 and above and PageMaker 6.0 and above. Whichever route you use to access and utilize PhotoCD images, be sure that you treat them with at least as much attention as you would a normal scanned image. Be sure to start out with good quality originals. During the initial scan, be sure that the proper film type information is used by the PIW site who performs the scan. Remember that PhotoCD scans are not automatically optimized for print production. Make sure that you properly adjust tone compression, gray map adjustments, and global color correction, as well as apply proper sharpening for print. These adjustments can all be made manually in Photoshop. But this process takes more time than some applications which are designed specifically for working with PhotoCD images. If you really like the PhotoCD format, you can even take non-PhotoCD images and create your own Image Pacs. PhotoCD is an inexpensive and highly flexible technology which will be increasingly used in multitudes of imaging applications. If you have not yet worked with this technology, it is worthwhile getting familiar with it.

Limitations of your scanner

Keep in mind that if you use a desktop CCD scanner there are some images which you will not be able to capture effectively. The dynamic range, that is, the range of tonal capture, of most desktop scanners is significantly lower (2.5 – 2.9) than that of PMT drum scanners (3.6 – 4.0). This means that images which have large tonal ranges and deep shadow detail may be beyond the ability of your scanner to capture completely. So be prepared to send images of black cats on white wedding dresses out to a service bureau which has a PMT drum scanner.

Scanning software

Good scanning software that gives you good control is the most important feature of a desktop scanner. Most scanners ship with at least some type of image acquisition software. Some provide you with only basic controls such as mode and resolution and the ability to save the image to disk with no view at all. Others are very sophisticated and provide preview with complete prescan image control. While I have not used all the scanning applications available (there are many good ones), here is a sampling of a few applications which I recommend. If you use an Apple scanner and you want to scan directly into Photoshop, I recommend Scantastic. MagicScan for UMAX scanners is also excellent. It provides you with a full range of prescan controls. If your scanning software does not provide you with robust scanning controls, there are several good third-party scanning software products. Here are a few that are available: ScanPrep Pro is an amazing "intelligent" automated scanning application which produces excellent results, supports a wide variety of scanners, and provides built-in calibration abilities; Binuscan's ColorPerfect is also excellent as is ArtScan Pro. Whenever you can, perform all of the image adjustments we have discussed on a prescanned image and let the scanner and its software apply them during the scanning process. This will save you much postscanning image editing in Photoshop or other image editing software. Adjustments you should make to a prescanned line art image include assignment of cropping, sizing, and resolution values. If you choose grayscale mode for detailed line art, you may also perform sharpening during the scanning process. The conversion to B&W through resolution enhancement and thresholdings will generally be done in in the postscan through Photoshop, unless you use an automatic scanning application like ScanPrepPro which will perform these functions for you.

Multipurposing of images

Although our discussions in this book center mainly on the preparation of files for prepress uses, we would be remiss if we did not briefly address some scanning guidelines for images which will be used for two or more output devices; that is, multipurposed. The more purposes for which you intend to use an image, the more general your scan settings should be. If you intend to use your images to output to RGB film and place them as well in WEB pages, then you may not want to perform some of the prepress-specific manipulations such as Gamut conversion, dot gain adjustments, and unsharp masking. The more manipulation you intend to perform in the postscan environment, the less restrictive your scan should be. If you intend to multipurpose your images, here are a few quick guidelines:

Multipurpose guidleines

1) Scan into a device-independent CIE color space like Lab.

2) Keep the original image unaltered in this form.

3) Make copies of this image to convert into other device-specific color spaces and file formats.

4) Make prepress-specific adjustments such as RGB to CMYK gamut conversion, dot gain adjustments, and unsharp masking on a copy of the image.

5) Images which will go to the Internet need to be kept in CIE space to retain their color saturation.

6) Limit all your gamut conversions to one step if possible to reduce loss of color saturation.

7) Compress images only as a final step before sending or archiving, and never compress an image more than once.

A final word

The more you work with scanned and RIPed images, the more you will develop a feel for how they work. Get in the habit of looking at your digital images on screen at high magnification. See how your scanning choices affect the pixels and their relationships. Before you scan, contact your printer to obtain the values they recommend for such items as neutral ink percentages, line screen, and dot gain. And remember that controlling resolution (and therefore file size), particularly of multibit per pixel contone images, is a critical tool in helping us to REDUCE & SIMPLIFY!

PAULINE'S FILE PREP TIPS

File Prep Hint #45

Image data changes during scanning from original image to 0s and 1s in RAM, to pixels on screen, to dots on paper. Original data is not 100 percent reproducible. All print images are constructed out of dots. Line art is constructed out of small touching dots or spots, while contones are formed from patterns of larger separated dots (constructed from groups of the smaller spots) called halftone dots. It is useful to imagine the changes which happen to your images because being able to visualize the changes will help you decide the best way to scan your images.

File Prep Hint #46

Up to 95 percent of data is lost (from 5000 visible tones down to 100 printed tones) during the transition from original scene to film to digital data to Postscript to print. We must capture and save the best possible 256 shades of gray or tones during the scanning process. Proper tone compression, setting the highlight and shadow points, is crucial for this. Be aware of the difference between setting your highlight dot on a specular versus diffuse highlight area. Specular areas are pure white and have no tonal values; therefore, they should be avoided as highlight choices. Tone compression should be primarily performed during the scanning process and not during the postscan in applications such as Photoshop.

File Prep Hint #47

Brightness and contrast adjustments through alteration of tonal curves can be used to correct your images and concentrate limited tonal data in those portions of the image which are most important.

PAULINE'S FILE PREP TIPS

File Prep Hint #48

Make sure you scanner is linearized so that you know that it will properly reproduce all values of grayscale and color. Use a gray scale target with known values to calibrate your scanner

File Prep Hint #49

To remove the color cast imposed on your images by your scanner, scan a target which contains a variety of neutral tones. Measure the neutral areas with an on-screen densitometer and create correction curves which can be applied to all scanned images.

File Prep Hint #50

Don't forget to compensate for dot gain before you print your final image. Compensate for dot gain during the scanning process. But if you intend to multipurpose your images, scan without dot gain compensation, make copies of your original images, and apply dot gain only to those images which will be used for print. Also, be sure to apply dot gain corrections which are specific to each print device you will use.

File Prep Hint #51

We print with impure process inks. This flaw must be compensated for when setting gray balance. In highlight: C/M/Y = 6/4/4; in midtone: C/M/Y = 60/45/45. This correction can be, and often is, done during the scan process, but if you intend to multipurpose your images, you should scan your images neutral, make copies of the original scan, and apply the correction for impure

Pauline's File Prep Tips

printing inks only to images which you intend to print. This color correction can be performed during the RGB to CMYK gamut conversion and should be specific to each printer you use.

File Prep Hint #52

All scanners soften images as they sample images when they capture them. In order to return an image to its original sharpness or even improve it, a scanned image must be sharpened. Always choose a sharpening tool such as unsharp masking, which preferentially sharpens higher contrast areas of an image. Sharpening can be, and often is, applied during the scan process; however, if you intend to significantly modify an image after it is scanned, save the sharpening for last.

File Prep Hint #53

We work in various color gamuts in electronic prepress such as CIE (Lab or YCC), RGB on scanners and monitors, and CMYK on press. This means color data is lost during the gamut conversion process from RGB to CMYK. In general, and particularly when we will be multipurposing images, we want to capture an image into as large a color space as possible (usually a CIE color space) and then convert copies of the original images into whichever color space we intend to use them. Limit your image gamut conversions to one step whenever possible to reduce color saturation loss which inevitably occurs during gamut conversions.

PAULINE'S FILE PREP TIPS

File Prep Hint #54

Don't judge color visually on a monitor. Always use an on-screen densitometer to measure tone and color data.

File Prep Hint #55

Be aware of the tonal capture range (dynamic range) of your scanner. Your desktop scanner may not be able to capture the entire tonal range of some images.

File Prep Hint #56

Most image adjustments should be performed during the scanning process, not afterward. Use a low resolution prescan technique to set cropping, scaling, tone compression, gray map adjustments, global color corrections, and sharpening to save time and preserve image quality.

File Prep Hint #57

Simple, crisp line art images should be scanned at high resolution 800 dpi or greater and then converted to outline files in a dedicated outlining application like Streamline. Rough line art can be scanned as low resolution (300 dpi).

File Prep Hint #58

Scanning resolutions for unscaled continuous tone images, which will be two times (2x) the lpi at which the images will be printed. A 1.25 – 1.4 (quality factor) x the lpi is sufficient for most unscaled images. Use the following formula

PAULINE'S FILE PREP TIPS

to determine the input scan resolutions for contone images: [1.25 – 2.0 x lpi times scaling factor]. Using smaller quality factors of between 1.25 and 1.4 will dramatically reduce the file size of the image. High quality factors approaching 2.0 need only be used for images with high contrast areas or when trying to capture subtle shadow detail.

File Prep Hint #59

Final resolutions (after scaling) for contone images which will be reproduced with FM, or stochastic screening methods such as on banner printers, need not exceed 100ppi, as FM screening processing does not require as much pixel information as AM screening.

File Prep Hint #60

Complex and fine detail line art images can be scanned as 8 bit grayscale images and then converted to 1 bit line art using sharpening and thresholding.

File Prep Hint #61

Visualize the effect of the entire scanning and production process on your image before you start. Scan with a final purpose in mind. For multipurpose images, create neutral uncorrected scans, but always tone compress and map during the scan.

13

Document Construction

As the Byte Turns continues...

Will Pauline only help Danny make the connection to his high-res files, or will they make another connection as well?

I copied my page layout file to the disk I sent you. All the graphics and fonts showed up fine just before I copied it. Why can't you print my document correctly? I have a proof to prove it right here!

Well, I don't know.

I wish I did know.

So why can't we print his file???

I can't print his files because the high resolution graphics and his fonts are not there. Danny needs to understand how his documents are constructed and linked.

DOCUMENT PLANNING & CONTROL

Planning

Planning your print project should be your first priority. With proper planning you can eliminate unnecessary mistakes as well as minimize the complexity of your document and the number of changes you need to make by having a standard set of guidelines to go by. Design and produce your document with the final output in mind. The tried and true practice of using thumbnail sketches (Figure 13.1) is still very useful. In fact, with all the document construction and typesetting controls available to us, the use of thumbnailing has become even more important.

Here are some general planning guidelines:

❧ Plan your document with thumbnails before you start laying out your document on the computer. On your thumbnails include characteristics such as page size and orientation, margins, facing or no-facing page design, flowing vs. nonflowing text areas, number of columns as well as width of and gutter between them, and list of master page and style sheet elements.

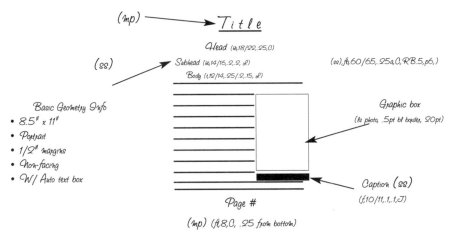

▼ Figure 13.1 Thumbnail Sketch

Creating rough thumbnail sketches before you begin work on the computer can save you time and editing. Notice that in addition to basic document information such as page size, orientation, margins, page facing, and auto text information, Master Page items (mp) and Style Sheets (ss) are marked and notated with formatting information. Even though I may ultimately adjust some of the formatting, this process helps to get me organized and dramatically speeds up my work.

- ❥ Plan to use graphic file formats which are appropriate for your project's final media. For most print projects use TIFF and EPS graphics whenever possible (more on this later).

- ❥ Plan to set aside some time to proofread your copy. It also helps to have more than one person proof the job. You can never proof a job too often. More on this in Chapter 18, "The Proof is in the Separation."

- ❥ Keep your document as clean as possible. Do not leave unnecessary boxes, lines, etc., lying around. Do not try to use white boxes to knock out an area. Be "code conscious" when creating your document. Choose the simplest way to accomplish your task; for example, move a text box instead of using the baseline shift to reposition an entire section of text.

- ❥ There are many graphics and documents which you can create on a computer which are difficult or impossible to print. Examples include complex masks, bright spot colors printed in CMYK, and overlapping blends. As a document designer and creator, you must keep this in mind as you prepare your files. The freedom you have as a computer-oriented designer must be tempered by your responsibilities to create files which are compatible with their final use.

We will be discussing all of the above topics in more detail throughout the book.

Document composition

Composite page layout

The composite document is the document which contains all of the various text and graphic elements which make up the final document. The composite application is used for formatting, arranging, and organizing all of these text and graphic elements, and is usually used for printing as well. The most common composite applications are page layout programs such as PageMaker and QuarkXpress. These applications are well suited for precise control of type as well as compositing pages. Some composite pages are produced in drawing applications such as Illustrator, Freehand, or CorelDraw. Using a drawing application for compositing single-page, graphic-intensive documents is acceptable, but one can construct longer, more text-intensive documents more effectively in a page layout application.

▼ Figure 13.2 Screen Font
This is a low resolution bitmapped screen font. The character is built out of dots, like a bitmapped graphic. Contrast this with the outline printer font in Figure 13.3, which is constructed out of lines instead of dots. The screen font file is used for the display of type onscreen. Screen fonts are not imbedded in a page layout document and must be sent with its printer font partner, as a separate file to accompany the page layout document in which it is used.

▼ Figure 13.3 Printer Font
This is a high resolution outline printer font built out of lines, unlike the screen font in Figure 13.2. The printer font file is used for scaling and printing. Printer fonts are not imbedded in the document and must be sent with the screen font partner as a separate file to accompany the page layout document. Printer fonts are like outline graphic files.

Graphics applications

Just as page composition and typesetting is best performed in page layout applications like QuarkXpress and PageMaker, most graphic elements are best created in graphics applications. There are basically two types of graphics applications: painting and drawing. Painting type graphics, also known as bitmapped or raster graphics, are created in applications like Photoshop or Painter. Paint images are constructed out of patterns of dots. Drawing type graphics, also known as outline or vector graphics, are created in applications such as Illustrator, Freehand, or CorelDraw. These graphics are constructed out of lines. Graphics are generally created in one of these graphics applications and then imported into page layout applications as elements for final document composition.

Page elements

Type

Text on a page is created through the use of fonts. While there are several varieties of fonts (more on this later), most fonts contain two types of information. First is screen font information (Figure 13.2), which is used for displaying type on a monitor; second is printer font information (Figure 13.3), which is used for printing the font. Screen font files are generally bitmapped files of low resolution (low resolution is all that is required for viewing on a screen). Printer font files are high resolution outline files which can be scaled to a wide range of sizes for printing. The screen font file and printer font files are linked to each other and to the document where they are placed. Both the low resolution screen font files and the high resolution printer font are necessary for creating, viewing, and printing type in a document. It is important to note that both the screen fonts and printer fonts are *external* files which *are not included* automatically within a page layout document when you copy or move the document to another disk. If you attempt to view or print a document which does not have access to the proper font files, the copy will generally be rendered on screen and printed as a default font, most often Courier. Therefore, when you move a document from one computer to another you must make sure that you send the font files, both screen and printer, for all of the fonts which you have used along with the document.

There is one concept which has helped me understand fonts and has removed some of the confusion and complexity surrounding them.

▼ Figure 13.4 Low Resolution Screen Image
This is the low resolution (72 ppi) screen image (55K) used for viewing an imported image. This low resolution file is imbedded in the page layout document and should be linked to an *external* high resolution file which will be used during printing. It looks pixilated when it is printed. Compare with the sharper high resolution image in Figure 13.5

▼ Figure 13.5 High Resolution Print Image
This is the high resolution partner to the file shown in Figure 13.4. This is a 300 ppi image (1.3MB) and is linked to the low resolution image when imported into a document. This image is used for printing. This high resolution file is *not imbedded* in the document, so it must be sent separately and linked to the internal low resolution image.

Fonts are often discussed as if they are file types or document elements completely separate from graphics. I prefer to think of fonts as being special types of graphic files. The bitmapped screen fonts are special types of paint or bitmapped graphics, and printer fonts are special versions of outline or vector files. Keep this comparison in mind as you work your way through the chapters on graphics and typesetting.

(Note: In Windows 3.1 the screen and printer font file equivalents are called .pfm and .pfb files. Also, this discussion of screen and printer fonts does not apply to TrueType fonts which combine these two components into one file. See Chapter 11, "A Tale of True Typesetting," for a more complete discussion of this topic.)

Graphics

Graphic elements are generally created within a graphics application and then imported into a page layout document for combination with type and other graphic elements. Like fonts, graphic elements have two components: a low resolution screen view component (Figure 13.4) and a high resolution print file component (Figure 13.5). The low resolution screen view component of the graphic file is, unlike fonts, actually imbedded in the page layout document. This means that when you move a page layout document which contains an imported graphic file to another disk or computer, the low resolution graphic file moves along with the document. So the screen view will always be there unless you remove it intentionally. The continual presence of the the low resolution screen view file can lead you to believe that the entire graphic file is present. But, in order to print properly, the high resolution graphic file component must also be present and linked to its low resolution graphic file partner. Because the low resolution screen view image is always visible, it is easy to forget, when copying or moving a document to another disk or computer, that the high resolution version of imported graphic files is not part of the page layout document itself. What will happen if you try to print a document for which you have forgotten to send along the linked high resolution versions of the imported graphic files? It will still print and you will see the graphic, but you will be able to reproduce only a low resolution version of the graphic. This generally results in the image being rendered with large pixels.

Native files

Most graphic application documents, such as Freehand or CorelDraw documents, are not directly importable into other applications in their original or native document format. Therefore, some types of

▼ *Figure 13.6 Native Document*
Original outline graphic is created as a document in a drawing application such as Illustrator, Freehand, or CorelDraw.

▼ *Figure 13.7: Exported EPS File*
This graphic is exported as an EPS file, which is then suitable for importing into a page layout application such as QuarkXpress or PageMaker.

graphic files, most notably EPS graphics which are produced in drawing applications, must be specifically *exported* as EPS files in order for us to be able to *import* them into other applications such as PageMaker or QuarkXpress (see Figures 13.6 and 13.7 for examples). The EPS file is sometimes not as editable as the original parent or native document from which it was produced and exported. As a result, when you are copying documents to a new computer or sending your files out to be printed, it is good practice to send along the native or parent graphic document as well as the exported EPS graphic file. This will allow whoever is printing the file to edit any aspect of the graphics file if it becomes necessary.

Document construction basics

Master pages

Master Pages are templates for placement of document elements (see Figure 13.9). Master Pages automatically place repetitive text and graphic elements and are especially useful for longer documents. Repetitive page elements such as page numbers and mastheads can be constructed in Master Pages and then applied to multiple document pages. Using Master Pages to locate repetitive document elements saves a tremendous amount of time and improves the consistency of element placement. The use of Master Pages also dramatically improves the editability of a document. Note that in the thumbnail sketch shown at the beginning of this chapter I have Master Page elements designated. (See Chapter 11, "A Tale of True Typesetting,-" for a more complete discussion of Master Pages.)

Style sheets

A style sheet is a template for type formatting (see Figure 13.8). A style sheet should be used to format any type which occurs repetitively throughout a document. As with the use of Master Pages, using style sheets saves time, improves consistency, and dramatically aids in the editing process. When I am sketching my thumbnails, I always include at least the initial names and basic formatting characteristics of the style sheets I intend to use. For more details on style sheets, see the Typesetting with Style section in Chapter 11.

Document management

OK, raise your hand if you have never lost a file. If you have your

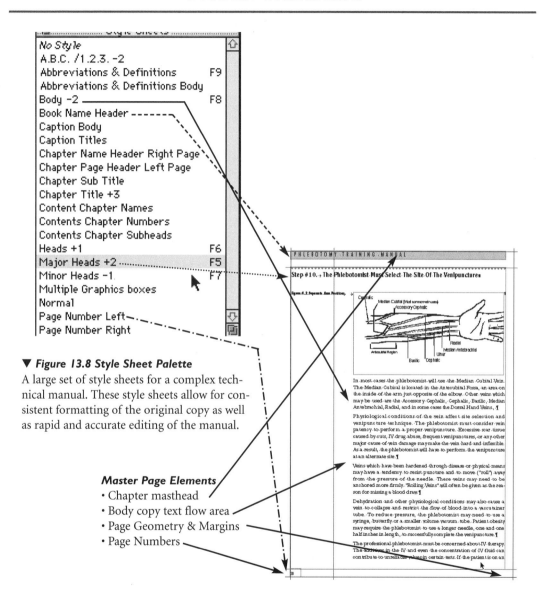

▼ Figure 13.8 Style Sheet Palette
A large set of style sheets for a complex technical manual. These style sheets allow for consistent formatting of the original copy as well as rapid and accurate editing of the manual.

Master Page Elements
• Chapter masthead
• Body copy text flow area
• Page Geometry & Margins
• Page Numbers

▼ Figure 13.9 Technical Manual Document Page Showing Master Page and Style Sheet Elements
The chapter name masthead at the top of the document and the page number at the lower left corner are set up on a Master Page. Each chapter has its own Master Page. Four style sheet text formats are used on this page.

DOCUMENT
Low Resolution Screen Images vs.

Low Resolution Screen Font File
- Low resolution (72ppi)
- Bitmapped file and image
- Used to display text on screen
- Not included in page layout document
- Must be sent along with document on disk
- Linked to external scalable outline printer font file

Screen Font Name
Palatino

Quark, PageMaker
Document

PAGE LAYOUT DOCUMENT

HEADLINE TYPE

Link to High Resolution Graphic File

Chicken

Imported PICT or Tiff Preview
- Low Resolution (72ppi)
- Included in page layout document
- Linked to external high resolution EPS graphic

72 ppi Screen Image = 18 K

Low Resolution Screen Image
- Low resolution (36 or 72ppi)
- ~18 K @ 72ppi
- Low Res bitmapped PICT or TIFF
- Used to display graphic images on screen
- Included in page layout document
- Linked to external high resolution graphic

▼ **Figure 8.11 Document Construction**
Page layout documents are shells into which proxies for type and graphics are placed. Low resolution versions of graphic images are stored in the page layout document itself. High resolution versions, used for printing, are stored externally to the page layout document. Font information is entirely external. All the external files need to be sent to your printer along with the page layout document itself. (See C-2)

CONSTRUCTION
High Resolution Printing Images

Link to High Resolution Printer Font File

Printer Font Name
PalatRom

High Resolution Printer Font File
- High resolution Postscript/Outline file
- Scalable
- Not included in page layout document pages
- Linked to external low resolution screen font file
- Not seen on screen, but used to print document
- Must be sent along with document on disk

Graphic Type

Editable Type

Chicken

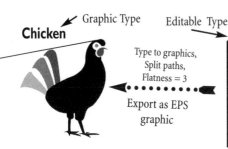

Type to graphics,
Split paths,
Flatness = 3

Export as EPS
graphic

Chicken

Original Parent/Native Documents
- Original Photoshop or drawing file
- High resolution pixel and/or vector image
- May contain layers, channels and/or editable type
- *NOT* included in page layout file
- Should be sent as separate unlinked graphic file along with page layout document and linked graphics on disk

Exported EPS Graphic
- Encapsulated Postscript
- Vector /Outline: Resolution independent
- For importing into page layout file
- *NOT* included in page layout document
- Must be sent along with document on disk
- Linked to low resolution preview

Drawing Document
- Freehand
- Illustrator
- Corel Draw

Flatten layers and remove alpha channels Export as TIFF or EPS Graphic

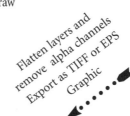

**200 ppi 4.34MB
RGB Photoshop Image**

High Resolution TIFF or EPS CMYK Printing Image
- High resolution (200 ppi – 300 ppi)
- 370 KB @ 200 ppi (No layers or channels)
- High resolution bitmapped TIFF or EPS
- Used for printing graphic images
- *NOT* Included in page layout document
- Sent along with document on disk
- Linked to low resolution graphic file

**200 ppi 370KB
CMYK Print Image**

hand in the air, you are either a blatant liar or a computer neophyte. In either case, lost or temporarily misplaced files are a pain in the rear and an event to be avoided. One often overlooked and crucial aspect of electronic publishing is the proper management of files. Develop a consistent folder and file naming system and use it. Always name a file properly and know where you are placing your files when you initially save them.

A good habit to have when working on documents is to periodically save multiple copies of your documents. This should be done in addition to or as a supplement to daily backup procedure. One of the easiest ways to accomplish this is to use the "Save as…" command (see Figure 13.10 for menu location) to create new sequentially named or numbered versions of documents. There are many advantages to using this procedure consistently. Most importantly, if your document becomes corrupted through a system crash or other mishap, you will have only lost a few hours of work rather than a whole day (or many days if you haven't done a recent backup). I always perform a "Save as…" prior to printing. I do this to protect my document from the intrusive printing process and to simplify my files. Figure 13.11 shows the dialog box you will see when doing a "Save as…" Simplifying files helps to make printing go smoother and faster. One other speed-enhancing suggestion is to consider reducing your long documents into smaller, more manageable ones. This is extremely important if your document is graphic-intensive.

Add sequential numbers to each document's name to save a sequence of versions of a document. When the document name area is highlighted in the dialog box, hit the Right Arrow key and type in the next number in the sequence.

▼ *Figure 13.10 "Save as" Menu Choice*
"Save as…" allows you to create a new document with a different name.

▼ *Figure 13.11 "Save as…" Dialog Box*
Use this to create multiple copies of working documents. Be sure to appropriately *name* and *place* each new document you create.

PAULINE'S FILE PREP TIPS

File Prep Hint #62

In addition to sending a composite page layout document such as an Xpress or PageMaker document, send all of the high resolution versions of any graphic images you have included (placed or imported) in your document. Remember that graphic images which are visible in page layout documents are only small, low resolution screen versions of the larger, high resolution graphic files. The high resolution graphic files exist as separate files from the page layout document.

File Prep Hint #63

Send original or parent document versions of EPS graphic files as well as the exported EPS graphics themselves which have been exported from drawing applications such as Freehand, Illustrator, or CorelDraw documents.

File Prep Hint #64

Send font files for all fonts used in your documents. Send both the screen and printer font files. Both are required for the proper viewing and printing of your file. View your fonts as just special types of preformed graphics.

File Prep Hint #65

Do not imbed the high resolution graphic images in a page layout document. Keep the high resolution files separate for easy access and editing.

14

Color Me Right

As the Byte Turns continues…

*Will Danny and Sam E. PAINT themselves into
a corner that Pauline can't PICT them out of?*

*Can you match this
metallic Pantone
with 4/c process????*

We can do it!!!

*Oh dear, what have I got-
ten myself into??*

Can't we ???

*You told them we could repro-
duce what with
4/c process !!!!
I'm gonna kill both
of them.
Just wait and see!!!*

COLOR BASICS

No such thing as a color computer!

You may be shocked to find out that you do not own a color computer! That's right. Although your computer was advertised as an 8 bit/256 color or 24 bit/16.7 million color machine, your computer, in fact, only truly understands two values: black and white. This is because you work on a digital computer and the digital nature of your computer restricts it to understanding only two signals, 0 and 1, or black and white. But wait! Before you rush indignantly back to your computer store to demand a refund for false advertising, think about this: having only two color values to worry about is a lot less complicated than keeping track of 16.7 million. The RGB and CMYK images you capture, create, and work with on your computer are really composed of grayscale channels, which in turn are composed of groups of black and white values. Color is always added outside of your computer. The color you see on your monitor is the result of the stimulation of red, green, and blue phosphors imbedded in the inside of your monitor glass. The color variations you see on screen are the result of different intensities of off and on signals (0s &1s) sent from your computer to each of the colored screen phosphors. Similarly, all hard copy output from a computer is black and white, with the color being added by an external device. Take a look at the film output from a "color imagesetter." It is four different sheets of black and white film, one for each of the process colors. The color in this case is applied through the application of Cyan, Magenta, Yellow, and Black (K) printing inks on a printing press. If you are still not quite convinced about the black and white nature of your computer, open up an RGB image in Photoshop. Look at each channel (R, G, & B) individually. You will see that each "color" channel is actually a grayscale channel with 8 bits or 256 shades of grayscale information contained in each pixel. Enlarge the image so that you can see the component pixels. Now bring up your on-screen densitometer/image information palette (F8) and explore the field of pixels from which the image is constructed. Keep track of the "K" values in the image information palette as you survey the image. Note that the values will vary from 0 to 256. This concept of working in black and white can really simplify working with color graphics. Instead of trying to relate to 16.7 million colors, it is easier and more accurate to think about and work with our color images as combinations of several grayscale images whose tonal values we will manipulate to adjust the final color output.

Basic Color Theory

Green

Center Point
White, (RGB)
Black, (CMYK)

Yellow

Red

Magenta

Cyan

Blue

Yellow

Additive RGB Color Space:
Used on Monitors and Scanners

Red, green, and blue light combine or add to create colors. Contrast this process with the subtractive process below which is used in printing.

Cyan Surface or Dot

R,G,B

G, B

Magenta Surface or Dot

R,G,B

R , B

Yellow Surface or Dot

R,G,B

R,G

▼ *Figure 14.1 Subtractive CMYK Color Space Used In Printing*

Transmitted (RGB) light is selectively absorbed by various combinations of the three process colors (C,M, & Y). The color(s) we see on a printed piece comes from the light which is transmitted and reflected rather than absorbed by the process colors (see C-5 for color plates).

Basic color issues

Several related issues need to be kept in mind when you are working with color images on an electronic publishing system and preparing files for print. The first is that we work in at least two different color spaces: RGB for our scanners and monitors, and CMYK when we go to press. The second issue is that we print with various combinations of inks, such as spot color inks and process color inks. Each color space or ink set has its own distinctive color values or gamuts, some of which are not reproducible in the other color systems. Because we work with different color systems, we must be very careful when we assign our color values as we create our electronic documents. We must always be mindful that the colors we create on-screen can be recreated in the final output color space and media.

Color concepts glossary

❧ **Color Space:** Color spaces are models we use to describe or define color. Color spaces generally involve ranges of color which occur within the visible spectrum. The volume of a specific color space depends upon how that color is produced. The two most important color spaces we work with are RGB color space, for scanning and viewing on monitors, and CMYK color space for printing.

❧ **Color Gamut:** The range of colors which a device such as a color printer or monitor can reproduce. Printers, which work in CMYK color space, typically have far smaller color gamuts than those captured by color scanners and reproduced by color monitors. This difference in color gamut often results in printed colors which look significantly different, usually darker and less vivid, than those captured by scanners and viewed on monitors.

❧ **Bit Depth:** The number of bits per pixel used to create the various grayscale values in an image. One bit images are black & white, 8 bit images have 28 or 256 shades of gray, 24 bit RGB images have 224, or 16.7 million colors. These are constructed out of three 8 bit grayscale channels, one for each color Red, Green, and Blue. CMYK images have four 8 bit grayscale channels and are therefore 32 bit per pixel images.

❧ **RGB Color Space:** The range of visible colors produced by adding various combinations of transmitted Red, Green, and Blue light together. These colors can only be viewed and must be converted for printing.

▼ *Figure 14.2 Percent Color Space Model*
This is a three-dimensional model of HSV (Hue, Saturation & Value) color space. Hue is represented by the outside rim of the cylinder. Saturation, or color purity or intensity, varies across any cross section of the cylinder with maximum saturation on the outside rim and minimum at the center. Value, which is a measure of gray scale value or brightness, varies along the vertical axis of the model cylinder, with 100 percent gray at one end and 0 percent gray at the other. The color picker diagram on the facing page is a cross-section view through the cylinder. The slider to the right of the pie changes the value or view position along the vertical axis.
Note: A color version of this image can be found in the Color Plate section.

▼ **Figure 14.3 RGB/HSV Color Picker**

To the right is the HSV color picker. By manipulating the sliders, you can create all of the colors which this monitor can display.

• The Hue, or basic color, is represented by the
colors on the *outside* edge of the color circle.
The values are recorded in percent of RGB.

• The Saturation is represented by the colors
inside the rim of the color circle. The colors
nearer the center of the circle are lighter, that
is,z less saturated, than the colors nearer the
rim. Progressive amounts of white are added to
any Hue (rim color) at positions tending away
from the rim toward the center. The center is
pure white or 100% Red + 100% Blue + 100% Green.

• Value is a measure of the percentage of grayscale which a color contains. Value ranges from 0% to 100%
and is controlled (added or subtracted) by sliding the large vertical slider up and down. In its current position, the value of this color is 0% grayscale. If the slider were moved all the way to the bottom of its track,
100% gray would be added to the color and it would be pure black.

Note: A color version of this image can be found in the Color Plate section in the center of this book (see C-6).

Color Models Available

▼ **Figure 14.4 Color Assignment Palette**

In most applications colors can be stored in and applied
through a palette such as this QuarkXPress color
palette. The three Pantone colors are spot colors. RGB
colors are monitor colors and should not be used for
printing. CMYK colors are used for building and printing process colors. The Registration color is assigned to
page elements such as crop, registration, and fold marks
which should occur on every separation.

Note: A color version of this image and Fig. 14.5 can
be found in the Color Plate section in the center of this
book (see C-6).

▼ **Figure 14.5 Color Models**

This is a list of the more common color matching systems which are used in graphics applications. The Pantone System is the most widely
used. The system labeled Pantone contains the
spot color guide colors. The Pantone Process
system contains the process color guide colors.
And the Pantone ProSim contains the closest
simulated process color matches for the spot
colors. The Focoltone, TruMatch, Toyo, and DIC
systems offer process color matching guides
similar to the Pantone Process system (see C-6).

▼ Figure 14.6 Color Gamut Comparison

The entire color picker circle shows the gamut of the RGB colors which can be seen on the monitor. The roughly triangular red area inside of the color picker circle is the limited range of those RGB colors which can be reproduced in the CMYK space. The black dot in the lower half of the color circle shows the position of the Pantone spot color 251 CV. Pantone 251CV is well out of gamut and will not be reproducible in CMYK. Note: A color version of this image can be found in the Color Plate section in the center of this book (see C-8).

☞ CMYK Color Space: The range of visible colors produced by subtracting various portions of Red, Green, and Blue light when it is reflected off of a media such as paper with CMYK color applied to its surface .

☞ Process Colors: The colors and inks used to recreate images on a printing press. The standard four process colors are Cyan, Magenta, Yellow, and Black. Additional colors can be added to expand the normally small process color gamut. Process colors are usually used to reproduce continuous tone color images. The process color gamut is much smaller than the spot color gamut and should not be used to attempt to produce exact matches with spot colors.

☞ Spot Colors: Commonly referred to as PMS colors (short for Pantone Matching System), spot colors are special mixtures of various combinations of 14 standard colors plus a transparent white. The 14 standard Pantone spot colors include: Pantone Yellow, Pantone Yellow 012, Pantone Orange, Pantone Warm Red, Pantone Red 032, Pantone Rubine Red, Pantone Rhodamine Red, Pantone Purple, Pantone Violet, Pantone Blue 072, Pantone Reflex Blue, Pantone Process Blue, Pantone Green, and Pantone Black C. Spot colors found on the PMS swatch charts are usually specific mixtures of only three of these colors, one of which is usually either transparent white or Pantone Black. The spot color gamut is much larger than the process color gamut.

☞ Color Calibration: The matching of color values from an original image to those captured by a scanner or other digital imaging device, viewed on a monitor, and printed on one or more printing devices. Each device in the link will capture, display, or reproduce color differently. The challenge is to adjust each device so that they will match each other's color reproduction. The three primary issues involved in color calibration are color space of each device, color gamut of each device, and the drift of each device's color characteristics over time.

☞ Assigning Colors: When choosing your working colors, choose colors which will be consistent with the final use of those colors. For instance, if you plan to print all of your colors in CMYK, use a CMYK color swatch book such as the Pantone Process Color System book instead of a spot color chart. Choosing initial spot colors which are later approximated with process colors can often lead to very disappointing results.

☞ Gamut Conversion: RGB color files need to be converted into CMYK color files (TIFF or EPS or DCS). RGB color files work fine on your computer, which uses the RGB color space to create and display colors on your monitor, but the printing process requires CMYK files. Files left as RGB images will often end up being printed as spot colors or grayscale images. The RGB to CMYK conversion/gamut mapping should be done specifically for each individual device.

▼ Figure 14.7: Color Choice Guides

Three basic types of color Swatch book choice guides appear here. From left to right they are: 1) Pantone spot color guide, 2) Pantone CMYK process color guide, and 3) Pantone process simulation (ProSim) color guide. The spot color guide shows a range of spot colors 250CV to 255CV. ("CV" means printed on coated stock and "U" means uncoated stock.) They are the same color but appear different because of the printing substrate. CVP designates process simulation of a spot color, while the S prefix indicates a color chosen from the Process color swatch chart. The process guide shows the closest regular Pantone process colors to these spot colors. As you can see, the match is not good, especially in the lighter, more saturated colors. The ProSim guide is a special collection of process colors built specifically to simulate, as close as possible, the Pantone spot colors. Look closely and you will see that the ProSim guide has color values designated by single and even half percent values rather than the standard 10% and 15% value changes. Even this specific, focused attempt to match the spot colors with process colors fails with the more saturated colors. *Note: All spot colors shown on this page are printed with process colors and are therefore not accurate. The above charts are meant to show the differences between the spot and process values for the same colors. A color version of this figure can be found in the color plate section (see C-7).

▼ **Figure 14.8 Color Gamuts**
Color gamut describes the
range of color that a particular
device can capture or reproduce. This diagram is a two-
dimensional slice through
three-dimensional color space.
Note how much larger the
visual gamut of the human eye
is (CIE area) than either the
RGB (monitor) or CMYK
(printer) gamuts. You will also
see that there are RGB colors
that will not reproduce in
CMYK and vice versa. In this
two-dimensional slice the
gamut ranges of RGB and
CMYK gamuts are of similar
extent, but in the entire three-
dimensional space the practical
CMYK gamut is much smaller
than RGB due to pigment
impurities and ink density limitations. Figure 14.9 shows a
clearer representation of the
difference between the extents
of the RGB and CMYK color
gamuts.
Note: A color version of this
image can be found in the
Color Plate section in the center
of this book (see C-8).

Color assignment

Describing colors: models

There are a number of different models which have been developed
to describe color. Defining color is not as easy at it may seem at first.
We know what the colors red, green, and blue generally look like, but
when we get down to the nitty-gritty of precisely defining colors, we
run into problems. One reason for our difficulties is that evaluation
of color is heavily dependent upon human perception of color. Our
perception of color depends upon a wide range of variables including lighting conditions, context (surrounding colors), and even what
we have eaten. On top of all this we all have different social and cultural color values.

In the digital printing world we typically work in two related but different color spaces: RGB and CMYK. RGB space is used when we are
working with devices such as monitors and scanners, which generate
their own light. CMYK is used when we work with light which is
reflected off of a surface, such as with printed material. When we
work on a computer, we work in RGB color space. When we print
and view our results, we work in CMYK color space. Regardless of
the color model in which we work, we commonly define a color by
describing its Hue, Saturation, and Value (HSV). Hue is the basic
color, such as red, green or blue, and is defined by the wavelength or
frequency of light. Saturation is the purity of the color and is a measure of the amount of white which has been added to a hue. The less
saturated a color is, the more white has been added, and the lighter
the color appears. Value is a measure of the amount of grayscale
which has been added to the color. The greater the value of a color,
the darker it is. Most current "color pickers" use this HSV model or
some variation to define colors. RGB colors tend to be more saturated and therefore brighter than colors reproduced through the CMYK
process. Note: A more universal color model known as CIE color
space is gradually being adopted and will probably eventually replace
HSV for many definition applications.

Types of colors

There are generally three basic types of colors which you work with
in an electronic document: spot colors, process colors, and tints. Spot
colors are solid colors made up of specific mixtures of inks. Process
colors, also known as built colors, are made up of screen combinations of between four and seven process colors. Currently, most
process colors are built out of the traditional four process colors:

▼ *Figure 14.9 Color Gamuts*
This diagram shows the color gamuts for three different color spaces: HyperColor, RGB, and CMYK. Note how the gamuts for RGB color space and the human eye are much more extensive than the gamut for CMYK printing gamut. HyperColor is a version of HiFi color which utilizes double hits of CMYK to increase the process color gamut. Other HiFi color systems use additional process colors to increase the gamut range of process color. Pantone Hexachrome adds green and orange to C,M,Y,K to achieve an enhanced gamut.
Note: A color version of this image can be found in the Color Plate section in the center of this book (see C-8).

cyan, magenta, yellow, and black (CMYK). Recently, an expanded set of process colors (violet, red, and green) known as Hi-Fi colors have been added to the process color tool box. This expanded set of process colors allows us to print an expanded and richer gamut of process colors. Tints are screens of single solid colors. An example would be the 70 percent screen of spot color Pantone 292 shown in Figure 14.4. All three of these types of colors are generally viewed in RGB space and printed CMYK color space.

Color choices

The most reliable way to choose a color is to use a color guide or swatch book. Examples of three common guides appear on page 177. The first guide shown is the spot color guide, the second is the process color guide, and the third is a process color simulation guide. The spot color guide should be used if you intend to ultimately have your colors printed as spot colors. Many people use this guide even if they intend to print them as process colors. This approach is wrong. When you choose a spot color and ask your printer to "match that color," you will often be disappointed with the results. The spot color guide contains a far wider range of colors than the CMYK process colors spectrum can reproduce. Most spot colors which you find in the spot color guides (such as Pantone's Color Formula Guide 1000) cannot be reproduced in CMYK printing; that is, they are out of gamut. If you intend your colors to print as process colors, then you should assign the color values from a process color guide (such as Pantone's Process color System Guide). Doing so will give you a clearer idea of how your color will look and reduce your disappointment with your final printed results.

Do not use your monitor to judge color unless you have a well calibrated monitor, and even then be very careful. Several factors work against a proper screen representation of colors which will be printed. First, your monitor works in RGB color space and you print in CMYK color space. RGB color space on your monitor is significantly larger than CMYK color space, so it is very easy to assign colors which look great on screen but will never print. Secondly, most high quality color monitors are 20–30 percent brighter than they should be, so even colors which can be reproduced on press will appear differently on screen.

▼ Figure 14.10 DTP System
Each component of a DTP system treats color differently. As an image is transferred from scanner to computer to printer, its color values may change. The object of a calibration/color management system is to adjust all of the devices and the files so that the image is rendered as equally as possible on each system component.

Color gamut conversion

Because we scan and view our colors in RGB color space and print our colors in CMYK color space, the colors which we create and view in RGB space must be converted into CMYK equivalents. Although RGB and CMYK color spaces are theoretically similar, the RGB color space which we view on our monitors is usually much larger than the CMYK color space we print in (see Figure 14.6). That is, RGB has a larger color gamut than CMYK. Impurities in ink pigments and limitations on ink densities on press significantly reduce the practical CMYK gamut. If we choose RGB colors which are outside of the CMYK color gamut, those out-of-gamut RGB colors will be significantly changed when they are converted to their CMYK equivalents. The color picker diagram in Figure 14.3. shows the vast practical difference between RGB monitor space and CMYK printing space. Red, Green, and Blue should not be assigned for printing colors.

Hi Fi color

Because of the practical limitations of color reproduction imposed by the use of standard 4/c process inks and techniques, many people have tried various ways of enhancing the process color gamut. One such approach is called Hi Fi color. Hi Fi color is actually a variety of color-enhancing technologies. These include, but are not limited to, new screening technologies, such as the stochastic screens discussed in the screening chapter, and the use of more than four process colors or four passes of process colors. Some companies such as Pantone, which has developed its Hexacolor system, use two extra colors in addition to the four process colors. Others have seven-color systems which employ the use of three additional colors– usually orange, violet, and green – which are added to the four process colors. Dupont has taken a different approach to Hi Fi color ink process. They use the standard four process colors, but they apply them twice, thereby increasing ink density. All of these approaches enlarge the standard process color gamut. Figure 14.9 shows the qualitative increase in color gamut which results with the use of the Dupont HyperColor system.

Consider the final use

Always consider the final use of your electronic document. If you are preparing your document for viewing only on screen, you have a great deal more latitude in your color choices than if you intend to print your document. Particularly if you are printing your documents, be sure to use the proper color guide to designate your colors. For maximum accuracy, your color guide should use the pigmented colors you intend to print with, should be printed at the same line frequency, use the same screening method you intend to employ, and should be printed on a paper similar to the one you will be using. Using the proper guide will help you minimize color gamut conversion problems and improve your calibration attempts.

Color management

▼ Figure 14.11 Q 60 IT8 Chart

This industry standard chart is used as a scanning target. During a calibration sequence this target would be scanned, viewed, and output. The monitor image can be measured with a spectrophotometer and adjusted. The printed image can be measured with a densitometer and colorimeter. These measurements are then used to create transfer functions or curves which will be used for adjusting future output to that specific printer. Similar calibration curves can be constructed for each scanner printer combination.

Note: A color version of this image can be found in the Color Plate section in the center of this book (see C-8).

The need for color management

Proper assignment of colors is the first step to controlling color in a print environment. To truly have control of your color reproduction, you must manage your color from start to finish, from image acquisition to the final printed piece. Controlling color on the desktop has always been a challenge. Unlike integrated proprietary systems such as Scitex and Barco (which have matched components and software from the start), open desktop systems frequently have hardware and software components from a dozen or more manufacturers all working, or not working as the case may be, together. While open systems provide us with the blessing of choice and upgradability, they also challenge us with the requirements of controlling tone and color in images which must pass through all of these unmatched components. The matching of images across these unrelated components is called calibration. Each component of an electronic publishing system captures, displays, or prints color differently. One of the more significant challenges is that some components work in entirely different color spaces. This means that color has to be translated from one color space to another. This is known as *gamut mapping*. The most common gamut mapping hurdle is from the RGB color space, in which scanners capture and monitors display color, into CMYK color space, in which most printers reproduce color. Because RGB and CMYK gamuts are inherently different, there will never be complete fidelity between them. Just the tonal range compression alone, compressed from about 1000 tones in a 35mm transparency to around 100 on a printing press, guarantees that, at best, a printed image will be an approximation of the original. The tonal compression is even greater with digital image capture (see Chapter 12, "Taming Your Scanner," for a more complete treatment of tonal compression). To make matters even more interesting, we are always adding new gamut mapping challenges. The use of PhotoCD technology as a prepress tool requires that we gamut map from YCC color space to CMYK (see pages 150 – 152, PhotoCD, for a discussion of YCC color space).

Calibration

The object of calibration is to adjust your hardware and software so that you will be able to pass a color image from one to the other without altering the color. Once set up to do this, the equipment should not be altered except for periodic adjustments to keep the components in line with each other. There are many variables which can affect the way color looks. But for us, all of these variables can be grouped into three categories of concern:

1) Each device and software application captures, views, or reproduces color differently.

2) Colors must be gamut mapped as they move from one device to another, most importantly from the scanner or digital camera to the printer.

3) All hardware devices drift with time. Scanner bulbs age and their output spectrum changes. Monitor phosphors age and change. Printer toners, inks, and other variables change.

All three of these issues must be addressed for effective calibration. There are basically two types of calibration systems, open and closed. Open calibration involves the use of general device characterization files or profiles to control output for a specific model of printer. These device profiles are constructed from a series of test prints which are made on a large number of printers of that model to determine the average output characteristics of that specific model of printer. These characterization files are then used to adjust and control the printing of images to this model of printer. The EFI color system uses these device profiles to help control color output. The beauty of these profiles is that they are easy to use and do not require a great deal of operator knowledge to use them. The shortcomings of this type of calibration are that they often do not include the scanner in the calibration system and the profiles are model- but not device-specific. So if you happen to have a non-average printer, the general device profile would not help very much. Some model profile systems allow the operator to adjust the profile to account for the peculiar characteristics of specific machines. However, if one is going to go to the trouble of "tweaking" the profiles, which is generally a time consuming process demanding color measurements of printouts, you might as well use the second type of calibration system, the closed loop.

Closed loop calibration is system- and device-specific. There are a number of closed loop systems. Ofoto was one of the first widely available desktop solutions, but they all have one characteristic in common. All closed loop calibration systems or procedures start with targets of known values–grayscale, color or both–which are scanned, printed, and then measured. The measurements of the prints are then compared with the original known target values. The differences between the originals and the prints are used to construct color lookup tables or calibration curves, known as transfer curves or transfer functions. These tables and curves are then used to adjust any images scanned and printed on those devices. These curves are similar in function to the model characterization curves used in the open system described above. The difference is that the closed loop system functions are developed for a specific combination of scanner, software, and printer. A different curve is developed for each scanner printer combination used. Over time, as equipment drifts or components and consumables are replaced or changed, the transfer functions can be changed to match those specific changes. All that is involved is a rescanning and printing of the known target with subsequent measurement and transfer curve creation.

▼ *Figure 14.12 CMS*
In a closed loop Color Management System (CMS), color transforms or profiles are created through analysis of scanned, viewed, and printed targets with known values, like a Kodak Q60 IT8 target series. Images and profiles are transformed back and forth through a device-independent reference color space (RCS), usually some variant of the CIE color space. The RCS serves as the primary point of reference or "touch stone" for images as they move back and forth across the system. The image is always referred back to the RCS regardless of where it is in the system.

PAULINE'S FILE PREP TIPS

File Prep Hint #66

Assign color properly. Use spot and process color designations properly. Assign spot color to only those items which will actually be separated as separate colors and printed as spot colors on the press cylinder. Assign process colors names to items which will print as process colors. Do not assign an item or area a spot color name and then ask the application or printer to convert it to process colors.

File Prep Hint #67

Use color swatch books to judge and assign colors values. Do not use your monitor! Use a spot color swatch book to assign spot colors, a process color swatch book to assign process colors, and the ProSim (process simulation) book to assign process colors which are the closest approximations to the various spot colors. Always note the difference between the spot color and its closest approximation. It is usually not too close.

File Prep Hint #68

Be sure that colors assigned to portions of imported graphics are included in the output application. Also be sure that any imported colors have names identical to the same colors used in the importing application. Also check to be sure that each color has its correct spot or process color designations. Use imported colors for assignment to prevent any duplication of colors.

Pauline's File Prep Tips

File Prep Hint #69

Delete unused colors in color palettes in all applications used – page layout as well as graphic applications. Delete colors from the color palettes of vector graphics before they are exported as EPS files from their parent applications.

File Prep Hint #70

Be aware of color gamut limitations when you assign colors. Remember that RGB and spot color spaces are far more extensive than CMYK color spaces. Therefore, many of the colors you can create on your computer and view on your monitor cannot be reproduced in CMYK printing.

File Prep Hint #71

Remember that RGB files must be converted into CMYK for printing. Your RGB-to-CMYK gamut conversion must be controlled and set as specifically as possible to produce CMYK images which match the gamut of every output device on which the image will ultimately be printed.

File Prep Hint #72

If you need to maintain color fidelity throughout the design and creation process, calibrate your system. Calibration is best achieved through the use of a closed loop calibration process. This process utilizes targets with known values which can be compared with scanned, viewed, and printed results and analyzed to create custom device-specific profiles for each component of your production system.

15

Application-Specific Tips

As the Byte Turns continues…

Oh woe is me! With all these different applications and updates to learn and keep up with, will there be any time left for Danny D'Ziner and Pauline E. Prepress to go Beyond Press?

You said you could take all of my files. You're the professionals. You're responsible for making them print !

We can do it!!!

Oh dear, what have I gotten myself into??

Can't we ???

I can't process these files. They are too complicated and pieces are missing. It's the customer's responsibility to prepare the file properly !!

APPLICATION-SPECIFIC FILE PREP TIPS

This section is designed to introduce you to some of the the the more commonly used applications and some of their file preparation specific tools. Some of the details of the dialog boxes may vary from one version of an application to another. I have tried to include tools which have been consistently included in the applications, as well as some new ones which I think will stay around for awhile. All these application-specific tools help us to satisfy our battle cry of REDUCE & SIMPLIFY!

QuarkXPress

Font usage utility

Use the Font Usage utility (Utilities Menu) shown in Figure 15.1 to check your fonts usage prior to collecting your files for output. The Font Usage utility will allow you to see which fonts are being used in your document. The Font Usage utility also has a search and replace capability which is a useful tool for changing the font assignments of large sections of text or as a tool for locating and replacing any stray characters such as spaces or punctuation marks which may have been incorrectly assigned. Using the Font Usage utility will simplify and clean up your font assignments in your document and help preempt any font problems during output. After you have imported text files, especially those translated from another operating system like Windows to Mac, check and use the the Font Usage utility for Courier or other substituted fonts. You can use the Find/Change utility (Edit menu) to remove unwanted spaces, tabs, and line returns from imported text files.

▼ *Figure 15.1 Font Usage Dialog Box*
This QuarkXPress dialog box can be used to see which fonts are being used in a document. The search and replace capabilities of the Font Usage utility is a useful tool for changing the font assignments of large sections of type or as a tool for locating and replacing any stray characters, such as spaces or punctuation marks which may have been incorrectly assigned. The Utilities menu where the Picture Usage dialog box is found is shown highlighted above the dialog box.

▼ *Figure 15.2 Pictures Usage Dialog Box*
This dialog box can be used to make sure that all your low resolution imported graphics are linked to their high resolution partners, are in the proper file format, and are set to print. It can even be used to find the location of a high resolution graphic file, although the entire location path is rarely shown. Note that most of the imported TIFF files are not properly linked to their high resolution files. Also note that the last graphic file is a PICT file, which should be converted into a TIFF file to facilitate printing. The Utilities menu where the Picture Usage dialog box is found appears highlighted above the dialog box.

▼ **Figure 15.3 Collect For Output**
The Collect For Output dialog utility, which is included in XPress, is located under the File menu in XPress. Collect For Output helps facilitate the collection of document components which need to be transferred to another site. Collect for Output will gather a copy of the document, the high resolution graphic files, and a document info file. The fonts are *not* collected.

Picture usage utility

Use the Picture Usage utility (Utilities Menu) shown in Fig 15.2 to make sure that all of your graphics are ready for output. The Picture Usage dialog box can make sure that your imported graphics are all linked to their high resolution versions, that they are of the proper file format, and that they are assigned to print. Picture Usage can also be used to find the location of a high resolution graphic file component. I also use the Picture Usage utility to check for PICT files which I have not yet converted to TIFF files. Specific font usage and graphics can even be identified and located within a QuarkXPress document.

Collect for output

As an aid in helping you collect file components use The Font and Picture Usage utilities and Collect For Output extension (under FILE menu) shown in Fig 15.3 to help collect files on a disk. These will help save a copy of the document, all associated graphics files, and a document data sheet to any folder which is designated. An example of the kinds of files collected when using Collect For Output can be seen in Figure 15.4. Remember, you will still have to collect the fonts separately, but the document data sheet will tell you which fonts to collect. Also, Collect For Output does not find and save the original or parent files from which an EPS was created. The EPS parent should be included along with Exported/Imported EPS graphics. This is particularly important when sending Freehand EPS files prior to version 3.11 to the service bureau in case the file needs to be altered. This procedure is most important for time critical jobs. One step better is to use a preflighting utility such as FlightCheck or PreflightPro which will troubleshoot your documents and collect font files as well. See Appendix E: File Prep Utilities for more information on these utilities.

▼ *Figure 15.4 Collected Output*
This is the collected output from this chapter. Copies of the document and the high resolution graphics, as well as a report document, have been created. The PICT files were not collected. Can you identify which graphic files in this document were still PICTs when this collection was made?

Keep graphics out of gutters in facing page documents unless you mean for that element to bleed from one page to the other. Crossover elements will sometimes cause a double download of graphics for both pages. Use filled graphic boxes instead of filled text boxes when creating tinted or screened boxes.

Blends in XPress

For the best quality blends, use the blend tool in QuarkXPress as an iteration tool only. Use the XPress blend creation tool to try out various blend variations. Create your final gradations and two color (CMYK) blends, especially long ones, in a painting, bitmap editing program like Adobe Photoshop using dithering and adding noise (see Photoshop section below). Blends created in painting programs are generally higher quality and they print faster.

Color assignments and separations

Be sure to check process separations in the colors dialog box (Edit – Colors+New or Edit) for each color you want to print as a process separated color even if you use the CMYK palette to create a color. Delete Red, Green, and Blue from the colors dialog box (Edit – Colors+Delete) when printing 4–color separations, unless you are using one of these colors as a spot color. Printing will be much faster. Illustrator and Freehand files brought into XPress with custom Pantone spot colors will separate those colors as process colors. If custom spot colors are to be maintained, the custom spot colors must be recreated in Quark using the colors dialog box (Edit – Colors) with exactly the same names as the colors in the Illustrator file. Send or request QuarkXPress preference file if custom traps have been set. (You should send it with your file anyway for versions prior to 3.2). QuarkXPress Version 3.3 and later will automatically update your

▼ *Figure 15.5 XPress Page Setup*
In QuarkXPress the proper PPD, or Postscript Printer Description, file is chosen in the Page Setup dialog box. Before you send your file out as a Postscript file, be sure you have the PPD for the output device at the location where the file will be output. Note that in the dialog box the Printer Type is an Agfa Selectset 5000, which in this case is an imagesetter at a printing company where the file will be output. The file can now be saved as a Postscript file by clicking on the Options button and choosing the print as a Postscript file option. Saving a file as a Postscript file should be done with care, as it is an essentially uneditable file in which changes are very difficult to make.

color palette to include the color names of files which you import, but check to make sure anyway, particularly if the imported spot colors are to be printed as process colors.

Printing

A complete range of printing options and controls are available in QuarkXPress's Print Dialog box. Before creating a Postscript file of a QuarkXPress document, be sure to choose the proper PPD on a Mac (Printer Description File) or Postscript printer driver in Windows in the Pages Setup and/or print dialog boxes. The PPD /printer driver you choose should be for the printer on which the final output will be done. If you are sending your file to a printing company or service bureau, this will generally be an imagesetter. Having the proper PPD/printer driver will ensure that the page geometry of your file will match that of the device on which your file will be printed. See Figure 15.5 for an example of the XPress Print Setup dialog box.

PageMaker

Save for service provider

The Save For Service Provider utility, found under the Plug-ins menu, is a useful and intuitive file component checking and collection utility included in Pagemaker Version 6.5. It will not only provide you with a complete list of file components (document, graphics, and fonts), but also will help you gather them up as well (see Figure 15.6 a and b). It will work with both application and Postscript files generated from Pagemaker 6.5. Save For Service Provider has a Package-making submenu which allows you to customize the collection of fonts and graphics. Even more extensive file troubleshooting and file component collection capabilities can be found in preflighting utilities such as FlightCheck and PreflightPro. See Appendix E: File Prep Utilities for more information on these utilities.

Save as: copy files for remote printing

In Pagemaker 6.0, if you perform a Save As from the File menu and choose Copy: Files for remote printing (6.0) or All linked Files (6.5) (Fig. 15.7), PageMaker will save a copy of your document in its present state as well as copies of all the high resolution graphics linked to the document. In addition, Pagemaker will create a tracking settings file which can be used by your service bureau when they launch your document. This Save As function is similar to XPress' Collect for

▼ **Figure 15.6a Save For Service Provider**
This Plug-in utility provides detailed information about a PageMaker 6.5 document and provides component checking and gathering capabilities (including fonts). It is much more powerful than the built-in Display Pub Info Addition/Plug-in utility.

▼ **Figure 15.6b Package Making**
This subset utility portion of the "Save For Service Provider" Plug-in allows you to customize the collection of file components such as the types of fonts, the updating of graphics, and the format of a document components information report.

▼ *Figure 15.7 Files For Remote Printing*
Use this Selection in the "Save As" dialog box in Pagemaker to save a copy of the document and high resolution copies of all linked graphics. Tracking tables for that document are saved as well.

▼ *Figure 15.8 Display Pub. Info*
The Display Publication Info utility is a PageMaker Addition, found under the Utilities menu, which helps you create a list of all the document components contained in a PageMaker document. Display Pub Info will not gather any file components together.

Output utility, with the exception that Pagemaker does not create a document information file. You can save the Display Publication information as a text file to create a document information file which you can send along with your files to your service bureau.

Display Publication Information

As a basic aid in helping you identify file components you can use the Aldus Addition or Adobe Plug-in Display Publication Information (under Utilities – Aldus Additions / Adobe Plug-ins menu & submenu shown in Fig. 15.8) to provide you with a list of all the fonts and graphics as well as other document components such as style sheets and colors used. Display Publication Information will provide you with a list of components, but not the components themselves. One item to note is that Display Publication Information will generally list the system fonts, as well as fonts actually used in the document, whether the system fonts are used in the document or not. I prefer using Save For Service Provider as a file information tool for PageMaker documents. It is more complete and less confusing.

Imbedded vs. linked graphic files

Graphic files should be linked to (attached to), but not imbedded in (included within) page layout documents. In Pagemaker do not select "Store copy in publication" when prompted by a dialog box. Keep graphics as separate external linked files. Use File -Links (Fig. 15.9) to check the linked status of external graphics. Keeping graphics as separate files will: 1) Keep your PM document smaller, 2) allow your ser-

▼ *Figure 15.9 Link Information*
The Link Information dialog box displays information about all linked graphics. It shows whether a high resolution version is stored in the Pagemaker document. It is generally best NOT to store any high resolution graphics inside of Pagemaker documents. Leave this option unchecked.

▼ *Figure 15.10 Link Options Defaults*
Be sure the Store copy in publication check box is disabled. This will discourage Pagemaker from including high resolution versions of graphics in its documents.

▼ **Figure 15.11 Removing Colors**
Prior to printing separations or sending your file out, use the Define Colors dialog box to remove any colors not used in the application.

▼ **Figure 15.12 PageMaker Print Dialog Box**
In PageMaker the proper PPD or Postscript Printer Description file is chosen in the Print dialog box. Before you send your file out as a Postscript file, be sure you have the PPD for the output device at the location where the file will be output. Note that in the above dialog box the Print to: is a QMS 410, which is the local network printer, but the Type: is an imagesetter, which in this case is the imagesetter at a printing company where the file will be output. The file can now be saved as a Postscript file by clicking on the Options button and choosing the Print as a Postscript file option.

vice company access to this graphic file if they need to edit the file during preparation for printing, and 3) allow for far easier updating of graphic files if you choose to edit them after they are placed in PageMaker. You can prevent PageMaker from including or attempting to include the high resolution versions of graphic images inside of a PageMaker document. Launch PageMaker, but do not open a document. Choose Link Options under the Element menu. Disable (uncheck) the Store Copy in the publication dialog box that appears. This will discourage PageMaker from attempting to store copies of the high resolution versions of graphics when you place a graphic in a document. If PageMaker ever presents you with a dialog box asking you if you want to store a copy in the application, just say no.

Removing unused colors

Removing unused or not to be used colors from your color palette is a good idea for several reasons. First, removing unwanted colors simplifies your color palette. Second, by removing colors which you do not want to inadvertently use, such as Red, Green, and Blue, you can prevent some color assignment mistakes. And, most importantly, removing unused colors in a document prior to printing will prevent the printing of unnecessary film during the separation process.

I remove Red, Green, and Blue from my color palette even before I begin construction of a document. Prior to printing access the Define Colors (Fig 15.11) dialog box (Elements menu) and click the Remove Unused button. Any colors not assigned to a document element will be removed from the list and therefore be prevented from printing. This is also a good time to check for duplicate colors (such as the same spot color being used with two different names, one assigned in Pagemaker, and one assigned in an imported graphic).

Printing Postscript

Before creating a Postscript file of a PageMaker document, be sure to choose the proper PPD (Printer Description File) in the Print Setup dialog box. The PPD you choose should be for the printer on which the final output will be done. If you are sending you file to a printing company or service bureau, this will generally be an imagesetter. Having the proper PPD will ensure that the page geometry of your file will match that of the device on which your file will be printed. See Fig. 15.12 for an example of the PageMaker Print Setup dialog box.

▼ *Figure 15.13 Photoshop Gradient Tool*
Check "Dither" in the Gradient tool palette when creating gradients in Photoshop to discourage banding from occurring when the gradient is printed at high resolution.

▼ *Figure 15.14 Photoshop Path Tolerance Setting*
To reduce the RIPing times associated with Path creation in Photoshop, pay close attention to the tolerance setting. Create a path to convert a selection into a vector-based line path. Lower tolerance settings result in tighter fits between the selection and the created path. But tighter paths also generally mean more control points, and more complex paths, which results in slower, more difficult RIPing processes. Experiment with various path settings to view the results. Choose a tolerance which creates fewer control points than a perfect fit. Then edit the existing points to correct the line placements.

Photoshop and other painting applications

Gradients and blends

Create gradients and blends in a pixel-based application such as Photoshop rather than in page layout or drawing applications. Bitmapped blends tend to print easier, faster, and with better quality. The banding which often occurs when printing gradients and blends at high resolution can be avoided when working in Photoshop by dithering them (check Dither in the Gradient tool palette see Fig. 15.13). To further reduce the possibility of banding on output, I also like to add one or two pixels of noise followed by an application of a 2 pixel blur (my favorite is gaussian blur) to help add noise and distribute grayscale values across the entire blended area. In addition, creating gradients and blends in Photoshop, and especially in Photoshop 4.0 and above, also gives you much better control and flexibility than creating them in page layout applications like QuarkXPress.

Clipping paths and silhouettes

The first step in creating a Silhouette usually involves selecting a portion of an image which is to be removed from its background. This can be done in Photoshop utilizing a variety of selection tools including the selection marquees, the Lasso, the Magic Wand, and several color selection tools. After a selection is made, this selection must be converted into a path, a vector-based graphic outline, and then further modified into a clipping path. The vector path is used to create a smooth edge around the portion of the image which is to be silhouetted. The creation of the clipping path turns the path into a "cookie cutter" which isolates the selected portion of the image from its background. Paths can be created directly using the pen tool, although this can often be a tedious and time consuming process. Using the magic wand to create a selection which you may then convert into a path is often faster, but can be fraught with problems related to the creation of complex paths. I often use several selection tools during this process, but I always have one goal in mind. My goal is to create as smooth and accurate a silhouette as possible with the simplest path possible.

This process of creating a silhouette using a clipping path creates a complex, compound image. This is considered a compound image because it has both bitmapped and vector-based graphic segments in the same image. Compound images are some of the most difficult to

▼ *Figure 15.15 Photoshop Clipping Path Flatness Ratios*
To reduce the RIPing times associated with clipping paths created and saved in applications like Photoshop, set the flatness ratios to at least "1" and preferably higher. Beware that flatness ratios above "5" often produce visible straight line segments along curved paths. When assigning flatness ratio values, be sure to use whole numbers such as "1" or "3," not fractions of numbers such as 1.5 or 0.75. These values will increase RIPing times.

▼ *Figure 15.16 Image Control*
When working in Photoshop select Levels (top) to set highlight and shadow points, and Curves (bottom) to make gray map adjustments, rather than using Brightness and Contrast controls, which tend to dramatically reduce image quality.

RIP because they combine the challenges of RIPing presented by both raster- and vector-based graphics in the same image. During this silhouetting process two decisions you make will determine how easily this clipped image will print. The first involves deciding how closely the path you create matches the original selection. This is determined by assigning a tolerance to the path during the path making step. When you make a path from a selection, the dialog box that you see in Fig. 15.14 will appear. Assigning a low tolerance number such as 0.5 creates a path which closely matches the original selection, but also often results in a path which has a large number of control points. Paths with large numbers of control points are more difficult to RIP. I generally select a tolerance between 1.5 – 2.0 which generates few control points with a fair fit. After the path is created and before I turn the path into a clipping path, I adjust the location of the control points and the curves they control with the pen tools to create a more precise fit. I will often remove unnecessary points during this editing process as well.

Flatness of clipping paths

When a path is converted into a clipping path, be sure to pay attention to the flatness ratio of your path (Fig. 15.15). The flatness ratio controls the number of tangents or line segments used to draw curves along your paths. Small flatness ratios, 0 – 1, create very smooth lines but very complex paths which are difficult to RIP. Larger flatness ratios use fewer line segments and are therefore easier and take less time to RIP. But be aware that a flatness ratio set too high will result in visible straight line segments along paths which should be smooth curves. The best flatness ratio depends upon the RIP being used, the type of curve being drawn, and the output resolution. As a starting place, try setting flatness at between 2 and 5. Avoid low flatness ratios of 0 – 1. Experiment with your equipment, but use only whole numbers for flatness values; using fractions, such as 1.5, dramatically increases RIPing times.

File resolution

The resolution of any contone bitmapped file which will be used for printing should depend upon the line screen (lpi) at which it will be printed. A good rule of thumb to follow for maximum resolution is that the resolution of an image in ppi should not exceed two times the line screen (2x lpi) of the final printed image, and often even less resolution. Most often 1x – 1.25x lpi is sufficient. For instance, a Photoshop contone TIFF which will be printed without scaling at 150

▼ Figure 15.17 Scanner Interface

The screen above shows the Photoshop scanner plug-in interface control of UMAX MagicScan software. Scans should be performed in two steps: An initial low-resolution preview scan followed by a higher resolution final scan. Cropping and other necessary adjustments are made during the preview or prescan and applied during the final scan. Note the final scan resolution is set at 150 lpi. A quality/multiplication factor of 1.5 has been set in a separate scanning preference dialog box, yielding a final scan and image resolution of 225ppi.

lpi need not exceed 300 ppi in resolution, and often 150–188 ppi is fine (see Chapter 8, "Resolving Resolution" and Chapter 12, "Taming Your Scanner" for more information on file resolution). Keeping resolution down is one of the key components of reducing file size in our continual quest to REDUCE & SIMPLIFY!

Contone color

Remember that scanned images of color continuous tone images which are intended to be used for print need to be globally color corrected to compensate for impure printing inks. A standard white highlight dot is typically corrected to yield the following CMYK values: C=6%, M=4%, Y=4%, K=0%. Corresponding midtone values might be C=60%, M=45%, Y=45%, K=25%.

Tone adjustments in Curves and Levels

When performing tone adjustments in Photoshop, use Levels and Curves rather than Brightness and Contrast. I use Levels to set highlight and shadow points and Curves to make any gray map adjustments after I have set my highlight and shadow points (see Fig. 15.16). Curves adjustments provide a continuous series of linked control points along the Curves graph line. When one point is adjusted, other points along the curve are incrementally adjusted as well, thereby creating smooth tonal adjustments with a minimum loss of data. But be aware that every time you make an adjustment, such as a change in the curves dialog box to a file in an image editing application, you are not only adjusting the data but also losing data. Keep your number of adjustments to a minimum (see discussion of scanning applications below and in Chapter 12).

Scanning applications

Prescanning

When scanning images, in particular continuous tone images, it is best to use a low resolution prescan technique (see Fig. 15.7). Use the low resolution prescan image to evaluate your potential scan image. Most of your image adjustments, such as cropping, scaling, tone compression, gray map adjustments, global color corrections, and sharpening, should be performed during the scanning process rather than as postscan adjustments in an application like Photoshop. Evaluation of the low resolution prescan image allows you to decide how the

▼ *Figure 15.18 Streamline Setup*

Streamline is terrific for creating easily editable and scalable outline files from bitmapped images. One of the potential problems with Streamline-created outline files is that Streamline tends to make long, complex paths which are difficult to RIP. To help reduce the complexity (number of control points) of a Streamline file, set the tolerance to loose. In most cases, Streamline will create a very accurate outline without too many control points.

▼ *Figure 15.19 Document In Layers*

Layers palette in Freehand shows how a document is constructed in separate layers rather than all in one plane. Each layer can be activated and edited separately.

adjustments need to be set during the high resolution scan. Using a prescan evaluation and high resolution scan adjustments save time and preserve image quality, because every postscan adjustment made in Photoshop deletes data from the image. *scan high resolution because data lost on tweaking*

Line art

Simple, crisp line art images should usually be scanned at high resolution, ≥ 800 ppi, and then converted to outline files in a dedicated outlining application like Streamline. Coarse-edged images with little edge detail can be reproduced very well with low resolution scans (~300 ppi). Complex and fine detail line art images should be scanned as 8 bit grayscale images and then converted to 1 bit line art using sharpening and thresholding. Be sure to scan line art at a multiple of the optical resolution of the scanner. This will result in more consistent edges which will be easier to Streamline.

Contones

Scanning resolutions for unscaled continuous tone images rarely need to exceed two times (2x) the line screen at which the images will be printed. Often using quality factors of 1.25 – 1.5 x the lpi is sufficient. If an image is to be scaled up or down either during the scanning process or afterward as a postscan manipulation, be sure to account for this when assigning the scan or input resolution. The resolution of a file, as determined by the above guidelines, needs to be adjusted either up or down by the percentage of the scaling. For example, if a 4" x 5" image is to ultimately be scaled and printed as an 8" x 10 image, the scan resolution will need to be doubled because both sides of the image will be scaled 200%. The following formula can be used to determine input or scan resolution: 1.25 – 2.0 x lpi x scaling factor. If we use 1.25 as our quality factor, 200 percent as our scaling factor, and 150 lpi as our printing resolution, then our input resolution should be 1.25 x 150 x 2 = 375 ppi (see Chapter 12 for a complete discussion of this issue). Here again the repeated hew and cry is to REDUCE & SIMPLIFY!

Streamlined/outlined files

Outlining preferences

When working with line art files, particularly if the line art has been generated as an outline from Streamline, you need to be cognizant of

▼ *Figure 15.20 Convert To Paths*
This is the Convert to Paths selection in Freehand. This command is used to convert type to graphic paths prior to exporting as an EPS, preventing the nesting of font files.

▼ *Figure 15.21 Illustrator Path Control*
Choose Split Long Paths to reduce the length of paths prior to creation of an EPS. Setting the resolution will determine the flatness and the length of split path segments.

PATH length and the number of control points along any given path. Streamline tends to: 1) create many control points, particularly if the original outlined graphic was low resolution or very detailed, and 2) create long paths. Both of these conditions increase the RIPing complexity of the graphic file. You can preempt having to perform corrective editing of the Streamlined path in an illustration application by initially creating a simplified version. Figure 15.18 shows how the tolerance can be set to Loose in the Streamline Conversion Setup dialog box. Experiment with the tolerance setting on various types of images to see how it affects the outlining of images. I set the tolerance to maximum for most images. (See Fig. 9.11 and 9.12 in Chapter 9, "Grappling With Graphics" for a comparison of a line art image which was converted using both tight and loose tolerance settings.)

Drawing applications in general

Build graphics in layers (see Figure 15.19) so that they can be constructed, edited, and troubleshot more easily if there are RIPing problems. Often, only a portion of an EPS file may be the cause of an output problem. For instance, one path in an illustration may be too long or complex. If a complex graphic is built in layers which can be individually viewed and activated, isolating and correcting the troublemaking paths can be easy. Editing the image in any way is easier if the graphic is built in layers.

Always adjust the flatness ratio in drawing programs like Illustrator, Freehand, and CorelDraw prior to printing or creating EPS files. Flatness ratios should always be greater than 0. A flatness range of 2–5 is a good starting place for most line art graphic files.

Use proper printer description files (APDs, PPDs, PDXs, PDFs) when printing a file (choice of printer in print setup box). When preparing EPS graphics to export for placement in another application such as a page layout, choose the printer description file of the highest resolution final output machine (imagesetter), even if you will be proofing on a lower resolution printer such as a laser printer. This will have the graphics program include flatness and path lengths which are compatible with the more memory intensive imagesetter RIP. Default PPD selections can also be done through the use of the LaserWriter Driver 8.x in the Chooser (Mac) .

▼ Figure 15.22 Object Control
The resolution of individual objects can be controlled in Illustrator by selecting an item and choosing Attributes under the Object menu. Controlling the resolution of an object in Illustrator is how the flatness is controlled. The default object resolution is 800ppi, which results in a flatness of 3 at 2400 dpi output resolution.

▼ Figure 15.23 Deleting Colors
Deleting unused colors should be done prior to exporting a document as an EPS graphic or printing. In Illustrator, choose Custom Color under Object menu to produce this dialog box. Select Unused color and Delete. This same procedure can be performed in all the major drawing type applications.

Setting type in drawing applications

Avoid setting a lot of type in outline graphics applications such as Illustrator, Freehand, and CorelDraw if you intend to export the graphic as an EPS for inclusion in a page layout application.

Create outlines of text in EPS files imported in page layout documents. This will improve printing speed and reduce font location problems. (Use ATM in Windows.)

To create an outline of some text characters, select the copy, make sure printer fonts and ATM are loaded, then choose a convert to paths or outline text option. This is available in nearly all drawing applications. An example is shown in Fig. 15.20.

See Chapter 19, "Managing The Mess" for some suggestions on when and how to create a print-ready exportable EPS file while retaining its editability.

Illustrator

To control the document-wide path lengths and flatness ratio in Illustrator use File –Document Setup (Fig. 15.21) and input the resolution of the output device you will be printing to, then check Split Long Paths. The resolution setting will determine the path lengths which Illustrator creates.

In Illustrator the flatness of individual objects may be controlled by adjusting its resolution on an object-by-object basis by selecting an object and choosing Objects – Attributes (Fig. 15.22) and setting a separate individual resolution for the selected graphic.

Unused colors may be removed from the list of colors in the color palette by choosing Object and selecting Custom Color (Fig. 15.23). Select All Unused and then choose Delete. This will reduce the size of

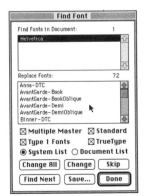

▼ Figure 15.24 Change Fonts
The Find Font utility in Illustrator is useful for making font lists and for finding and removing unwanted fonts.

225

▼ Figure 15.25 Delete Utility
Use Delete utilities in Freehand to remove unused colors and text boxes prior to printing or creating EPS files.

▼ Figure 15.26 Output Options
Freehand allows you to control the splitting and flatness of all paths through its Output Options dialog box. Set flatness between 2 and 5.

▼ Figure 15.27 Flatness Control
Individual Path flatness can be controlled though the Inspector Palette in Freehand by selecting the path and choosing the geometric symbols in the palette.

the color list which allows for faster importing and printing of the graphic file and prevents the printing of unwanted pieces of film during separation output. Illustrator also has a nifty Find Font utility (Fig. 15.24) which allows you to view all the fonts used in the document, select one, and change it to another font globally. This utility is very useful for making font lists when gathering fonts for sending your file out. It is also useful for searching and replacing fonts that you do not want in the document, such as those pesky spaces and paragraph returns which did not get selected when you changed the formatting of some copy.

Freehand

Freehand provides for deletion of unused colors through several avenues, but the easiest to access is the Delete submenu under Xtras menu (Fig. 15.25). To remove extraneous colors from the color palette prior to export as an EPS file in older versions of Freehand (prior to 5.0), select all elements on a page which you wish to export and copy them to another page. Only the colors which you have used will be copied and placed in the new document.

Path length and Flatness ratio can be controlled in several locations in Freehand. Global control can be exercised through the selection of the Output Options choice under the File menu (Fig. 15.26). Check Split Long Paths. Set Flatness to greater than 0 (try 2–5). Control of flatness for individual objects is accomplished through the use of the Inspector Palette (Fig. 15.27). Select your path and then click on the geometry symbols.

One of the most useful and flexible file prep tools available in Freehand is the Simplify tool (Fig. 15.28). Use Simplify to reduce the complexity of a path created or opened in Freehand. Simplify gives you complete control over how much simplification (how many control points will be removed) will be applied to a line. This type of control can dramatically reduce the RIPing times required to process a path. This is a good tool for simplifying complex paths which may be created by Streamline or other outlining applications.

PostScript files

What is a PostScript File

When we construct our documents we usually save them, at least initially, as application files in native document formats such as PageMaker, and QuarkXpress files. These native file format docu-

▼ *Figure 15.28 Simplify Paths*
One of the best file prep utilities in Freehand is the Simplify Control. The Simplify dialog box allows you to add or subtract a point from a path. The path on the top is a very complex path with hundreds of control points. The path on the bottom is the same path after Simplify has been applied with a setting of 10. As you can see, the integrity of the path has been maintained, but the number of control points has been reduced by over 95 percent. The Simplified path on the bottom will RIP/print much faster than the unsimplified path on the top.

ments are full viewable and editable with most of their document components such as high resolution graphics and font files being maintained as linked but separate and easily editable external files. These are made for document creation, viewing, editing, and printing.

An alternative to saving your documents in native file formats is to save your file as a PostScript file. A PostScript file is a text based document which contains, if properly constructed, all the document information, including imbedded font and graphic files, required for printing that document. A PostScript file is a print-oriented document format. PostScript files are not easily viewable without a special PS file viewer or editor, and they are not editable without a special PostScript file editor. The entire object behind creating a PostScript file is the creation of a complete file made primarily for printing, not editing. The greatest strengths of a PostScript file, its completeness and uneditable nature, are also its greatest weaknesses. If you construct a PostScript file correctly it will print correctly no matter who prints it. However, if you make any mistakes in the construction of your document, or the creation of the PostScript file, those mistakes get printed too.

Use of PostScript files

PostScript files are often created and used when the the person who creates a document either does not want their document to be edited when they send it out to be printed, or they are sending their document file to someone who needs to print their document but does not have the application which was used to create the document.

PostScript files are created by preparing your file as if you were about to print your document, but instead of printing your document to a printing device, you print your file to a disk.

Once you are sure that your document is constructed properly you must pay close attention to properly configuring the various print setup dialog boxes provided by your application before your actually "print" your PostScript file to your disk.

Creating a proper PostScript file

On the next page you will see some typical print setup dialog boxes. These are from QuarkXPress 4.0.4, but your application and version will have similar dialog boxes. Different applications and versions have different dialog boxes, but the key variables must always be set for proper printing to occur. Following is a list of typical PostScript file setup variables:

Document setup variables (Fig.15.29)

- Page range to print: All is typical, but if you want only a portion, you need to specify which pages you want to print.
- Separations: "On" for imagesetting or "Off" for composite desktop printers.
- Page sequence: "Odd" "Even" or "All."
- Registration: On or Off depending upon whether your file will be separated or not. Turn "On" for separations.
- Bleed: If and how much.
- Spread: Whether facing pages will print together.

Setup choice variables (Fig. 15.30)

- PPD for Mac, and Printer Driver for Windows (choose the highest resolution device on which the final document will print). This is a crucial setting.

Figure 15.29 Document Setup Print Dialog Box

▼ *Figure 15.30 Setup Choices Print Dialog Box*

▼ *Figure 15.31 Output Print Dialog Box*

▼ *Figure 15.32 Print Options Dialog Box*

▼ *Figure 15.33 Printer Dialog Box*

- Paper size and width: Should match the output device.
- Enlargement: Usually best set at 100%.
- Orientation: Landscape or Portrait.
- Paper Offset and Gap: You should get this information from your printing company.

Output choices (Fig. 15.31)

- Type of plates: Spot and/or process separations to print.
- Resolution: Choose the resolution of the highest output device. 2400 is typical for many imagesetters. 300 -1200 dpi is typical for most desktop printers.
- Line screen (lpi), or frequency, at which halftones will be printed: 150lpi - 200lpi is the typical range for commercial offset presses. 60lpi for 300dpi laser printers, 85lpi for 600 dpi laser printers and 110lpi for 1200 dpi laser printers.
- Screen angles used to print: There are many options here depending upon the RIP which is used.
- Spot color screen angles: The default screen angle is generally the same as the K (black) ink angle (generally 45°). Screens or tints of spot colors which overlap should be set at different screen angles to prevent the creation of moiré patterns.

Print options variables (Fig. 15.32)

- Picture quality: Usually set to "High Resolution" or "Normal."
- Picture data: Usually Binary for imagesetters. Some Windows networks prefer ASCII which is larger but more compatible.
- Overprint options: Generally turned on.
- Whether a positive or negative print image is needed.

PostScript file variables (Fig. 15.33)

- Destination: "File" instead of "Printer."
- Format: Set to "PostScript."
- PostScript Level: Either "One", "Two," or "Three," depending upon RIP and work flow.
- Data format: Binary for most high resolution imagesetter output.

Some Windows networks handle the ASCII file format better, which is a larger but more compatible format.

- Font Inclusion: Be sure to select "All" here. The default is often "None." If "None" is chosen, none of the font files you used to create your document will be included in the PostScript file. Other font files will be substituted with the result being different looking type and reflowing of type.

Ask your printer

The settings, variations, and options I have discussed and recommended for PostScript files above will work in many circumstances. However, it is always a good idea to check with the printing company or service bureau who will be printing your PostScript files for recommendations which are unique and/or specific to their equipment, Rips, and/or workflow. Some of the settings we discussed here such as line screen and screen angles may be set or overridden at the RIP. In most print dialog boxes you can save a set of settings and recall them later. This is called a "Print Style" in these dialog boxes. Print Styles save valuable time and prevent print setup errors.

PDF: the portable document format

What is PDF?

PDF, or Portable Document Format, is a non-native file format which is viewable and has limited editability. PDF requires only a PDF viewer in order to see the document. PDF is a file format created by Adobe Corporation as a document format which is independent of the platform, application, or computer on which it was created. PDF was designed primarily for viewing and printing of documents without needing the native application installed on a computer. PDF even has font character simulation capabilities to aid in the viewing and printing of documents. PDF has many advantages but also some liabilities. If you are aware of both, and create and use PDF document properly, it is a powerful, flexible, and very useful document technology.

PDF advantages

PDF is portable, that is, it is application- platform- and OS-independent and does not require the native application for viewing and printing. A PDF document, like a PostScript file, can contain all fonts and graphics if properly constructed. But unlike a PostScript file it is easily viewable and at least somewhat editable.

PDF also contains high quality easy-to-RIP and print normalized Postscript information. PDF files also tend to be very compact, with much smaller files sizes. File size reduction of up to 90 percent, compared to a PostScript file can be obtained. PDF files are also page efficient. PDF documents are built a page at a time and can therefore be processed that way: RIPing, trapping, imposition, etc.. PDF can be used for a variety of purposes including proofing, exchanging, and editing prior to printing. It is also an excellent document archiving and retrieval tool.

For production purposes, PDF documents can contain job ticketing information with document and job information. This is a huge work flow advantage. PDF is also extensible, which means that many extensions can and have been built for PDF and more are on the way. For example, Forms extensions allow variable data input to PDF files. And, finally, PDF is Web safe/compatible, which makes PDF an easy and dependable way to send files across the Internet.

PDF challenges

Most of PDF's challenges relate to printing problems, especially in high resolution separation environments. PDF files are generally created from PostScript files. Therefore the quality and completeness of the PDF document depends upon the quality and completeness of the PostScript file from which it is constructed. PDF was originally designed primarily for viewing documents in an RGB environment, not printing them in a high resolution CMYK-oriented separation environment. Therefore, PDF is not inherently separation compatible, and currently, (version3.0), requires the plug-ins in order to work effectively with PDF files in a prepress environment. PDF has a fairly complex print preparation interface, and not all RIPs will process print PDF files. If there are problems with the PDF file, they are not as editable as an application file. PDF is still a relatively unknown format, although I think this will change rapidly.

Preparing PDF files for print

Preparing a PDF file for print requires the same attention as creating any print document. We must be aware of missing fonts and graphics, or corrupted components such bad PostScript code, fonts, or graphics. Improper geometric manipulation (resize, crop, rotation) may cause slow RIPing. We should avoid white "cover-ups" and provide the proper graphic file formats for print by using TIFF and EPS graphics and avoiding PICTs, WMF, PMP CAD formats, etc.

PDF preflight

Like PostScript documents, PDF files need to be set up properly if you want them to print correctly. Here is a short list of the most common PDF page construction bugaboos:

• Correct trim size

• Bleeds properly defined

• No hairlines

• Proper graphic file format

• Color space conversions: RGB will not convert to CMYK

• All font files included

• Rules & borders properly positioned

• No blank pages

• Color assignment

• Trapping properly applied

• Total ink coverage not exceeding 340%

Distiller setup

Distiller is the Adobe application through which a PostScript file is processed in order to create a PDF document. One of the most common errors when creating a PDF document is using the default "Job Option" setting in Distiller. Distiller's defaults settings are RGB view oriented, and most are inappropriate for printing. To have our PDF files print properly we must configure the Distiller Job Options correctly through the PDF "Job Options" dialog box. This is particularly true if you are sending your PDF files out for printing (see Fig. 15.34).

▼ *Figure 15.34 Distiller Job Options Menu Choice*
Select and configure the Job Options prior to Distilling a document into PDF format.

PDF "Job Options"

There are four tabbed subsections of the PDF "Job Options" dialog box. Following are some issues and setting recommendations for print, and particularly for prepress.

General options (Fig. 15.35)

• Usually set Compatibility to Acrobat 3.0; some older versions of the Viewer and Exchange will only read Acrobat 2.1.

• Pay attention to Page Size. Some printing companies prefer a 8 3/8 (8.375)" x 10 7/8 (10.875)" over the default 8.75.

• Only use the ASCII setting when instructed by your printing company or if you are having problems printing your PDF file across your network. The ASCII version is generally more compatible, but is a larger file size.

• Set resolution to the highest output device to which you will be printing. This is usually 2400 dpi for an imagesetter and 600 dpi for a laser printer.

Compression options (Fig. 15.36)

• The safest way to create a PDF file which will print properly and without problems is to turn off all the compression. Doing so, however, will create much larger files. If you are sending your files in on a disk, the file size increase may not be a problem.

• If you are sending your PDF files across the Internet, the large file size created by uncompressed text and images may be a problem. Check with your service bureau or printing company who will be printing your files for compression guidelines.

• If you do compress your images here are some of the safer suggestions:

* Check Compress Text and Line Art (this is a safer lossless compression).

* DO NOT Down-sample or Subsample your images.

* DO NOT choose Automatic Compression.

* DO select Manual compression and high quality JPEG or 8-bit LZW.

• Check with your service bureau for compression compatibility for imaging with their RIP.

▼ *Figure 15.35 Distiller General Preferences*
In General settings, pay particular attention to the page size. Some printers do not like the default 8.5" x 11" size. Check with your printing company for specific values to place here.

▼ *Figure 15.36 Distiller Compression Preferences*
The safest way to create a PDF file which will print properly and without problems is to turn off all the compression. Doing so, however, will create much larger files.

▼ *Figure 15.37 Distiller Compression Preferences*
The safest way to create a PDF file which will print properly is to embed all the font files. This will create a larger but more accurate printing document. If you are using your PDF strictly for on-screen proofing or viewing purposes and send your PDF file across the Internet, subsetting may be a good option.

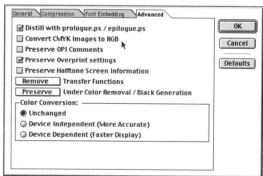

▼ *Figure 15.38 Distiller advanced preferences*
These advanced preferences vary from printing company to printing company. I have set this up for a typical output print. You will want to consult your printing company or service bureau for their specific requirements.

Font embedding options (Fig. 15.37)

• Part of the advantage of the Acrobat technology is the ability to substitute font proxies for missing fonts. But this also leads to documents which do not print exactly like the original.

• For best results, check the "Embed All fonts" check box.

• Also, place "99%" in the Subset fonts dialog box.

• Including all the font files will make the resulting PDF document larger – but the text will print more reliably.

• If you are just using the document for on-screen proofing or viewing and/or sending your PDF file across the Internet, you may not want to embed the fonts for that purpose. In this case, un-check the "Embed All Fonts" and use the Acrobat default value of 25% in the Subset dialog box.

Advanced options (Fig. 15.38)

The advanced tab in the Distiller Job Options setup is easily the most cryptic and confusing. Here are some guidelines:

• Check/activate the "Distill with prologue.ps / epilog.ps" so that spot colors will separate properly.

• UNCHECK "Convert CMYK Images to RGB." This is checked/activated by default and should be deactivated.

• Uncheck "Preserve OPI Comments" unless instructed to turn this on by your printing company.

• Check/activate "Preserve Overprint Settings" to make sure that any colors assigned to overprint will do so.

• UNCHECK "Preserve Halftone Screen Information" if the Halftoning is set at the Rip. Check/activate this preference if you have set your halftoning information in Photoshop and want it to be honored.

• Choose the "Remove" "Transfer Functions" option unless you are sure that you want a transfer function you have created in Photoshop to be applied.

• Choose the "Preserve" "Under Color Removal/ Black Generation" option to make sure the the color conversion functions you have chosen in Photoshop will be applied. If these functions are addressed in a different separation application at the RIP, then this function should be set to "Remove" instead of "Preserve."

• Check/activate "Unchanged" button color conversion section.

Ask your printer

The settings, variations, and options I have discussed and recommended for either PostScript files or PDF will work in many circumstances. However, it is always a good idea to check with the printing company or service bureau who will be printing your PostScript or PDF files for recommendations which are unique and/or specific to their equipment, Rips, and workflow.

PAULINE'S FILE PREP TIPS

File Prep Hint #73

Graphic elements placed or imported into page layout documents should be manipulated (scaled, cropped, rotated, or skewed) for design iteration purposes only in those applications. Final editing choices should be applied in the original graphics application. Use Publish and Subscribe to speed up these updating chores.

File Prep Hint #74

In QuarkXPress use Collect for Output and Font and Picture Usage to help identify and collect document components. Extensions such as The Bundler provide even more extensive help.

File Prep Hint #75

In Pagemaker use the utility Save For Service Provider and Save as Files for remote printing to help identify and collect document components. Plug-ins such as Document Info may provide additional help.

File Prep Hint #76

Use the Link Options menu choice under the Element menu to prevent Pagemaker from automatically including high resolution versions of graphic images in its documents.

Pauline's File Prep Tips

File Prep Hint #77

Create all blends in bitmapped editing applications like Photoshop. You will have more control, they will be of higher quality, and will print faster. Use Dithering and add Noise and Gaussian blur to blends to prevent banding on output.

File Prep Hint #78

When creating clipping paths in Photoshop, be sure to create simple paths with few control nodes by setting tolerance at 2.0 and above during the creation of the path from a selection. Also set the flatness ratio to 3.0 or above to facilitate output at high resolution.

File Prep Hint #79

Use Levels and Curves in Photoshop instead of Brightness and Contrast controls to make tonal adjustments on photographic images.

File Prep Hint #80

When adjusting the resolution of a contone image in Photoshop, do not merely add resolution to a file. This will destroy your image. You can safely increase the resolution of a contone image by reducing its dimension while holding the file size constant in the image size dialog box.

PAULINE'S FILE PREP TIPS

File Prep Hint #81

When scanning always use a two-step scanning process which includes an initial low resolution prescan. This scan is used to analyze and adjust settings which will be applied during a second high resolution scan.

File Prep Hint #82

Before converting bitmapped images to vectors using Streamline, set the tolerance to a high number, usually 4–5, to reduce the number of nodes generated by Streamline.

File Prep Hint #83

Construct complex images in layers in both painting and drawing applications. This makes both initial construction and subsequent editing and troubleshooting much easier. Save native copies of the original layered images prior to export as printable TIFFs and EPSs.

File Prep Hint #84

Convert type set in drawing documents to graphic outlines prior to exporting the file as an EPS document. It is also a advisable to limit the amount of type which is set in any document slated for conversion to an EPS. Avoid converting small (≤20pt) and serif typefaces.

PAULINE'S FILE PREP TIPS

File Prep Hint #85

Be sure to remember to split long paths and set path flatness ratios to at least 3 prior to export as an EPS in all vector-based documents.

File Prep Hint #86

In general, use applications for the purposes for which they were intended. Perform layout and typesetting with applications like QuarkXPress and Pagemaker, draw with applications like Illustrator, Freehand, or CorelDraw, and paint with applications like Photoshop and Painter.

File Prep Hint #87

For highly complex paths, use your drawing application's ability to decrease the path complexity by reducing the number of control points which occur along the paths.

File Prep Hint #88

Learn a small number of applications very well, rather than trying to learn several varieties of each kind. Become expert at one page layout, one drawing, and one painting application. Experiment with others after you are well grounded in your primary applications.

DTP 401

Finishing The Project

SCREENING

P

T

TRAPPING

PROOFING

DISK PREP

Client Disk

Separations

CYAN

MAGENTA

YELLOW

BLACK

16
Screening Your Images

As the Byte Turns continues…

*Will Danny learn to scan his images for the proper lpi, or
will Pauline screen more than his images the next time Danny calls?*

Why don't the printed versions of my photos look more like the originals ?

Well, I'm not sure?

I wish I understood how a scanner worked.

Can't we make them better?

Danny's original images are continuous tone, while the printed versions are halftone dot pattern equivalents. Plus, Danny did the original scans and sent us only raw scan files.

IMAGE REPRODUCTION: SCREENING TECHNOLOGY

Reproducing images with dots

Dots

There are four basic kinds of images which need to be reproduced on a printing press: text, line art, tints, and continuous tone images. Most of our current printing technology uses dots to reproduce these images. There are basically three kinds of dots: *laser dots, halftone dots,* and *stochastic dots.* Laser dots, sometimes referred to as laser "spots," are the small individual dots created by a laser imaging engine such as a laser printer or an imagesetter. The size of the dot produced by a print engine depends upon the resolution of that particular printer. A 300 dpi desktop laser printer creates laser dots which are 1/300" x 1/300" square. A 1200 dpi imagesetter creates laser dots which are 1/1200" x 1/1200" square. Some printers have the ability to create more than one size of laser dots, which allows them to print at more than one resolution. The density of the dot pattern which a laser printer or imagesetter is capable of producing is determined by the resolution of the device. A 300 dpi laser printer can create a pattern of identical dots using 300 dots arranged vertically and horizontally in every square inch (90,000 dpi^2). Any combination of these 90,000 dots can be placed or "turned on" on a page. If all 90,000 dots are placed, a solid 1" black square will result. If none of the 90,000 dots are placed, a solid 1"white square will result. This is how text and line art images are created, by either placing or not placing dots at various places on a page. Halftone and stochastic dots are used to reproduce tints and contones and are constructed from groups of laser dots.

Reproduction of solid text and line art images, such as the solid "P" shown in Fig. 16.1 is fairly straightforward. Solid images can easily be reproduced by merely placing identically sized laser dots end to end and/or side by side in whatever shapes or sequences are required to recreate the image. The size of the dots used is determined by the resolution of the printer. The smaller the dots used to reproduce an image (that is, the higher the resolution of the printer), the finer the detail and the sharper the images which can be reproduced. The solid black "P" shown in Fig. 16.1 is a good example of how dots can be arranged to create a text character or line art image. Notice how higher resolutions will create images with sharper edge detail. Colors can be applied to those solid dot patterns if required.

Image Example *Expanded View Of Printed Image*

Solid Text and Line Art Images

Text and line art images which are solid, that is 100 percent grayscale or black, can be reproduced by placing solid laser dots end to end with no space in between. Only black and white tones need to be produced. Any solid colors can be assigned to either the black or white area during the printing process. The size of the dots and the stairsteps depend upon the resolution of the image. Higher resolution equals smaller dots.

Screened/Tinted Text and Line Art Images

Images such as this 25 percent grayscale image which are *not* solid images (images of less than 100 percent gray) require the use of spaced halftone dots. These are collections of dots rather than individual dots to simulate the effect of grayscale images. In a halftoning system the halftone dots are equally spaced, and the size of the dots is modified to simulate various shades of gray.

Gradations / Degradés / Blends

A gradation from one shade of gray to another is the simplest kind of contone image. Images such as this 0 -100% grayscale blend, known as a gradation, gray ramp, or degradé, are simulated by generating rows of halftone dots of gradually increasing or decreasing sizes. Blends can be created by forming two overlapping gradations. Often a different color will be assigned to each gradation.

Contone Images

This is an example of a complex contone. Complex contones have a wide variety of grayscale areas grading one into another. These complex areas are reproduced using a complex pattern of equidistant halftone dots of various sizes. The sizes vary according to the lightness or darkness of various parts of the image.

▼ **Figure 16.1 Laser Spots and Halftone Dots**
Small individual dots are all most laser printers and imagesetters have to create images with. Solid areas like the top "P" are fairly easy to construct. A printer lines up laser spots end to end to fill a solid area or create a continuous line. Tones can be reproduced by producing patterns of closely spaced dots, called halftone dots. Traditional halftoning creates patterns of equally spaced dots and varies the size of the dots to produce various shades of gray. Each halftone dot is constructed out of numerous laser spots.

Image reproduction gets a bit more challenging when we try to reproduce a tint or tone (an area filled in with one shade of gray), and particularly when we try to reproduce a continuous tone (*contone*) image where tonal values vary continuously across an image, such as in a blend from one shade of gray to another or in a photograph of a person's face.

Why screens?

To fully appreciate the challenge of reproducing a continuous tone (contone) image, we must remember that we are restricted to the use of dots when we want to reproduce an image on a printing press. We do not have the luxury of directly creating shades of gray or colors as we can in photography. Postscript laser printers and imagesetters are essentially dot production machines. At any given position on a piece of film or paper, an imagesetter will either place a dot or not place a dot.

Since we cannot directly create tints or shades of gray, we are forced to use patterns of dots called **screens** to *simulate* grayscale values. This simulation takes advantage of the limited ability of the human eye to resolve or distinguish small dots which sit next to each other. Traditionally, we have created dots of various sizes placed closely beside each other to simulate the impression of a grayscale value. These variable-sized dots are called halftone dots. Halftone dots are composite dots constructed out of combinations of laser dots. By using combinations of laser dots to build halftone dots, we can construct halftone dots of various sizes. Unlike laser dots, most halftone dots are separated by space because they are created in a grid pattern known as a halftone grid. Unless the individual halftone dots are large, they do not touch. We generate patterns of halftone dots to simulate the appearance of shades of gray in printed images. Small halftone dots are used to simulate low grayscale or screen percentages such as 10 or 15 percent. Large halftone dots create high tonal or screen values. Larger halftone dots require greater numbers of laser dots or spots to construct them. An area filled with halftone dots of all the same size will create a *tint* of one tonal value such as a 25% tint or screen. This area will appear to the human eye as an area filled with 25% gray. An example of a 25% tint and an enlargement of the screen pattern used to create it appears in Fig. 16.1. Color can be applied to this area to create a 25% tint of that color. That same area filled with halftone dots of gradually varying sizes creates a graduated screen such as that seen in the third "P" shown in Fig. 16.1. A constantly varying pattern of dot sizes will simulate a continuous tone image; that is, one where the grayscale values vary across the image. This is

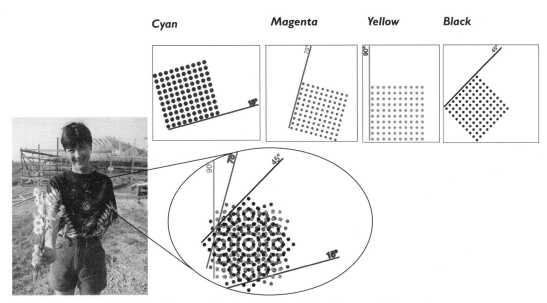

Cyan **Magenta** **Yellow** **Black**

▼ *Figure 16.2 Color Contone Images: Overlapping Four Color Process Halftone Screens*

Complex color contones such as this photograph are reproduced using a complex pattern of four overlapping screens of halftone dots. There is one screen pattern for each process color. Each color is printed at a different angle to avoid the generation of moiré patterns. Colors are separated as much as possible across the available 90°. The three strongest colors – Black, Cyan, and Magenta – are each separated by 30°. The fourth and weakest color, Yellow, is separated from two of the other colors, in this case Cyan and Magenta, by only 15°. When all four color screens are combined, a continuous tone color image simulation is produced. Note the rosette pattern which results when the four screens are in perfect registration.

Note: A color version of this image can be found in the Color Plate section (see C-9).

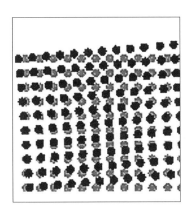

▼ *Figure 16.3 Moiré Pattern Generation*

When two or more overlapping screens are printed out of registration, repeating geometric patterns known as a moiré pattern can result. Printing each screened color at a different and optimum angle helps reduce the occurrence of moire patterns. Because Yellow is separated from Magenta and Cyan by only 15°, it tends to form moiré patterns with them. In a dark image any yellow moiré is not very noticeable, but in light images areas such as tans and pastel greens these moirés may be apparent. It is the repeating pattern of halftone dots which makes conventional screening technology prone to the development of moiré patterns. The use of frequency modulation screening technology, where dot placement rather than dot size is used to create tonal variations and the image dots are more randomly placed, removes this problem of moiré pattern development.

Note: A color version of this image can be found in the Color Plate section in the center of this book (see C-9).

▼ Figure 16.4 Dot Technologies
These are two different dot manipulation methods for generating tonal values from patterns of dots, AM and FM screening. Here we see magnified views of a tint or screen of one tonal value produced by both methods. On the left is a magnified view of the pattern of equally spaced halftone dots which is characteristic of AM screening technology. On the right is a magnified view of a tint generated by randomly spaced dots used in FM screening technology.

how grayscale photographs (such as the girl's image in Figure 16.1) are reproduced through printing. The gradual change in tonal values across in a person's face is constructed from a gradually changing pattern of various size halftone dots (see Chapter 8, "Resolving Resolution," for a detailed discussion and example of how a halftone dot is constructed).

Color contones

Meeting the additional challenge of reproducing color as well as tonal variation is accomplished through the use of four overlapping halftone screen patterns. Figure 16.2 shows how a pattern of four overlapping halftone patterns, which have the four process colors CMYK applied to them, are used to create a halftone simulation of a continuous tone color image. The enlarged view shows a highly magnified view of the four overlapping patterns of halftone dots, each with a separate process color applied to it. Halftone dots can form various shapes–some are round, others are square, elliptical, or even diamond shaped. The halftone dots shown in Fig. 16.2 are round dots.

This process of creating halftone dots was traditionally accomplished by taking a high contrast photograph of a continuous tone image (another photograph) which was covered with a special photographic screen. The resultant high contrast image would contain a pattern of dots, called halftone screen, which had dots varying in size to correspond to the grayscale value of that portion of the underlying image from which that dot was created. In a Postscript-based electronic publishing system, this screening process is performed by the Postscript RIP (Raster Image Processor). Until a digital contone is actually processed by the RIP, the image information retains grayscale values.

Screening angles

Overlapping patterns of halftone dots are usually printed at varying angles from each other. When contone color images are printed with the process colors Cyan, Magenta, Yellow, and Black, each color is printed at a different angle to help prevent the pattern of dots from interfering with each other. The conventional angles used for printing the four process colors are 90° for yellow, 75° for Magenta, 45° for black, and 15° for Cyan. These angles provide the maximum angular distance between each color, which should minimize the geometric interference between them when they overlap during the printing process. This scheme of separating the angles at which colors are printed helps dramatically, but it is not perfect.

▼ Figure 16.5 Halftone Tint
Above is a magnified view of a tint or screen produced by conventional AM screening technology which employs equally spaced halftone dots. Note the regularity of dot pattern. Creation of tonal variations is accomplished by varying dot size. AM screening is prone to the development of moiré patterns due to the regularity of the dot spacing.

▼ Figure 16.6 Stochastic Tint
Above is a magnified view of a tint or screen produced by Stochastic or FM screening technology which employs randomly spaced dots. Note the irregularity of dot patterns. In FM screening technology dots are randomly placed within an area. Creation of tonal variations are accomplished by varying the density of the dots rather than their sizes. FM screening technology is less prone to moiré creation.

If one or more of the screen patterns is misaligned during the imaging of printing process, the screen patterns can interfere with each other. When this interference pattern occurs, it forms a repeating pattern of dot groups called a moiré pattern. Figure 16.3 shows a moiré pattern and how it can be produced by two misaligned screens. Moiré patterns tend to be more obvious in lighter areas such as yellows and tans than in darker areas of an image such as browns and dark greens. This is because the misaligned dots forming the repeating pattern tend to be closer together and in some areas form darker sections of the patterns which will be more obvious when applied to a more lightly colored area. Over the years there have been numerous attempts to decrease the occurrence of moiré patterns by developing more sophisticated   screening algorithms. Screening technologies such as rational and irrational screening, Adobe Accurate Screens, Linotronic HQS, and Agfa's Balanced screening technologies use custom screen angles to improve upon the quality of halftoned images and reduce the occurrence and impact of moiré patterns. All these technologies, however, use equally spaced halftone dots. Because of the regularity of their placement, they will always be prone to moiré formation.

Conventional screening

Conventional screening refers to the use of regularly-spaced halftone dots. The key word here is regularly spaced. In conventional screening we vary the size or amplitude of equally spaced halftone dots to simulate various shades of gray. Technically, this is called amplitude modulation, or AM screening, because we are varying the size or amplitude of the dots to affect our creation of tonal value reproduction. In AM screening technology the center of each dot is equidistant from all surrounding dots. AM screening works similar to AM radio. With AM radio we are varying the Amplitude or size of the radio wave to change a channel. In the case of AM screening we are varying the size of the halftone dot to change the simulated tonal value. As mentioned above, this regular spacing of halftone dots has some inherent problems of moiré pattern development, which are difficult to completely overcome. We are not, however, limited to amplitude modulation for accomplishing our tone reproduction.

Stochastic screening

Stochastic screening, also known as FM or frequency modulated screening, uses *irregularly* or *randomly* spaced dot patterns. With FM screening we vary the *placement* rather than the size of the dots to create tonal variations. Light tonal areas of an image will have widely

▼ Figure 16.7 Gradations
Above are two gradations. The one on the left is generated with conventional AM halftone dots where the dot size is varied to create the changing tonal values across the gradation. The gradation on the right was produced with FM screening. Note how the dot density rather than the dot size increases from top to bottom.

spaced dots, while darker tonal areas will have more closely spaced dots. One of the several advantages of FM screening is the elimination of moiré patterns created when you have misalignment of two or more regularly-spaced dots patterns. We also find the FM screening provides smoother gradations from one tonal value to another. FM screening also requires less image information and therefore lower resolution images as well as smaller file sizes to produce a quality equivalent to that of a conventionally halftoned screened image. Because of these advantages, many of the newer desktop printers use this new FM screening. I predict that FM or stochastic screening will largely replace conventional screening as the standard screening method for the reproduction on tonal values. Figures 16.4–16.6 show comparisons of AM and FM screening technologies.

Dot gain of screened images

Any tonal image which is reproduced as patterns of dots will be affected by a phenomena known as dot gain. Dot gain is the tendency for dots to grow in size when they are reproduced on a printing press. Dots of ink grow in size when printed on paper for much the same reason that a drop of colored water will expand when dripped onto a paper towel. The printing ink, like the colored water, is absorbed into the paper and spreads out as it does so. In addition, since the dots of ink are being pressed onto the page by the press, they tend to spread out. Some dot gain can occur during the plate making process, but most of it occurs during the application of the ink onto the page.

Dot gain values and variables

Dot gain values are expressed in percentages and are usually measured at the 50% dot. The 50% dot is used because 50% is generally the point of maximum dot gain, with dot gain values generally decreasing toward the high light and shadow regions of an image. Dot gain percentage varies with the kind of paper on which you print. Coated papers generally exhibit smaller dot gain values than uncoated papers. Coated stock dot gain values will typically vary from 10% to 20%, while coated stocks will exhibit dot gain percentages varying between 20% and 30%. Some newspaper stocks exhibit even higher dot gain values.

There are a number of variables which affect dot gain characteristics: paper stock, ink characteristics, press setup, screening technology, screen frequency, and paper moisture. Dot gain values often vary with different types of ink and may even vary within a set of inks. For

Original Contone Image

Pixels from scan

50% Pixel

50% Dot at RIP

70% Dot at print

20% Dot Gain on press

Final Image Darker & Lower Contrast

▼ **Figure 16.8 Effects Of Dot Gain**

This sequence shows what happens to contone image data as it is scanned, RIPed, and printed. Dot gain occurs during printing. Here, a 20% dot creates a final image which is darker and lower in contrast than the original.

example, each of the four process colors (C,M,Y,K) exhibit slightly different dot gain characteristics. Dot gain tends to be greater with FM screened images than with AM screened images due to the larger surface area-to-volume ratio characteristic of FM screens smaller dots. With AM screening technologies, higher screen frequencies also tend to create larger dot gain functions than lower screen frequencies, again due to the smaller dots used. Consult your printer to discuss what dot gain characteristics you can expect with the paper stock, screening, and printing setup to be used with your images.

Controlling dot gain

Otherwise high quality images can be ruined when affected by dot gain. Images which are not dot gain corrected tend to look dark and have lower contrast than they should. Midtones, in particular, tend to look dark due to the high dot gain characteristics at 50%. A 20% dot gain at 50% will push midtone values up around 70%, thereby darkening the entire image. Figure 16.8 shows the progressive changes a contone images experiences as it proceeds through a digital production process, where dot gain occurs, and the effect dot gain can have on an image. If you are creating your own final high resolution images, you should always adjust for dot gain to help assure that your images look good when they are reproduced on press.

Grayscale contones

There is no automatic method in Photoshop of applying a dot gain correction to a grayscale contone. There are two easy ways to adjust for dot gain, however. The first method, making a gamma curve adjustment in the Curves dialog box, permanently alters the image. The adjustment is easy. Obtain the 50% dot gain figure from your printing company, open the Curves dialog box, then click on the middle of the gamma curve at the 50% mark and pull it down to the 30% mark. Use the In/Out reading at the bottom of the dialog box to help you place the new point. Figure 16.9 shows how a 20% dot gain adjustment would look in Curves. Note how this gamma curve adjustment results in a maximum dot gain compensation at 50% with gradually decreasing values toward the high light and shadow end of the curve. The advantage of making a dot gain adjustment with Curves is twofold. First, you see the results of the adjustment on screen, and second nothing else has to be done to the image for the dot gain adjustment to be applied. The disadvantage of the Curves adjusted dot gain control is that the change is permanent and specif-

▼ Figure 16.9 Curves Dialog Box

Dot gain on a grayscale contone image can be adjusted using the Curves dialog box in Photoshop. Here is a correction for a 20% dot gain at 50%. The midtone point is depressed to 30%. On press this will return to 50%, rendering the image in its proper tones. The percentage of dot gain adjustment decreases toward the highlight and shadow ends of the tone curve.

▼ Figure 16.10 Transfer Functions

Transfer Functions from Photoshop can help adjust for dot gain on a grayscale contone image. Here is a correction for a 20% dot gain at 50%. The midtone point is again depressed to 30%. On press this will return to 50%, rendering proper tones. The percentage of dot gain adjustment decreases toward the high light and shadow ends of the tone curve.

ic to that print job. If you use a Curve adjustment to compensate for dot gain you may want to save a copy of the image before you apply the Curve adjustment. It is also a good idea to label the two images differently so you can easily distinguish them. I add a w/C onto my images to indicate they are saved with a Curve correction. For example, an original image may be named Portrait CMYK 200.Tiff and the Curves adjusted image I would name Portrait w/C CMYK 200.Tiff

If you intend to multipurpose an image (use it for several different purposes), you may want to utilize a second alternative for applying a dot gain correction: Transfer Function. To create a Transfer Function in Photoshop, choose Page Setup from the File menu, then click on the Transfer button in the lower left portion of dialog box. Tab through the grayscale percentage data areas until you reach the 50% box. Enter the dot gain value, 20%, in the 50% box and a gamma curve identical to the one you created in the Curves dialog box will be created. Save this Transfer Function. The next step is to save your image as an EPS file along with the transfer curve you just created. You will notice that your image will not be altered on screen. The transfer Function will be applied only when the image is RIPed. (Refer to Figure 16.10 to see an example of the creation of a Transfer Function curve in Photoshop.)

Again, the advantage of using a Transfer Function is that the curve is applied only when the image is RIPped and does not alter the original image. Another advantage to using a Transfer Function is that if you have more specific dot gain data which you need to apply to percentages other than 50%, it is easier to create these custom curves as Transfer Functions due to the tab -through nature of the Transfer Function dialog box. If you will be printing your image on several different printing devices, such as a desktop printer for proofing, a banner printer for making a poster, and then finally on an offset press, you can apply a different Transfer Function curve for each printer and never alter the original image.

Color contones

The control for dot gain of a color image can take place as early as during the scan of the image, and this may be desirable if an image is only going to press and will be printed only once on a particular paper stock and on a specific press. However, in the age of multipurposing of images, it is better to adjust for dot gain later in the production process, either when the image is converted from RGB to CMYK, or through the use of a transfer curve when going to press. Photoshop allows you to adjust for dot gain when you convert an image from

RGB mode into CMYK mode. Prior to the mode conversion, you can assign a dot gain value in the Printing Inks Setup dialog box, which will then be applied to the image when it is converted from RGB to CMYK. (See Figs. 18.5 and 18.7 in Chapter 18, "The Proof Is In The Separation," for more information on assigning dot gain during separations.)

With color contones, as with grayscale contones, the advantage of using a transfer curve is that the curve is only applied when the image is RIPed and does not alter the original image, and custom curves are easier to construct. Images which utilize transfer curves must be saved in EPS format out of Photoshop in a fashion similar to how we saved the grayscale images in the previous section.

PAULINE'S FILE PREP TIPS

File Prep Hint #89

Remember that your color images will be separated into individual pieces of film and plates for printing. Be sure to assign your colors properly and print test or proof separations to check your color breaks. Printing separations is really the only way to check to see if your colors will separate properly.

File Prep Hint #90

Be sure that your individual spot colors are assigned different screen angles, particularly if those colors will be overlapped, or moiré patterns will likely result. If you consistently have trouble with moiré patterns when printing colored patterns and images, consider trying an FM screening method rather than conventional AM halftoning.

PAULINE'S FILE PREP TIPS

File Prep Hint #91

Be sure to adjust for dot gain before you send a contone image to press; otherwise, your images will
look darker and in lower contrast than you expected. Use Curves or Transfer Functions to adjust for
dot gain in grayscale images. For color contones,
apply dot gain adjustment during the RGB to CMYK
conversion process.

File Prep Hint #92

Contone images and other patterns with tonal values will be printed as a pattern of dots called a
screen. Visualize how your image will print as a
screen and avoid pattern assignments which cannot
be effectively screened. Avoid assigning grayscale values or patterns to thin lines because they will be
imaged only as a discontinuous series of dots when
printed.

File Prep Hint #93

Choose a screening technology which matches the kinds of images you are
trying to reproduce. We will increasingly have choices of different screening
technology. Also know which technologies work best on the print device you
will be using. Contone images often look better when reproduced with FM
screening technology, particularly when printed on desktop banner printers,
while solid area images reproduce better with AM screening technologies.

17

Feeling Trapped?

As the Byte Turns continues…

Will Danny D'Ziner and Pauline E Prepress live happily everafter? Or will they begin to feel TRAPPED by their too-numerous Postscript errors?

Why did those lines occur around some of the colored type on my last printed piece?!

Looks like the graphics were not trapped.

What a mess!!!

Why were Danny's files not trapped?

You said he would be responsible for providing us with RIP-ready files and that he would do his own trapping!

TRAPPING

What is trapping?

Ink trapping

Originally (and still in some contexts) in the world of print, the word "trapping" referred to the relative tendency of one ink to stick or "trap" onto another during the printing process. This amount of stick or trap is important to know when determining what the size of the various printing dots should be when overlapping process colors are being printed on top of each other. Controlling the size of the original image dots on the film and printing plates and being able to predict the amount of increase or decrease in dot size, dot gain, or loss when it is printed on by a press is important. The final size of the various color dots affects both the color and the darkness of an image which is being printed. The greater the stickiness of two overlapping inks, the smaller the size of the dots of the overlapping colors needs to be.

Object trapping

The second and currently more common use of the word "trap" refers to the amount of overlap which occurs between two areas of adjacent touching colors. The trap or overlap of two colors is usually measured in thousandths of an inch, but is sometimes measured in points as well. For the remainder of the discussion on trapping in this book, "trapping" will refer to this second definition: object trapping.

Why do we need trapping?

Trapping or overlapping of two adjacent colors may be necessary if those adjacent colors, which need to touch and fit snugly against each other, are applied by two separate cylinders on a printing press. Color elements which are supposed to touch on a page can sometimes end up being slightly separated during the printing process. This separation is generally caused by slight misalignments which can occur as paper is transported through a printing press. Other variables such as imprecision of image placement during film making and dimensional stability problems of the film itself can also contribute to misalignment problems. The amount of separation is usually small – only a few thousandths of an inch. But if two dark colors which are supposed to be touching are separated by even the smallest hairline, the generally light colored paper or other media will very obviously show through, ruining the intended nature of the border between the two colors. Preventing this appearance of inappropriate light lines between objects is why we overlap, or trap, objects of different colors on a printed page. Not all touching objects need to be trapped. Only those objects whose inks are applied by different or non-common press cylinders need to be considered for trap.

Trapping basics

There are four basic ink application and trapping terms and techniques with which you need to be familiar: spread, choke, overprint, and knockout. But before we define and apply these specific techniques, it will be helpful to first discuss object relationships.

Object relationships

To prevent confusion and facilitate communication about the relationship of overlapping objects and their traps, it is helpful to agree on a frame of reference. The frame of reference we use in trapping is foreground and background objects. Keeping the concept of foreground and background clear is the key to keeping trapping relationships straight, particularly in complex documents with many layers. When determining trapping or overlap relationships, we always choose an object which we designate as the foreground. Then we determine the overlap or trapping relationship which that object has with all of the background objects with which it intersects. If that first object is in turn overlain by any other objects, then it will be considered a background object to all those overlying objects. Figure 17.1 on page 263 shows a sequence of foreground and background relationships. When two objects meet edge to edge with no clear foreground or background relationship, one will need to be arbitrarily designated as the foreground object. In reality, any object created in a graphics or page layout application is constructed and will exist in its own layer. This construction layer relationship helps determine foreground and background relationships for objects which meet only at the edges.

Trapping concepts

There are four ways in which a foreground colored object can be printed in relationship to a background object. A foreground object can be spread into, choked by, overprinted onto, or knocked out of a background colored object. Trap values are always assigned to foreground objects.

Spreading

Spreading occurs when a foreground object expands or spreads out into or over a background color. Spreading the foreground object slightly increases its size as it spreads out over the background object. Spreading is an appropriate technique when the foreground color is lighter than the background color. Assignment of a spreading relationship between a foreground object and its background results in the assignment of a positive trap value to the foreground object; that is, the foreground object is expanding and its edge is moving out.

Choking

Choking occurs when a background object moves into or chokes the foreground object. Choking the background object slightly increases the area of the background object as it expands over the foreground object. To keep clear as to whether an object is spreading or being choked, always be clear on the foreground and background relationship between the objects. Foreground objects can only spread, and background objects can only choke. Assignment of a choking relationship between a foreground object and its background results in the assignment of a negative trap value to the foreground object; that is, the background object is moving into the foreground object. Its edge is moving into the foreground object. Remember that the trap value is always assigned to the *foreground* object, so even though the background is expanding, the foreground objected is being invaded; hence, the concept of the choke and the assignment of a negative trap value.

Overprint

Overprinting is the easiest of the trapping concepts to understand and control. With overprinting, a foreground object is printed directly over or on top of the underlying color, hence, the name overprint. This ink application technique is appropriate when you are printing very dark colors with grayscale values above 95 percent. Overprinting colors with grayscale values lighter than 95 percent should generally be avoided as this will generally make a significant visible change in the color of the overprinted object. The color of the underlying object will be mixed with the overprinting object's color, resulting in the generation of a new and generally darker color. There are, of course, no positive or negative values associated with an overprint because edges do not move.

▼ Figure 17.1 Knockout
This figure shows a knockout. The Cyan area under the black T is removed or knocked out from behind the T. If the T is considered the foreground object, then a choke trap would have the Cyan background move in, or choke in, around the T. A spread trap would enlarge or spread the T out into the Cyan background. An overprint would print the black T directly on top of the background without removing any of the Cyan. Overprinting is the safest way to trap because there are few alignment problems. However, overprinting will result in color alterations of the overprinted object unless it is very dark (>95 grayscale value). Note: A color version of this image can be found in the Color Plate section in the center of this book (see C-10).

Knockout

Knocking out is not really a trapping technique at all. In fact, knocking out implies an absence of trap or overlap altogether. A foreground object is said to be knocked out of a background area; that is, an area which is the exactly the same size and shape of the foreground layer is knocked out of or removed from the background object. In this way the foreground and background objects will just touch along their borders; they will not overlap. Boundaries between objects formed from knockouts are prone to misalignment problems which result in light media-colored lines showing through along the edges. Knockout can be most effectively applied when one or both the foreground or background object color is very light. If at least one color is very light, a media color which might show through will not be as apparent. Figure 17.1 shows a knockout.

Trapping rules of thumb

As a general rule, light colors should move into dark colors. Avoid too much trap; it will create edge changes in the trap zone or area of overlap. This is particularly true along edges where light colors overlap. Too much trap along the boundaries between light colors will create darkened edges. Some good trapping applications will allow you to decrease dot percentages of the two overlapping colors within the trap zones to prevent this darkening. Too little trap will result in light lines showing through between the edges of intersecting colors. Ask your printer for the standard trap values and use them.

Who should trap?

There is a long term and ongoing debate over who should be responsible for trapping. In the best of all possible worlds the clients would perform all the trapping chores because a file is most easily trapped when it is created. Then the printing company would not have to worry about it. In the real world, however, clients do not have the technical knowledge or skills necessary to assign traps correctly, and a poorly trapped file is more difficult to deal with than one with no trapping assigned at all. I come down in the middle of the debate. In general, I think it is best to let the output service bureau or printing company define the traps on files they will be printing. However, as a creator of files you should be knowledgeable enough about trapping to avoid creating difficult trapping problems. If you are not trap savvy, especially for process color traps, you will need to consult with the production staff of your printing company to determine some preferred ways of constructing your file. It's easy to construct absolutely beautiful color graphics files which are nearly impossible to

▼ Figure 17.2 Trap Example
Different applications use different methods for applying trap, but they all spread, choke, knockout, and overprint in one way or another. The Freehand trap dialog box shows the foreground T being spread by 1 pt. If the reversed button were activated, then the background would choke. Note: A color version of this image can be found in the Color Plate section in the center of this book (see C-10).

trap and RIP. Consult with your printing company during the design and construction phase of your documents so as to avoid the biggest problems. Following are some tips on avoiding trapping problem in the files you construct.

Trapping tips

• You can avoid the need for trapping between adjacent colored areas when you are working with process colors if you build adjacent touching elements with colors which have at least 15 percent of one dominant common color. Use Cyan (C), Magenta (M), or Black (K) for your common color. Avoid using Yellow (Y) as it is too weak a color to serve as an effective trap mask. Doing this will eliminate the need for trapping. For instance, if two touching elements contain at least 15 percent Cyan, these two elements will not need to be trapped because the Cyan plate will apply color across the trap boundary. Sharing two or more colors in adjacent colors will reduce the need for trapping at their boundary even more.

❧ As a general rule, move lighter colors into darker colors when you trap. This creates fewer noticeable problems in the overlap area or trap zone.

❧ If you do trap, note it on the document information sheet. You can print the window of a file job as a check disk content list.

❧ If you intend to apply trapping to a file, be aware of which portions of your document can be trapped by the application in which you are working. Most page layout applications such as QuarkXpress and PageMaker will not allow you to trap imported graphics. Also, you will generally not be able to trap page elements created in page layout application such as type on top of an imported element such as an EPS graphic. Assign traps for EPS graphics in the original drawing program (ie., Freehand, Illustrator, or CorelDraw). A good rule of thumb to know is that you can apply traps only to those items which are created in the application in which you are working.

❧ If you set chokes and spreads in a drawing application, be aware that most drawing applications stroke lines and outlines symmetrically; that is, they put half the stroke on either side of the line or outline. If you assign a 1 pt. stroke to line in your drawing application, you are really creating only a .05 pt overlap or trap.

❧ Note the trapping capability of your program to flag those areas which may require or be favorable to traditional methods. Some examples of trouble traps: trapping on top of indeterminate

▼ Figure 17.3 Trap Palette
This closeup of the Freehand trap palette indicates an application of a .25 pt trap. In addition, a trap nuance called tint reduction is also being applied. The tint reduction will decrease the screen value of the overlapping colors within the trap zone, or area of overlap to decrease the darkening which occurs where the two colors overlap.
Note: A color version of this image can be found in the Color Plate in the center of this book.

(multiple) background colors; trapping on top of color TIFFs in a page layout application.

❥ Avoid spreading type, especially small serif type faces, because the enlargement will ruin the geometry of the typeface. In fact, it is a good idea to try and avoid either spreading or choking small type at all. Overprint type whenever possible to retain the typeface's original geometric integrity.

❥ Design with trapping requirements and challenges in mind. Avoid, if you can, the creation of elements which are difficult to trap. Designs which include multiple overlapping blends are examples of designs to be avoided if possible.

❥ Note that trapping amounts are press-sensitive. A successful trap setting on one press may not work on another. Check with the production staff at your print company.

❥ Always consult with your printer for the preferred trap values before you start assigning trap values. Ask the printer if trapping is even necessary. Some single cylinder digital presses don't require trap creation.

❥ Ask your printer about an automatic trapping application. If the printer uses one, you may be wasting your time assigning traps because the automatic trapping application will probably just overwrite your trapping assignments.

❥ Be wary of sending PostScript files instead of a document files. Postscript files are unalterable and therefore fixed. Fonts and graphics are imbedded, but this fact makes for a much larger file, so be careful. Also, be aware that text imbedded in the included EPS file may not print. There is no room for error when you send Postscript files; what you send is what you get.

❥ Never set white to "OVERPRINT." White background areas should knockout to show the color of the underlying media, which is usually paper.

❥ Take a field trip to your favorite printing company and have the folks there walk you through the printing process. Be sure to visit the stripping room to see how film is composited and discuss trapping with one of the strippers. Such a field trip will enlighten you in so many ways about what happens to the files you send.

PAULINE'S FILE PREP TIPS

File Prep Hint #94

You can avoid the need for trapping between adjacent colored areas when you are working with process colors if you build adjacent, touching elements with colors which have at least 15 percent of at least one dominant common color, either Cyan or Magenta.

File Prep Hint #95

As a general rule, move lighter colors into darker colors when you trap. This creates fewer noticeable problems in the overlap area or trap zone.

File Prep Hint #96

If you set chokes and spreads in a drawing application, be aware that most drawing application stroke lines and outlines symmetrically; that is, half the stroke goes on either side of the line or outline. If you assign a 1 pt. stroke to line in your drawing application, you are really creating only a 0.5 pt overlap or trap.

File Prep Hint #97

Note the trapping capability of your program to flag those areas which may require or may prefer with traditional methods. Some examples of trouble traps: trapping on top of indeterminate (multiple) background colors; trapping items such as type on top of color imported graphics in a page layout application.

PAULINE'S FILE PREP TIPS

File Prep Hint #98

Avoid spreading type, especially small serif type faces, as the enlargement of the characters will ruin the geometry of the typeface. In fact, it is a good idea to try and avoid either spreading or choking small type at all. Overprint type whenever possible to retain the typeface's original geometric integrity.

File Prep Hint #99

In general, you will probably want to leave the trapping chores to your printing company, but some of these guidelines will help you avoid creating trapping problems. Always consult your printing company prior to building in traps to make sure you know to build them properly and that you use trap values appropriate for the printer's film and presses. Improperly assigned traps can be more of a problem than assigning no traps at all.

18

The Proof Is In The Separation

As the Byte Turns continues…

After all the Postscript heartaches, can Pauline E. Prepress and Danny D'Ziner endure the challenge of Separation?

My print job looks different from the file I sent you! I didn't send a proof, but what difference does that make ??

I'll check to see what happened.

Oh dear, not again. Why do I always get stuck in the middle??

Why can't she print Danny's file correctly?

Good grief! I can't look at a disk and tell what's on it. Even when we launch a document, we cannot be sure that it is correct without the most recent proof!

▼ Figure 18.1 Color Palette
This is the color palette from QuarkXPress showing the four process colors, a Pantone process color, a custom process color build using the four process colors, one Pantone spot color, and a varnish. There will be six individual separations printed on individual pieces of film from this list of ten colors. RGB col-should not be used in the printing process and should be removed. The varnish will be applied and separated, like a spot color. The process colors will be combined to create built process colors such as the Pantone process color and the custom Process color, as well as any contone color images existing in the document. The registration color should be applied only to items such as crop, trim, registration, and fold marks which need to be placed on each separation. Note: A color version of this image can be found in the Color Plate section in the center of this book (see C-10).

Separations

Why separations?

Separations are required for multi-color printing. Each color which you need to print has to be applied by a different cylinder on a printing press. Each cylinder requires a separate plate which carries the portion of the print image to be printed in that color. The image on each plate is created by exposure of light which shines through a separate piece of film created specifically for that plate. Increasingly, the film portion of this process, and in some cases even the plate portion, is being eliminated in favor of direct imaging on plates and press cylinders. But whether an image goes through a film-to-plate-to-press cylinder process or is directly imaged on cylinders, color images need to be separated into their component parts so that separate inks can be applied to the proper portions of an image in order to build the image properly on press.

Types of separations

There are basically three kinds of separations: spot, process, and finishes. When you prepare a file for output, you need to make sure that all elements on your page are assigned the proper color separation values.

Spot colors

Spot colors are composed of specific mixtures of usually three ink colors. Each color is applied by its own cylinder on a printing press. The spot color gamut is very large. Spot colors are used when you want a very specific and usually bright color to print (see Chapter 14, "Color Me Right" for a detailed description of color systems). For each spot color which you want to print, a separate press cylinder will be required. This can become an expensive printing proposition in a hurry.

Process colors

The traditional process color system includes only four colors: Cyan (C), Magenta (M), Yellow (Y), and Black (K). These four process colors are used together in many different combinations to create a wide spectrum of colors. Unlike the spot color system where each spot color is applied independently of other colors, process colors are designed to work or build together to create other colors. So each color built with process colors will contain percentages of C,M,Y, and

▼ Figure 18.2 Separation Setup
This is the Print dialog box with separation setup. Note that only six separations will be printed from the ten colors listed in the color palette in Figure 18.1. Here the SEPARA-TION submenu choice is activated. This in turn activates the list of separations shown in the PLATE submenu.

▼ Figure 18.3 Spot Color Separation
This QuarkXPress edit color dialog box demonstrates how to designate a spot color to separate as a spot color. Here the spot color 3395 is assigned from the Pantone spot color swatch chart mode. Note the Process Separation check box near the upper lefthand corner is *not* checked. If this box is checked, Quark XPress will separate all items assigned to this color on the four process color plates. Note: See color plate section C-10.

K. CMYK builds are particularly useful for recreating continuous tone color images like color photographs. If we tried to reproduce a color contone image with spot colors it would take thousands of colors, and therefore press cylinders, and would be astronomically expensive. Using the process color system, we need to use only the four process colors to recreate a continuous tone color image. Figure 18.1 shows a demonstration of an image constructed two different ways: one with spot colors and one with process colors.

Coats and finishes

Although they are not colors, finishes, like varnishes, will be applied on a printing press just like colors are. In terms of how they will be applied and separated, finishes should be thought of and treated just like spot colors. Coats and finishes are assigned to their own separations and therefore press cylinders, just like spot colors. Those areas of an image which need to have finish applied should be selected and designated for application just like a spot color. A finish is assigned a label just like a color and applied as a top layer on whichever items require a coating. Figure 18.2 shows an example of a finish item added to a color list.

Figure 18.4 shows an example of a seven-color chicken built out of both spot and process colors. While the spot color chicken will provide us with a more vivid chicken, the process color chicken will be a great deal less expensive to print.

Separate where?

A file may be separated into its various color components in any of several places including the original graphics application where a graphic was created such as Adobe Photoshop; from a page layout application which has separation capabilities such as QuarkXPress and PageMaker; from a dedicated separation application such as Adobe separator; or even at the RIP.

The first step in performing a separation is to decide who will perform the separation and then determine where. If your printer or service bureau is performing your high resolution scans for you and creating all of the original art work, then they will generally be responsible for performing the separation. If you are doing your own scanning and art generation, then you may want to be responsible. In any case, have a discussion with your printer or separator to determine responsibility. If you will be performing the separation, seek your printer's advice on the best separation application and setting to be used for printing your files with their system.

Separating spot colors

The generation of spot and varnish separations is very straightforward and will often occur from the application where the page composition is occurring. This is often a page layout application such as QuarkXPress or PageMaker but may also be from a drawing program such as Illustrator or Freehand if the page layout is performed there. The main problem to look out for with spot separations is to be sure that each spot color is set to print out on its on individual piece of film and that none of the spot colors is designated to be separated as a process color. Each application has its own way of indicating whether a color is destined to print as a spot or a process process color. Figure 18.3 shows how to designate a spot color in QuarkXPress. Note that you always want to make sure that the "Make Process" designation is never applied to a spot color. And just a reminder from the color chapter: Always choose your spot colors from a spot color swatch book. Don't depend upon the screen look of the colors when you are choosing colors as the screen view is often unreliable.

Built process colors

Graphic and other document elements which are assigned built process color values are some of the easiest images to separate. They are easy to separate if you have constructed the color values using color names from a process color swatch book such as the TruMatch or Pantone Process colors swatch books. With built process colors, there is never any question as to whether the colors will be on separate spot plates or on the process plates; they will always separate on the process plates. Always choose your built process colors from a spot color swatch book. Your monitor display of color is rarely dependable (see Chapter 14, "Color Me Right," for a full discussion of this problem).

Separations from Photoshop

The separation of process colors used to reproduce color contone images originally created in RGB color space (such as scanned or any digitally created images) is more complicated and demands much more attention than do spot color separations. The heart of the RGB contone separation problem centers on the difference in color gamuts which exists between RGB and CMYK color spaces. The separation of an RGB image into a CMYK image always involves a gamut compression (see Chapter 14 for a full discussion of this problem). The best rendition of RGB color into CMYK color space will occur if we map the original RGB image to the gamut of the specific

7/C Chicken built with 7 Spot Colors

7/C Chicken built with 4 Process Colors

Pantone 213 Plate

Pantone 2726 Plate

▼ *Figure 18.4b Process Color Palette*

All seven of the colors used here are created from various combinations of CMYK. Since only four sets of separations, film, plates, and cylinders are required to print this image, it is much less expensive to print than its spot color "equivalent." Note that all the extraneous colors have been removed from this pallet to avoid confusion. See color plate C-11.

Pantone 389 Plate

Pantone Black Plate

Pantone 252 Plate

▼ *Figure 18.4a Spot Color Palette*

Each of the assigned spot colors seen in this palette will be printed on its own plate. Each differently colored portion of the image is separated and has a specific spot color applied to it from a different press cylinder. Note that all the extraneous colors have been removed from this palette. While multicolor spot color printing like this allows you to use vivid custom colors, it is far more expensive than using combinations of process colors to produce the many color variations. (See color plate section C-11).

Pantone 3395 Plate

▼ *Figure 18.4a & b Spot vs. Process Separations*

This seven-color chicken is built and separated first with seven spot and then with four process colors. Note how the spot colors requires the use of seven separations and therefore sheets of film and press cylinders, while the process build requires only four of each. See color plate section C-11.

Pantone 486 Plate

▼ Figure 18.5 Printing Ink Setup (SWOP)

Before converting from RGB to CMYK, you should pay close attention to: 1) the ink color set chosen, and 2) the dot gain percentage. Contact your printer to obtain both. The dot gain percentage, should be for the dot gain at 50%. The values set here will affect the appearance of the Separation Setup dialog box shown below.

▼ Figure 18.6 Separation Setup

The values set in the Printing Inks setup dialog box above affect the curves shown here. Your choice of UCR or GCR will also affect the separation curves. The Black generation begins at the three quarter tone for the UCR and at the quarter tone for the UCR curve. The overall placement of the UCR curves is lower due to the differences in the beginning of the Black generation. Compare and contrast these curves with those used for other types of printing devices. See Color Plate section C-12.

CMYK device on which the image will be printed. This process is known as device-specific gamut mapping. Although this type of device-specific gamut mapping occurs infrequently today with our open DTP system, it will become more common in the future. But even if you cannot choose a device-specific gamut mapping, you can at least apply some industry standard settings which will place your image well within the ballpark of where you need to be, and maybe even in the infield. We will use the settings and dialog boxes in Photoshop to demonstrate the process of properly converting an RGB image to a CMYK file. In Photoshop there are two dialog boxes which are particularly important to the process of creating separations. These are the Printing Ink Setup and Separation setup dialog boxes, both of which are found as submenu choices under the Preferences choice of the File menu. Be sure that you correctly configure these preferences *prior* to performing an RGB to CMYK conversion; these controls will be applied only during the gamut conversion and will have no effect after the conversion is complete. Call your printing company and ask for suggestions on the specific values which you should enter into the following variables.

Printing ink setup

The Printing Ink Setup dialog box (Figs. 18.5 and 18.7) is used to assign two key parameters of a color separation: 1) the ink set used, and 2) the dot gain. In the Printing Ink Setup menu you should choose the device which most closely matches the device on which you will be printing. Many printing companies use the SWOP (Standard Web Offset Press) Coated and SWOP Uncoated ink sets as defaults, but ask your printing company to be sure. The ink set choices you make here will affect the position and relationship of the curves in the Separation Setup dialog box. Note the difference between the two sets of curves shown in Figs. 18.6 and 18.8 which, respectively, correspond to the selection of SWOP Coated and Canon Laser Copier Printing Ink selections scene in Figs. 18.5 and 18.7. The differences between the two curves result from the color difference, impurities, and behaviors which exist between the transparent inks used in SWOP printing and the thermoplastic toners used in color laser printing.

Dot gain

Dot Gain is a measure of the amount by which a halftone dot of ink will grow when it is applied by a printing press (see Chapters 12 and 16, "Taming Your Scanner," and "Screening Your Images" for more complete discussions of dot gain). When you perform an RGB to

▼ Figure 18.7 Printing Ink Setup (4/C Laser)
Here the Printing Ink Setup is being set for a four-color laser copier. Note the increase in dot gain to 33% from the 20% standard for the SWOP coated shown in Figure 18.5.

▼ Figure 18.8 Separation Setup
These curves show the Separation Setup curves applied to an image to be color separated for printing on a four-color laser copier using thermoplastic toners instead of the transparent inks used on a printing press. Note the difference in the starting positions and the effects of the Black generation curves in the UCR and GCR variations. Obtain values for Black Ink Limit and Total Ink Limit from your printer. These curves will be applied to an RGB file when it is converted to a CMYK image, so be sure to make and set the correct choices and values in both dialog boxes prior to performing that conversion. See Color Plate section C-12.

CMYK conversion in Photoshop, Photoshop will automatically apply the dot gain percentage entered into the Printing Ink Setup dialog box. For the SWOP setup shown in Fig. 18.5 the default dot gain is 20%. The dot gain of 20% refers to the dot gain which will be applied to a 50% halftone dot. A 50% dot will therefore be reduced to 30% and be expected to grow to 50% when printed on a printing press. Since the dot gain for most images is generally at a maximum around the 50% dot, a symmetrically decreasing dot gain curve is applied to dots as they approach the highlight and shadow points.

Dot gain varies with paper, ink, screen technology and frequency, and press conditions. Ask your printing company what dot gain percentage they recommend you assign for the press, paper, screen, and ink conditions which will be used for your job.

Using the dot gain function in the Photoshop Printing Ink Setup dialog box will provide you with some generalized controls for dot gain. While this general control is much better than ignoring this setting, more precise control over dot gain can be achieved. If you want to gain more precise control dot gain, you can construct your own dot gain transfer curves and save them with the file (see Chapter 16, "Screening Your Images").

Separation setup

Configuring the Separation Setup dialog box (Figs. 18.6 and 18.8) is the second step in preparing an RGB image for conversion and separation into a CMYK image. The curves you see in the Separation Setup dialog box are controlled partially by the choices you make in the Printing Ink Setup dialog box and partially to the choices you make and values you assign in this Separation Setup dialog box. In Fig. 18.6 note how different the SWOP curves look compared to the Canon Color Laser Printer. The difference between the two curves is primarily due to the different color characteristics of the transparent SWOP inks and the opaque thermoplastic toners used in the Canon Color Laser. You should notice that in the SWOP ink curves, the Cyan curve is much higher than the Magenta and Yellow curves. This disparity in curve strength is constructed to compensate for the impurity and therefore relative weakness of the Cyan ink due to its contamination with Yellow and Magenta inks (see Chapter 12, "Taming Your Scanner," for a discussion of this phenomenon).

Besides selecting a UCR and GCR mode, you should pay close attention to the Black Ink Limit and Total Ink Limit assignments. These numbers affect the amount of ink which will be applied to the paper by the press. The Black Ink Limit will generally vary between 90 per-

C
Y
A
N

M
A
G
E
N
T
A

Y
E
L
L
O
W

B
L
A
C
K

▼Figure 18.9 UCR Separations

Four separations are created here. Top to bottom, C,M,Y, & K using UCR Black generation. Note how the Black plate does not have as much tonal range as does the GCR Black separation in Figure 18.10. Also note how the C,M, and Y plates are darker than their GCR counterparts.

cent and 100 percent. The Total Ink Limit will generally range from 230 to 320 depending upon paper stock and press conditions. Again, here it is prudent to call your printing company and ask them for the values you should use.

UCR and GCR

An obvious difference between an RGB file and a CMYK file is that the CMYK image has four colors and therefore channels, while the RGB image has only three. A simple gamut conversion from additive color space to subtractive color space involves a three-color conversion from RGB to CMY. When a CMY image is printed on an offset printing press using conventional inks, images tend to be murky and lack contrast, especially in the shadow areas. The transparent and impure nature of process inks makes it difficult to create high contrast images with them. Black shadow areas tend to look muddy brown. In addition to the low contrast issue, when printing with high percentages of all three CMY inks in shadow areas the three inks tend to merge together, destroying shadow details.

The time honored solution to both the contrast and shadow detail challenges in process printing has been to substitute Black or "K" for various portions of CMY ink percentages. [By the way, "K" stands for Key color, because Black is the color to which printers have traditionally keyed the placement of all the other color inks during the printing process.] The substitution of Black for CMY works because in subtractive color space equal portions of Cyan, Magenta, and Yellow create Black.

There are two basic options we can choose for accomplishing this Black substitution for CMY. The first option is called Under Color Removal, or UCR, and the second option is known as Gray Component Replacement, or GCR. The effects of both methods on the separation curves for SWOP conditions can be seen in Fig. 18.6. The top curve is the UCR curve and the bottom, the GCR built curve. The fundamental difference between UCR and GCR separations is the grayscale percentage where black substitution begins. In UCR-separated images the substitution of K for C, M, and Y does not begin in earnest until the three quarter tone. In GCR-separated images the substitution of K for C, M, and Y begins at the quarter tone. Look at the Black generation curves in Fig. 18.6 to confirm this. Consequently, UCR images have most of their Black substitution in the shadow regions of the image, while GCR images have Black substitution throughout the tonal range from the quarter tone through the shadow region. Each method has its uses and proponents. Both methods

C Y A N

M A G E N T A

Y E L L O W

B L A C K

▼ *Figure 18.10 GCR Separations* Four separations created, top to bottom, C,M,Y & K using GCR black generation. Note how the black plate has a much broader tonal range compared with the UCR black separation in Figure 18.9. Also note how the C,M, and Y plates are lighter than their UCR counterparts.

will reduce ink volumes and provide better contrast and detail in the shadows. I generally prefer GCR for contone photographs because GCR provides improved contrast and reduces the total ink throughout the entire tonal range of the image. This tends to brighten and sharpen up the midtone areas of images which can easily become muddy. Be sure to ask your printer which method would be most appropriate for your images. Some printers use only one method and do not like to print images separated with the other. The difference between the effects of UCR and GCR can be seen in the separations shown in Figures 18.9 and 18.10. Note how the black plate generated with GCR shows density all the way down to the quarter tone, while the UCR-generated Black plate displays most of its density from the three quarter tone through the shadow. You can also see less density displayed in the GCR-generated Cyan, Magenta, and Yellow plates.

UCA

One often unknown and overlooked section of the Separation Setup dialog box is the area labeled UCA (short for "Under Color Addition"). UCA is available only when you choose the GCR Black generation method. UCA is used when you are trying to produce a solid cover of a shadow region rather than preserve contone image detail. UCA is the opposite of and has the opposite effect of UCR. Applying a UCA percentage will increase the C,M,Y colors in the shadows in addition to the Black being applied by the GCR. Adding more ink will, of course, tend to plug up the shadows and reduce shadow detail. With most contone images this is a disadvantage, but when the shadow region is dominated by solid areas instead of image detail, UCA can be an advantage. All the process colors including the Black "K" are transparent, so they are not able to provide rich, high density Blacks to cover solid areas. Solid Black areas created with process Black tend to look anemic compared with regions covers by spot color Black inks containing more pigment and are more opaque. Through the use of UCA, all four process colors are bumped up in the shadow region to provide richer Blacks for area coverage. Use this feature carefully; a little bit goes a long way. UCA should be used selectively on an image-by-image basis.

Some separation tips

- Remove unnecessary color from color palettes both in original graphic documents and from page layout documents. This will prevent confusion and extra plates from printing out during the final creation of film separations. Removing unused colors is also a good way to check your color assignments to see if you have assigned some colors you did not intend to or if you have goofed up some reassignment of colors during a design or editing change. It is a good idea to remove RGB from your color palette for all your print jobs.

- Make sure that all colors on your color palette are properly designated as spot or process colors. Also be sure that each element has the proper spot or process color value assigned to it. The only way to be sure is to print your own set of process separations on your proof printer. For long documents, it is not necessary to print out color separations of every single page. Choose a couple of representative pages which contain all of the colors used in that document and print separations of them. If they separate properly on those pages, they will likely separate properly on the other pages. We can again see the value of using standardization tools such as Master Pages and Style Sheets. If most elements are created as Master Page and Style Sheet items, then they will be consistent throughout the document.

- Avoid assigning spot color values to elements and then asking your printer to "match" it with process color values. It rarely works. If you want an element to be printed with process colors, create or build it originally out of process colors; that is, assign it process color values to begin with.

- Note spot and process colors carefully and choose separations instead of composite files if you want to print separations.

- Don't rename DCS files after they are created. Master DCS will not recognize renamed versions of its separate files.

- Do not set the line screen information in Photoshop (File – Page Setup) for Photoshop files exported from Photoshop for placement in another application such as QuarkXpress or PageMaker. Photoshop settings will override the importing program settings. Do not check Save Halftone Screen when saving a Photoshop file for this purpose.

- Pay attention to the Separation and Printing Inks Setup dialog boxes in Photoshop (under File:Preferences) prior to converting any RGB image to a CMYK image.

➤ Be sure to apply dot gain correction manually to your grayscale contone image using either the Curves dialog box, or save your grayscale image as an EPS with a dot gain transfer curve.

➤ Blends created between two spot colors in the same area will be separated as process colors. But blends between tints of the same Pantone spot color will be printed as a spot plate. If you want to create a blend between two different overlapping spot colors, you must do two things: 1) clone and identically overlap the area into which you want the overlapping blend to occur and, 2) assign the separate spot color gradations to each overlapping area. Be sure that the gradations you create are constructed entirely out of the spot color. Do not blend a spot color into black or white. Use 100 percent or 0 percent of the spot color instead.

➤ When creating EPS files out of Photoshop, do not save the line screen and frequency information along with the file unless you want that information to override the screening information set in the output application or the RIP software. If you are sending your files out to be processed, it is best to let the output bureau set the screening information.

➤ The Registration color (generally Black) included on many color palettes should be applied only to items such as crop, trim, registration, and fold marks which will occur on each separation. The Registration color should not be applied to regular text and graphic items used to construct document pages.

PROOFING YOUR PRINTS

Why proof?

Prior to the age of electronic publishing, we as clients produced full scale mechanical artboards to deliver to a printer. Proofing was done by printers because they were the first ones to actually produce a composite print. Now, however, with computer-based document creation, the compositing is being done as we create the file. The good news is that by creating a digital file we have reduced the number of steps that we go through. The bad news is that by removing the mechanical artboards that we deliver to the printer, we remove the only complete hard copy that the printer could look at to see what we had created.

As nifty and wonderful as computers are, they also have their own set of challenges. One of those challenges is that we cannot see digital files. Another challenge is that once a file leaves one computer and is opened up on another computer, the nature and structure of that file may be altered. Sometimes these changes are significant and obvious, like a missing graphic or a major change in the display of a font in a headline. Other changes may be more subtle, like a few shifts in line breaks or a change in the font of a caption or footnote. In either case, your printer will not know if what is on the screen and what prints off of the printers is correct or not unless an actual hard copy proof printed by you from the file you have goes with the disk. Your hard copy proof replaces the mechanical artboards of old in terms of a visual check of what you expect.

Quality proofs checklist

Producing good quality, accurate proofs is a key to making your job run smoothly. Here is a checklist of some features and characteristics of a good quality proof:

❑ Laser proof should be the most recent version of a file. Don't make changes to a file after you have created your final proof. If you make changes to a file, plan on creating another set of proofs.

❑ Make a composite of the entire file.

❑ Print color separations as well so you can check your color breaks and see how your separations will print (see Figure 18.2).

❑ Color breaks should be noted on composite, at least on simple files.

❑ Delete colors which will not be used from the file. Otherwise, the unused colors will still print out as separate plates when separations are printed.

❑ Indicate spot and process colors clearly.

❑ Note crop mark creation and location using the proper page size and bleeds. Make sure crops and separation descriptions are on the proof.

❑ Indicate Bleeds. These should be at least 1/8" past the page trim size as determined by crop or cut marks.

❑ Note percentage (%) of reduction.

❑ Send marked up laser for changes after initial blueline has been received and corrected.

❑ Edit graphics files properly. Don't add lines to fill in spaces between two boxes which are supposed to touch.

❑ Creating a proof or a set of proofs should not be a last minute affair. Leave some time to check your proofs for mistakes or any corrections/additions/changes. The creation of proofs is an aid to both you and your output service company. Creating proofs allows you to carefully check what the final product will look like. Very often you will find mistakes in how color breaks have been assigned when you create color separations on a laser.

❏ Using your own electronic publishing system to create your files is a great boon to you in terms of the freedom and control it allows you over the creation and production processes. But with this freedom comes responsibility. Since you are creating the files, you are primarily responsible for creating and preparing those files correctly. Creating complete proofs is one of the best tools to help you prepare your file correctly for print production.

PAULINE'S FILE PREP TIPS

File Prep Hint #100

Create composite and color separated laser proofs of the most recent version of your documents. Use these lasers as your proofing tool. Your proofs replace the mechanical boards of old as visual guides for how you want your jobs to print. The proofs you send to your printer should be of the final corrected versions because they will be used to proof screen and film versions of your files.

File Prep Hint #101

Plan time in your production schedule for proofing. No one can proof his own work, so provide time for others to proof the jobs. Use a proofing checklist so that a complete job is done.

File Prep Hint #102

The registration color is a composite Black which should be assigned only to document elements which should appear on all separations such as create crop, trim, fold, and registration marks.

PAULINE'S FILE PREP TIPS

File Prep Hint #103

For publications which will be reused with only type changes, consider designing them with replaceable type areas and assigning a separate color to change-able text which will print on its own separation. This approach reduces the need to reprint all plates for a copy-only change.

File Prep Hint #104

Create printer spreads on separate pages. *Do not* create side-by-side pages on a single sheet, like two 8.5" x 11" pages on an 11" x 17" sheet. Create two separate 8.5" x 11" sheets.

File Prep Hint #105

Mark up your proofs. Indicate bleeds, FPO and live images, and the percentage of scaling at which the proof was printed, if any, as well as crop, trim, fold, and registration marks.

PAULINE'S FILE PREP TIPS

File Prep Hint #106

Prior to converting an RGB image to a CMYK in Photoshop, you need to first configure the Printing Ink setup and Separation setup dialog boxes. It is imperative to choose the correct set of inks, and the appropriate dot gain values for the inks, paper, and press with which your documents will be printed. Also, prior to the gamut conversion, you need to designate which kind of Black generation curve will be used – UCR or GCR – as well as assigning ink percent values. Call your printing company for guidance in configuring these two dialog boxes and configure them before you complete the mode/gamut change.

File Prep Hint #107

It is extremely important to fill out your EFIS prior to sending your file out to be processed. Your EFIS contains crucial information about what your file contains and how it was constructed. This information is an important aid in helping your service bureau output your document. Remember, no one can see what is on your disk and your proofs. An EFIS provides the service company with the guidelines and information needed to process your files properly. When you fill out your EFIS, be sure to indicate the number of colors/separations which you expect. Indicate whether you have a spot color job, a four-color job, or a combination of four-color plus spot colors. Always clearly indicate the spot colors to be used.

19
Managing The Mess

As the Byte Turns continues…

Oh, what a mess Danny D'Ziner and Pauline E. Prepress find themselves in…with all those fonts and graphics to collect.

What do you mean, some of my fonts are missing? I'm sure I sent them all. Did you lose them??

Ah… well, that's what they told me in production.

I hate being in the middle!

Are you sure we don't have them??

Read my lips Sammy baby; WE DO NOT HAVE ALL OF THE FONTS!!! AND NO, WE DID NOT LOSE THEM!!!

FILE HANDLING GUIDELINES

Gathering file components together

The file gathering and organization challenge

In Chapter 13, "Document Construction," we explored how an electronic file is put together. When a page is constructed in a page layout application like QuarkXpress or PageMaker, most of the actual printing data (the high resolution graphics and fonts) is located outside of the page layout document. In the case of graphics, only low resolution proxy files are resident in the page layout document. For fonts, both the low and high resolution files are external to the page layout document. It is due to this multifile nature of most electronic documents that file gathering and organization is a critical and oftentimes laborious task. If any of the external files are missing, the page layout document will not print properly. It is important that all of the *original* graphic and font files actually used to construct the document are sent along with the document which is to be printed. It is not acceptable to ask your printer if he has fonts with the same name as your fonts and then expect the printer to use them to print your file. Remember, fonts are just special preformed versions of graphics. Name similarity is no guarantee that the printer's fonts will look or print the same as your fonts. Different revisions of the same font may have different kerning pair information and even different character stroke and counter shapes and sizes. Therefore, plan to send *all* of the components you used to construct your file. It is sometimes important to send along preference and tracking information files or extensions from the applications you used. Ask your printer what he requires for the specific applications you have used.

How to organize your fonts and files for sending

Before sending or delivering a file to your printer or service bureau, put the file and all associated fonts and linked graphics into one folder. Include all screen and printer fonts and non-imbedded graphic files with documents to be printed. Keep graphics in the same folder as the document for easy access by the application in case of lost links. Most applications will automatically relink with graphics which are located in the same folder as the document. In a similar manner, place the screen and printer fonts in the same folder so that they will be easily linked for viewing and printing. Include preference and data files for H&J and Kerning and tracking specifications, etc. Include all sep-

Disk to Send Out
• Label disk with file and company names
• Write file and company name on disk

File Organization
•Docs & Graphics Folder
  - Document
  - All imported graphics: TIFFs and EPS preferably
  - Native or parent EPS documents
  - Report document from Quark or Pagemaker

• Font Folder (Preferably Type 1 fonts)
  - Screen Fonts (preferably in a suitcase)
  - Printer Fonts (matches to screen fonts)

Notes: The composite page layout document and its associated imported graphics need to be in a common folder. Also place Screen & Printer fonts in a common folder.

Screen Font Suitcase Content
All the screen fonts are placed in a suitcase instead of being loose. This helps keep the fonts organized and makes them much easier to activate and deactivate using font utilities. This organization also allows you to open the font suitcase and compare screen and printer fonts side by side.

▼ *Figure 19.1 Disk File Organization*
These illustrations show how a page layout document and its associated external linked files should be organized. The two folder technique works well. One folder is for the page layout document along with all the linked high resolution graphics. Placing the page layout document and the linked graphics in the same folder will allow the high resolution graphics to automatically link to the document when it is launched. The same applies to the fonts. Placing the screen and printer fonts in the same folder allows the printer fonts to be linked when the screen fonts are accessed.

▼ Figure 19.2 Empty Font Suitcase

Keep an empty font suitcase in your fonts folder. This allows you to always have an empty font suitcase available to place screen fonts into when preparing a disk to send out. Before you place any fonts into it, copy the empty suitcase either to a disk or to a folder on your desktop. This keeps the original empty suitcase free for future use.

arated files (see Figs. 19.1 and 19.2 for examples of recommended file organization).

Fonts specifics

Macintosh fonts

If you work on a Mac, keep an empty font suitcase labeled "Screen Fonts" or labeled with your name ("Tazmanian Screen Fonts") in your screen fonts folder. This empty suitcase will be ready for you to copy onto your outgoing disk. Using a font suitcase allows you to place all of your screen fonts into this one suitcase to keep them all together, organized, and easily accessible. This tidies up your screen fonts and even more importantly allows you and your printer to access all of your fonts at one time by just accessing this one screen font suitcase (see Fig. 19.2). Refer to Chapter 11, "A Tale Of True Typesetting" if you are having difficulty identifying screen and printer fonts.

Windows fonts

If you work on a Windows OS-based machine, you have the same necessity of sending the screen and printer font versions of your fonts. As described and shown in Chapter 11, "A Tale Of True Typesetting," the Windows versions of screen and printer fonts are .pfm and .pfb files located in the ps fonts folder (subdirectory). One of the greatest challenges of working with fonts on a Windows machine is identifying the fonts because they are limited to a three-character suffix on the end of the file to specify the font name. I highly recommend the use of FontMinder as a font management tool for Windows. FontMinder is a nearly indispensible utility which helps you easily identify, group, and manage your fonts.

Be sure to place all of your printer fonts in the same folder with your screen fonts or your screen fonts Suitcase (Mac). Doing so will allow the automatic linking of your printer fonts to the screen fonts when the screen fonts are accessed. By labeling your screen font suitcase with your name, your service company can easily identify your fonts when accessing them.

Graphic specifics

Place all of your high resolution graphics along with the page layout document in a folder called Docs & Graphics. Placing the layout document and graphics in the same folder will ensure that the high resolution graphics will link to the page layout document when it is launched. You may want to create a third folder called "Parent To EPSs." In this folder you can place any drawing documents (Illustrator, Freehand or CorelDraw documents) which are the parents to any EPS file you have created. It is always a good idea to send along a fully editable parent document version of any EPS file you create. And the more complex your EPS , the more important it is to send along the parents (see EPS file preparation procedures below for a full checklist on producing printable EPS files while retaining the editability of the originals).

Vector and pixel graphic file preparation procedures

Both pixel and vector based images need to be simplified for RIPing. Combination pixel and vector graphic files are some of the most difficult and demanding files to RIP. Therefore, it is often wise to direct a little bit of extra attention toward the preparation of all of our graphic files. As we discussed in Chapter 9, "Grappling With Graphics," it is a good idea to perform certain file preparation functions in drawing application documents such as Freehand, Illustrator, and CorelDraw files, and to Photoshop images as well , in order to make them easier to RIP. Performing vector-specific adjustments such as splitting long paths, converting type to graphics (AKA convert into paths), and increasing path flatness ratios will go a long way toward satisfying our File Prep battle of REDUCE & SIMPLIFY. Removing layers and alpha channels from pixel-based Photoshop type graphics will make these type of images more RIPable as well. This type of output-specific file preparation will create a file which is very ready to print, but also ruins much of that file's editability. For example, splitting closed paths into segments makes them much more difficult to edit. When type is converted to outlines, the characters can no longer be edited as type, they must be edited as a graphic. When constructing your initial drawing document, be sure to construct your document in separate layers. These procedure not only makes the creation of the file easier but also makes easier any troubleshooting and editing of the file. Also be careful to limit the amount of type you set in any drawing document which you intend to export as an EPS. Converting large volumes of type to paths will creates hundreds of individual paths That situation can create output problems which are more daunting than the nested type problem you are trying to solve. Following is a suggested procedure for creating graphic files ready for printing and an original parent document file that remains fully editable:

Graphic construction checklist

❏ Construct the original drawing (vector) and photo (pixel) graphic document in separate layers.

❏ Perform a "Save As" and add "Print" to the end of the file's name preserving the original file in its fully editable form.

❏ Flatten layers and remove alpha channels from Photoshop images.

❏ Limit the amount type set in the drawing application document if you intend to export the file as an EPS.

❏ Remove unnecessary items such as extra text boxes.

❏ Make sure colors are properly designated as spot or process.

❏ Remove unused colors.

❏ Simplify paths (reduce # of control points).

❏ Convert type to paths.

❏ Split paths.

❏ Set the flatness ratios at between 2 –5.

❏ Set the proper PPD and, if appropriate, line screen information for the printer (often an imagesetter) which will ultimately be used to output the file.

❏ Export the "PRINT" document as an EPS file; be sure to include the .EPS suffix.

▼ Figure 19.3 Postscript File
Creating a Postscript file is an easy process to perform. The same PRINT dialog box is generally used as for normal printing. You are essentially printing your document to a disk instead of to a printer. In the above Freehand PRINT dialog box, you just choose FILE instead of PRINTER in the DESTINATION portion of the dialog box. While creating a Postscript file is easy, it is not always advisable to do so. A Postscript file is completely self contained and essentially uneditable. Always consult your printer before you send them a Postscript file, because you will want to set the proper print information before you create the file.

Send the original fully editable parent document as well as the exported RIP-ready EPS to your printer or service bureau. This procedure will give you both a print version and a fully editable "native" or "parent" version of your drawing document. It is a good idea to send along both versions of the file – the print-ready EPS and the original drawing version – particularly if you think the printer may have to perform some editing on the file. This type of attention to technical detail goes a long way toward our general goal of REDUCE & SIMPLIFY.

Creating PostScript and PDF files

Two other options for saving your document are to save it as a Postscript file or as a PDF document. Creating a PostScript file means printing your file to disk (usually your local hard drive). Creating a PDF document involves processing your PostScript file through an application called Adobe Distiller. A Postscript file is a text file which contains a complete description of all of the elements which compose the document, including all the page geometry, copy and its placement, and formatting information, and all font and graphic files. The advantages of saving your final file as a Postscript file is that all of the information which you need for printing the file is automatically included in the PostScript file. The disadvantage of using a Postscript file format is that it is essentially locked; it cannot be altered. Unless the file is exactly correct, it will not print properly. Most service printing companies or service bureaus need to make minor corrections or at least setting alterations in the files you send them. The adjustment may be as minor as changing the printer description file or changing the line screen and separation information. But if your file is a Postscript file format, none of these instructions can be easily changed. If you use this file format, make sure that your file is complete and correct. PDF files have the advantage over PostScript files of being viewable and somewhat editable, although not as editable as a standard application file like a QuarkXPress, PageMaker, or InDesign document. Communicate with your printing company to make sure that you have the most recent printer description files and that all of your color breaks, trapping, graphic resolutions, and graphic file formats and sizes have been set properly. Using Postscript file print utilities such as PS Express by Transoft can help speed up this process considerably. By the way, I always make a copy of my file by performing a "Save As" prior to creating a Postscript file or PDF document. If something happens to my file during the print-to-disk procedure, I still have a complete, undamaged version. (See Chapter 15, "Application Specific Tips," for more detailed information on creating PostScript files and PDF documents.)

Preparing your EFIS
(electronic file information sheet)

What on earth is an EFIS? EFIS is short for Electronic File Information Sheet. These are the forms which your printing company asks you to fill out to help output your file. There are a number of items related to your electronic file which are not immediately obvious. The more your printer knows about your file, the easier the printer can output your job, and the faster and better quality job he can do. The EFIS serves as an important information sheet for the service company production staff. Keep in mind that the service production staff knows nothing about a file when they first receive it. The EFIS is your opportunity to inform the production staff about your file. Be sure to note any special instructions on the EFIS. Each job you send to an output service company should be accompanied by a separate EFIS. We know its takes a little time to fill it out, but doing so can save a great deal of time and lots of heartache. A good EFIS serves as a checklist for you to use when you are preparing a file to send out. Below is a list of some of the essential items which you tell your printer. Also see Appendix D for an example of a well designed EFIS.

EFIS checklist

Here are some items which will help your printer process your files:

❑ Your name

❑ Your company name

❑ Your phone and fax numbers (to contact you with questions and send you corrections)

❑ Job name

❑ Basic job characteristics: e.g., 4/c 25pg catalog

❑ Media delivered: e.g., 200MB Syquest cartridge

❑ Page #s or range of pages to be printed: Pages 1–4 and Pg 15

❑ Page layout application used and especially the version #: e.g., XPress 3.31r5s❑ Graphics applications used and their versions: e.g., Photoshop 3.01 and Freehand 5.5

❑ Graphic file type present and the numbers: e.g., 25 TIFFs, 15 EPSs

❑ Typefaces (Fonts) used and their style: e.g., B helvetica bold Type 1

❑ Number of colors to be printed and their separation type and names. Clearly distinguish spot from process colors: e.g., 2 spot colors 256 and 3395; plus 4/c

❑ Send both composite and color separated proofs: composite for content and placement, color separations for color assignments

❑ On your proofs be sure to note bleeds, FPO graphics, color breaks, and the percentage reduction at which proof is printed

❑ Any special instructions or problem areas of which you are aware

Note for printing companies: Refer to Appendix D for an example of an EFIS sheet. This EFIS would be a good starting point if you work for a service bureau or printing company and you do not currently have an EFIS or you would like to upgrade yours. The two keys to an effective EFIS are simplicity and good design. A good EFIS should ask about all of the basic information in a file: applications/versions, fonts used, graphics, and colors. But it should avoid asking too much detail such as imagesetter output resolution or emulsion position. Too many technical details complicate the EFIS form, confuse your clients, and discourage them from filling out the EFIS sheet.

File preparation utilities

Because of the tediousness, opportunity for mistakes, and the possibility of forgetting components involved with the manual gathering of document components, I highly recommend the use of file gathering utilities.

If you use QuarkXPress, use the Collect for Output menu choice located under the FILE menu. Collect for Output will collect the page layout document itself and all of the linked graphics; then it will prepare a document report that lists all of the graphics, font, color, and other details associated with the document. This is a very handy utility which comes free as part of QuarkXpress. Collect for Output does not collect fonts. If you are a PageMaker user, you can use the Save As and File for remote printing to help gather your document components. For gathering PageMaker document information, you can use the Document Info Addition/Plug-in which comes free with PageMaker, but I recommend the more complete plug-in, "Save for Service Provider." Document Info is a bit confusing and not as complete as "Save for Service Provider." "Save for Service Provider" also comes free with PageMaker 6.5 and above and will do a content preflight and collect the document components, including the fonts. (See Chapter 15, "Application-Specific Tips" for a view of the menu access and Appendix E: Utilities for a list of valuable DTP file prep utilities and brief description about their use.)

I highly recommend using preflight utilities, FlightCheck from Markzware or PreFlight Pro from Extensis. Both provide extensive troubleshooting of your files, collect documents, fonts and graphics, and include detailed document reports.

Dry run technique

I use this following procedure to test my file gathering for completeness, particularly with complex files. I create a folder (subdirectory in Windows) on my desktop to collect all of the files I intend to send out. Then I close all system fonts using the ATM Deluxe (Mac and Windows). I have only four fonts: Geneva, Monaco, Chicago, and Symbol in my System folder. The rest of my fonts I locate outside of the System folder so that I can activate them or deactivate them at will. Then I access the fonts I have collected for my document, again using ATM Deluxe, and launch the document I have collected and will be sending to the printer. This process simulates what the printer will do after copying your files over onto their hard disk. This procedure will allow you to test the completeness of your collection. When you launch your document, your application should warn you of any missing fonts or graphics. I always check any font and graphic utilities to make sure all the fonts are available and that all the placed graphics are linked to their high resolution partners. This easy-to-do dry run procedure will help guarantee at least that all the components needed for printing will be present. Missing pieces is still the number one complaint about customer files. By making sure that you send all the proper pieces, you will be making your printer happy and, as a consequence, even more cooperative.

PAULINE'S FILE PREP TIPS

File Prep Hint #108

Organize the files you send out so that your page layout file and its associated graphics are in one folder and your fonts (both screen and printer) are in another folder. Place your screen fonts in a suitcase, if possible.

File Prep Hint #109

Keep an empty suitcase labeled with your name in your fonts folder on your hard drive. This empty suitcase will be available to quickly and easily copy to your traveling disks and will serve as a readily available traveling font collection site during font gathering chores.

File Prep Hint #110

Place original, fully editable parent files, such as nonsplit Illustrator documents with editable type and unflattened Photoshop format files, in a separate folder labeled 'Parents Documents.' Place the original unaltered application documents in this folder. If text, path, or layer troubleshooting or editing needs to be performed on an image, the printer has the option of using these fully editable documents.

File Prep Hint #111

To test your file collection, collect files to a folder on Desktop and launch your collected files using only the collected fonts and graphics. This simulates what your printer will do.

PAULINE'S FILE PREP TIPS

File Prep Hint #112

Label your disks with your name, company, job ID, and even your phone and fax number. Disks can get misplaced; make yours easy to identify.

File Prep Hint #113

If you send a Postscript or PDF file to your printer, make very sure that it is well prepared and that no changes will be necessary. Select your printer's PPD instead of yours prior to creating the Postscript file. A Postscript file is essentially uneditable; what you send is what you get.

File Prep Hint #114

While it is better to work with uncompressed files, if you do send in compressed graphic files, be sure to indicate this on your EFIS and send in a decompression utility along with your disk.

File Prep Hint #115

Create a separate Print file for complex drawing documents which you may want to edit later. Keep the original or parent document as is. Simplify, split paths, adjust flatness, and remove colors from the Print version before you export the EPS. Send all three files to the printer.

PAULINE'S FILE PREP TIPS

File Prep Hint #116

Fill out your printer's EFIS (Electronic File Information Sheet) completely and send it along with your job and proof prints. A properly completed EFIS greatly improves the chances that your file will print quickly and easily, thereby allowing your printer to get your job done on time and on budget.

File Prep Hint #117

Develop a good working relationship with your printer or service bureau. The creation and printing of Postscript files is a joint effort between you and your printing company. It is better to establish a good relationship with one or two printers so that you each learn each other's requirements and characteristics. Negotiate year-long contracts at attractive prices. You will save money and so will the printer. Choose printing companies which have well training digital and Postscript-savvy sales, customer service, and production staffs. Visit the company and tour the production facility.

File Prep Hint #118

Use preflight utilities such as FlightCheck for Markzware or PreflightPro for Extensis to help you troubleshoot your documents and collect and organize your page layout files and their associated fonts and graphics.

20
Taz's 118 Tips

Here is a tabulation of all of terrible Taz's terrific technical prepress tips!

TAZ'S TIPS

This section is a compilation of all of Pauline's file prep hints.

File Prep Tip #1

Take a field trip to your favorite printing company or service bureau and have staff members take you through and explain the production and printing process in detail. This will be an enlightening experience. Have them show you how they handle customer files and what they check for. By doing this you will more fully understand the challenges printers face when they try to reproduce your work. When you are on your tour, don't be afraid to ask plenty of questions. Make sure you understand the entire production process. This is also a good way to establish a relationship with the folks in the electronic prepress production department, the people who actually output your work!

File Prep Tip #2

It is important to learn the fundamental terms and concepts associated with electronic publishing. Knowing the terms will help you to communicate more effectively with your service companies as well as your other colleagues. Knowing the concepts will make you a more effective creator and preparer of electronic documents. Some of the key terms and concepts you need to understand include: resolution, dpi vs. ppi vs. lpi, spot vs. process colors, color gamuts, RIPing, RAM vs. virtual memory, image spot vs. halftone dot, halftone cell, AM vs. FM screening , raster vs. vector, pixel depth, master pages, style sheets, preferences, Postscript, Postscript files vs. document files, paths and clipping paths, flatness and tolerance, splitting paths, TIFF vs. EPS vs. JPEG vs. PhotoCD, document vs. native file, halftoning, screen vs. print fonts, tracking, leading and kerning, compression, SWOP and trapping, and preflighting.

File Prep Tip #3

Communicate with your printer. Work with the staff during the planning and construction phases of your job, not just when your job is completed. You will want to ask about items such as the press sheet size (which will affect the size and dimensions of your designs), the lpi at which they print (which will determine the resolution at which you scan images), and the file formats which they prefer (which will determine how you save your digital files). Working with your printer throughout your job design and creation will help avoid output problems and having to redo things later. In fact, if you have any questions about how to construct your file, ask at any time. An ounce of prevention is truly worth several pounds of cure in the digital world. The Postscript business is a constantly changing environment with new information becoming available all the time. Ignorance is not a sin, but staying that way is.

File Prep Tip #4

Purchase reliable hardware, and most importantly, keep the hardware up to date and tuned up. Make sure your power is clean. Install isolated lines. Use high quality cables from one manufacturer. Keep your publishing environment clean and cool. Imaging equipment hates dirt and high temperatures.

File Prep Tip #5

Know the basic components of your electronic publishing system and how they operate. You definitely need to know what RAM and storage memory are and how to effectively manage both. Be sure that you keep at least 20 percent of the RAM that you assign to any application free so that your application has room to expand. Never assign all of your RAM to open applications, as your system needs RAM space in which to expand. Optimally, your hard drive space should remain at least 50 percent free. The more you know about your system, the more effective an operator you will be and the more troubleshooting skills you will be able to develop.

File Prep Tip #6

Know the versions of all the applications which you use to create files. Be sure to supply version numbers to your service bureau when you send your files out to be printed. Each version of an application has its own quirks, and knowing the version numbers of the creating applications can be a big help when setting up and troubleshooting files. It is a good idea to keep up to date on your application versions. You don't have to buy the latest version as soon as it available, but don't get more than one application version behind. You should, however, have the latest revision (r.) of whatever version you use. Revisions are generally brought out to fix problems which become apparent after a version is released.

File Prep Tip #7

Remember that any software which you place on your computer complicates your computer. To help keep your system operating at its peak, limit the amount of software you put on your publishing system. Be especially brutal about removing software which installs files into your system folde;, these are the most intrusive and performance-robbing softwares. Yes, that means get rid of those cool screen savers, sounds, and games. Put those on your home computer. Use resource management utilities such as font and system file management tools to help you streamline your system resources.

File Prep Tip #8

All text and graphic images in a digital file are constructed out of two values: zeros (0s) and ones (1s). The fundamental building block of graphic images is the pixel, which in its simplest form is assigned a single bit value of either a zero (0) or one (1). More complex pixels can be assigned multiple bit per pixel values. The basic building block for text is a Byte which contains eight (8) bits. Each Byte represents one character such as an "A" or a "b." Graphic images and text are composed from combinations of bits and Bytes. It is useful to think of your text and graphic images as combinations of bits and Bytes; this will facilitate your understanding of how your text and graphic tools work when you are constructing and editing digital documents.

File Prep Tip #9

When sending a text file to be output, be sure that your service bureau or printer can interpret or "read" your text file format. It is best to send an unformatted ASCII or "Text Only" file which can be universally recognized and interpreted. If you need to send formatted text, be sure to confirm the platform, application name, and version of the application used to create the text file, e.g., Windows version 5.0, WordPerfect. If you are unsure of compatibility, send the text file as an ASCII or text only file. Another option is to use RTF or Rich Text Format which is a commonly translatable form for formatted text. Even simple formatted text files can change when opened up on another computer, so if you send formatted text, it is a good idea to send a laser proof of the text to provide a visual example of what you intended.

File Prep Tip #10

A computer is a great tool, but it needs management and maintenance like any other system. Keep your system up to date and be a minimalist. Remove unnecessary software from your system. Be sure to save regularly and perform "Save As" documents several times per day. Save copies of your preference files after you configure your computer, perform regular backups to protect your data, and archive regularly to remove inactive files so as to keep your active drive free for current use.

File Prep Tip #11

Removable media like floppy disks, Zip disks, optical disks, and syquest cartridges are too slow and undependable to be used for active work. Use them for storage only. So don't work off of floppies and do not use removable media as scratch disk space.

File Prep Tip #12

Don't be a mouser. Work from your keyboard. It's faster and less stressful. Working from the keyboard is 100 – 400 percent faster than mousing around. Working more from the keyboard will also help reduce the incidence of carpal tunnel syndrome

File Prep Tip #13

Keep your resolution concepts and terminology straight to help reduce the confusion which surrounds us when we discuss resolution. We capture, create, and view pixels, and we print dots. Therefore, all input resolution, such as when we paint in Photoshop or capture images with scanners and digital cameras, should be discussed in terms of pixel per unit area, such as ppi (pixels per inch) or res (pixels per mm). By contrast, we print with dots, both single dots (more correctly called spots) and compound dots, which are created through the combination of groups of the smaller spots, called halftone dots. Individual dots or spots recreate single tone text and line art images. The larger halftone dots are used to recreate contone images.

File Prep Tip #14

Three variables affect file size of an image: image dimensions, pixel depth, and resolution. Increases in any of these variables will increase an image's file size and therefore increase the production demands of a number of variables including: storage space, CPU resources, RIP time, and transportation and storage resources. Image dimension and pixel depth are determined by the document design, so resolution is often the only variable which we can adjust to decrease a file's size. The goal is to decrease file size as much as possible without affecting the output quality of the image. Understanding the basic concepts of resolution helps us understand that resolution is a square and not a liner function. Therefore, whenever we double the linear resolution of a file – for example, from 300 ppi yo 600 ppi – we quadruple the file size.

File Prep Tip #15

When discussing resolution with your printer, distinguish between input resolution (ppi) and output resolutions (dpi and lpi). Find out at what resolution your files will be output and create or adjust your file resolutions accordingly. Resolutions for pixel-based line art images should be between 600 ppi and 1200 ppi. Final resolutions of contone images should never exceed 2 x lpi (see Chapter 12, "Taming Your Scanner," for more advice on this topic).

File Prep Tip #16

There are two basic types of electronic graphic images: bitmapped/raster images which are constructed out of pixels, and vector/outline images which are constructed out of lines. Choose the type of image which best suits your needs. Vector images are preferred for simple line art which needs to be rendered with sharp edges. Vector-based images have the benefit of scalability without alteration of their resolution. The raster basis for an image is preferred when great detail is present, such as in complex line art and contone images.

File Prep Tip #17

Match graphic file format with end use. TIFF and EPS are the preferred file formats for use in Postscript printing. Use TIFF format for high detail and continuous tone images. Use EPS format for low detail images and for scalability, or for contone images which have additional information stored with them such as clipping paths and transfer function data. Do not use PICT or PCX files for print pieces. These are screen format files. Stick to using EPS and TIFF file formats whenever possible for files to be printed.

File Prep Tip #18

Outline simple, low detail, one bit line art TIFFs to create outline graphics in EPS format graphics. EPSs have smaller file sizes and are resolution-independent, scalable images. Use EPS file format to reduce file size and improve editability (especially scaling and skewing) of line art files. Use dedicated outlining applications such as Adobe Streamline to accomplish this task. Your control and results will be better than using the built-in outlining capabilities of your drawing application.

File Prep Tip #19

Create blends in bitmapped editing applications like Photoshop instead of in vector-based drawing or page layout applications. You will have more control over your blends and they will print faster and better. A pixel-based application like Photoshop allows you to add noise to your blends which helps reduce banding upon output.

File Prep Tip #20

Choose the proper pixel depth of your image depending upon how it will be used. Remember, increasing pixel depth increases file size. Use 1 bit for line art images, 8 bit for grayscale images, and 32 bit for process color images.

File Prep Tip #21

Vector-based (EPS) images are inherently more difficult to RIP than pixel-based (TIFF) images. Vector-based EPS files need to be specially prepared. Simplify (reduce the # of control points), split long or complex paths, and set "Flatness" ratio for paths between 2 and 5 prior to creation of an EPS file. Attention to these three variables will make your vector-based images much easier to RIP.

File Prep Tip #22

Exercise care when creating outline paths. When creating an outline in applications like Streamline, set "Fit Tolerance" preference to "Loose" prior to conversion to assure a simpler file with fewer nodes. This will make it easier for a Postscript RIP to process the paths created.

File Prep Tip #23

When converting paths from selections in Photoshop, be sure to choose a tolerance which results in few path control points, usually ≥ 2. Also, when converting a path to a clipping path in Photoshop, select a flatness ratio ≥ 3; this will reduce the number of line segments used when the path is drawn during printing. This is similar to what we discussed in File Prep Hints 18 and 19, and will help simplify the vector-based portion of these primarily contone images for easier RIPing!

File Prep Tip #24

Do not assign "Hairline" widths for lines because they are inconsistent and usually too thin. Always assign a specific, unambiguous thickness value to a line. Do not assign any line thickness values less than 0.25 points.

File Prep Tip #25

Do not assign patterns or grayscale values to thin lines (≤ 4 pts), as these patterns or values will be rendered as halftone dots during RIPing and printing and will be displayed as discontinuous blotches on paper.

File Prep Tip #26

Find out in which file formats your printer or service bureau prefers for your files. While TIFF and EPS are certainly the universal formats, there are often several choices for saving a file within these two general formats. For instance, 1 bit line art images can be saved as TIFFs or converted to vector-based EPSs. Color contone images are perhaps the most variable. Find out if you should send in your file as a CMYK TIFF or a 5-file DCS. You should avoid creating single file CMYK EPS files, as these are very time consuming to RIP.

File Prep Tip #27

If your printing company or service bureau performs scans for you or otherwise creates original graphics, be sure that when they send the file back to you, you know if it is a high or low resolution version of the graphic. If you intend to edit, correct, or otherwise perform pixel level alterations of the image, be sure you receive the high resolution version. The low resolution version is useless for this purpose. A low resolution version will be useful only for placement purposes. In either case, and particularly if you receive a low resolution FPO (for placement only) image, do not change the name in any way. If the printing company has sent you a low resolution image, they have the high resolution image which will be used during the actual RIPing stored on their drive. If you change the name, your FPO image will not be recognized as a match for the high resolution print version when you return the image, and a low quality image will result during printing.

File Prep Tip #28

If you compress your file, generally choose the JPEG format because it results in little image degradation. Be aware of the image degradation which will occur when you compress an image. Always save JPEG images which you may need later for print in the best or Maximum Quality mode. A 5/1 to 10/1 compression with JPEG is generally fine. PhotoCD is another useful compression format, although it is less "open" and more proprietary that JPEG.

File Prep Tip #29

Remove unnecessary elements from your document pages. Don't just cover them up. All elements within active margins will be processed by a RIP which processes a page from the bottom up, and it has no idea what is on top. The concept of out of sight, *but* not out of RIP applies here. To help find extraneous items, I set my view on "Fit Spread In Window" so that I can see my entire page as well as the paste board. Then I scroll through the document and check for items on the paste board. Another trick is to select all the items on a page. This will activate the handles of any extra items which are underneath foreground items.

File Prep Tip #30

Create complex and especially line art EPS graphics created in drawing applications in separate layers. Doing so will allow you to more efficiently create and allow your printer to more easily troubleshoot and edit the graphic.

File Prep Tip #31

Make sure you can RIP and print every graphic you create on your low resolution desktop laser printer before you send it out to be RIPed by someone else on a higher resolution RIP. If it won't RIP and print at low resolution on your laser printer, it certainly won't RIP and print on a more demanding higher resolution RIP. However, be aware that the fact that an image RIPs and prints on your system does not guarantee that it will RIP and print on another system.

File Prep Tip #32

Avoid including the high resolution version of graphic images in your page layout documents. Including the high resolution images makes the page layout document much larger and more unwieldy. It also makes troubleshooting, editing, and updating the file while it is imbedded impossible. Send along the high resolution images as separate files.

File Prep Tip #33

Nesting is for the birds! Be conscious of not nesting text and graphic elements in your documents because nested elements are difficult for RIPs to locate and process. Avoid placing previously created EPS graphics inside of a drawing document when you intend to later export that document as an EPS file. Type set in a drawing document to be exported as an EPS should be outlined/converted to a graphic prior to creation of the EPS. Saving entire document pages as EPS files will generally create nested elements and should be avoided when possible.

File Prep Tip #34

Use thumbnail sketches to plan your document prior to constructing a document. Using thumbnails will help you construct your document in the most efficient manner. Your thumbnails should include characteristics such as page size and orientation, facing vs. nonfacing design, margins, number of columns, text flow, list and placement of master page elements, style sheets, and notes about document-specific preferences you need to set.

File Prep Tip #35

Use Master Pages for repetitive page elements and Style Sheets for repetitive text formatting. Using Master Pages and Style Sheets enhances the consistency and speed of document creation and dramatically improves the accuracy and speed of editing.

File Prep Tip #36

Use Postscript Type 1 rather than Truetype fonts. If you use Truetype, use them exclusively; don't mix Truetype with Type 1 in the same document.

File Prep Tip #37

Choose typeface styles from the font menu rather than from keyboard shortcuts or font style palettes. This will prevent the creation on-screen of fonts which do not exist.

File Prep Tip #38

Be careful about adding too many fonts to your documents. This is both good design and technical advice. Each font increases the complexity of your document.

File Prep Tip #39

Avoid reversing small and serif typefaces because the character shapes are difficult to create and maintain when they are printed.

File Prep Tip #40

Do not baseline shift large blocks of text. Move the entire text box or area. Baseline shift should be used to adjust individual characters or words.

File Prep Tip #41

When making custom adjustments to character spacing, work at high magnification on screen so you can see small changes in space adjustments. Track first to make coarse adjustments, then kern individual characters to fine-tune the look. Avoid massive kerning adjustments to body type.

File Prep Tip #42

Assign leading absolute values rather than using auto leading. Auto leading may create inconsistent leading when individual characters are baseline-shifted (such as when using superscripts and subscripts).

File Prep Tip #43

Your computer is not a typewriter; it is a sophisticated typesetting tool. Don't use multiple spaces and returns to control the horizontal and vertical placement of type. Use paragraph formatting and tabs to position type. Read Robin Williams' Book, *The Mac Is Not A Typewriter*. I think this is the single best introduction to typesetting ever written.

File Prep Tip #44

Snap body copy type to baseline grids when working with multicolumn text pages. This will keep the baselines of your body copy consistent from one column to another.

File Prep Tip #45

Image data changes during scanning from original image to 0s and 1s in RAM, to pixels on screen, to dots on paper. Original data is not 100 percent reproducible. All print images are constructed out of dots. Line art is constructed out of small touching dots or spots, while contones are formed from patterns of larger separated dots (which are constructed from groups of the smaller spots) called halftone dots. It is useful to imagine the changes which happen to your images, as being able to visualize the changes will help you decide the best way to scan your images.

File Prep Tip #46

Up to 95 percent of data is lost (from 5000 visible tones down to 100 printed tones) during the transition from original scene to film to digital data to Postscript to print. We must capture and save the best possible 256 shades of gray or tones during the scanning process. Proper tone compression as well as setting the highlight and shadow points is crucial. Be aware of the difference between setting your highlight dot on a specular versus diffuse highlight area. Specular areas are pure white and have no tonal values and therefore should be avoided as highlight choices. Tone compression should be primarily performed during the scanning process and not during the postscan in applications such as Photoshop.

File Prep Tip #47

Gray map adjustments through alteration of tonal gamma curves can concentrate limited tonal data in those portions of the image which are most important.

File Prep Tip #48

Make sure your scanner is linearized so that you know that it will properly reproduce all values of gray.

File Prep Tip #49

To remove the color cast imposed on your images by your scanner, scan a target which contains a variety of neutral tones. Measure the neutral areas with an on-screen densitometer and create correction curves which can be applied to all scanned images.

File Prep Tip #50

Don't forget to compensate for dot gain before you print your final image. Dot gain compensation can be done during the scanning process, but if you intend to multipurpose your images, scan without dot gain compensation, make copies of your original images, and apply dot gain only to those images which will be used for print. Also be sure to apply dot gain corrections which are specific to each print device you will use.

File Prep Tip #51

We print with impure process inks, so we must compensate for this flaw when setting gray balance. In highlight: C/M/Y = 6/4/4; in midtone C/M/Y = 60/45/45. This correction can be and is often done during the scan process, but if you intend to multipurpose your images, you should scan you images neutral, make copies of the original scan, and apply the correction for impure printing inks only to images which you intend to print. This color correction can be performed during the RGB-to-CMYK gamut conversion and should be specific to each printer you use.

File Prep Tip #52

All scanners soften images as they sample and capture images. In order to return an image's original sharpness or even improve it, a scanned image must be sharpened. Always choose a sharpening tool such as unsharp masking, which preferentially sharpens higher contrast areas of an image. Sharpening can be and often is applied during the scan process; however, if you intend to significantly modify an image after it is scanned, save the sharpening for last.

File Prep Tip #53

We work in various color gamuts in electronic prepress such as CIE (Lab or Ycc) and RGB on scanners and monitors or CMYK on press. This means color data is lost during the gamut conversion process from RGB to CMYK. In general and particularly when we will be multi-purposing images, we want to capture an image into as large a color space as possible, usually a CIE color space. Then we convert copies of the original images into whichever color space we intend to use them. Limit your image gamut conversions to one step whenever possible to reduce color saturation loss which inevitably occurs during gamut conversions.

File Prep Tip #54

Don't judge color visually on a monitor. Always use an on-screen densitometer to measure tone and color data.

File Prep Tip #55

Be aware of the tonal capture range (dynamic range) of your scanner. Your desktop scanner may not be able to capture the entire tonal range of some images.

File Prep Tip #56

Most image adjustments should be performed during the scanning process, not afterward. Use a low resolution prescan technique to set cropping, scaling, tone compression, gray map adjustments, global color corrections, and sharpening, to save time and preserve image quality.

File Prep Tip #57

Simple, crisp line art images should be scanned at high resolution (800 dpi or greater) and then converted to outline files in a dedicated outlining application like Streamline. Rough line art can be scanned as low resolution (300 dpi).

File Prep Tip #58

Scanning resolutions for unscaled continuous tone images, which will be reproduced with conventional AM halftone dots, should not exceed two times (2x) the lpi at which the images will be printed. And 1.25 – 1.4 (quality factor) x the lpi is sufficient for most unscaled images. Use the following formula to determine the input scan resolutions for contone images: [1.25 – 2.0 x lpi x scaling factor]. Using smaller quality factors of between 1.25 and 1.4 will dramatically reduce the file size of the image. High quality factors approaching 2.0 need only be used for images with high contrast areas or when trying to capture subtle shadow detail.

File Prep Tip #59

Final resolutions (after scaling) for contone images which will be reproduced with FM or stochastic screening methods, such as on banner printers, need not exceed 100 ppi; the FM screening process does not require as much pixel information as AM screening.

File Prep Tip #60

Complex and fine detail line art images can be scanned as 8 bit grayscale images and then converted to 1 bit line art using sharpening and thresholding.

File Prep Tip #61

Visualize the effect of the entire scanning and production process on your image before you start. Scan with a final purpose in mind. For multipurpose images, create neutral, uncorrected scans, but always tone compress and map during the scan.

File Prep Tip #62

In addition to sending a composite page layout document such as an XPress or PageMaker document, send all of the high resolution versions of any graphic images you have included (placed or imported) in your document. Remember that graphic images which are visible in page layout documents are only small, low resolution screen versions of the larger, high resolution graphic files. The high resolution graphic files exist as files separate from the page layout document.

File Prep Tip #63

Send original or parent document versions of EPS graphic files, as well as the exported EPS graphics themselves, which have been exported from drawing applications such as Freehand, Illustrator, or CorelDraw documents.

File Prep Tip #64

Send font files for all fonts used in your documents. Send both the screen and printer font files. Both are required for the proper viewing and printing of your file. View your fonts as just special types of preformed graphics.

File Prep Tip #65

Do not imbed the high resolution graphic images in a page layout document. Keep the high resolution files separate for easy access and editing.

File Prep Tip #66

Assign color properly. Use spot and process color designations properly. Assign spot color only to those items which will actually be separated as separate colors and printed as spot colors on its own press cylinder. Assign process color names to items which will print as process colors. Do not assign an item or an area a spot color name and then ask the application or printer to convert it to process colors.

File Prep Tip #67

Use color swatch books to judge and assign colors values; do not use you monitor. Use a spot color swatch book to assign spot colors, a process color swatch book to assign process colors, and the ProSim (process simulation) book to assign process colors which are the closest approximations to the various spot colors. Always note the difference between the spot color and its closest approximation; it is usually not too close.

File Prep Tip #68

Be sure that colors assigned to portions of imported graphics are included in the output application. Also be sure that any imported colors have names identical to the colors used in the importing application. Also check to be sure that each color has its correct spot or process color designations. Use imported colors for assignment to prevent any duplication of colors.

File Prep Tip #69

Delete unused colors in color palettes in all applications used – page layout as well as graphic applications. Delete colors from the color palettes of vector graphics before they are exported as EPS files from their parent applications.

File Prep Tip #70

Be aware of color gamut limitations when you assign colors. Remember that RGB and spot color spaces are far more extensive than CMYK color space. Therefore, many of the colors you can create on your computer and view on your monitor cannot be reproduced in CMYK printing.

File Prep Tip #71

Remember, RGB files must be converted into CMYK for printing. Your RGB-to-CMYK gamut conversion must be controlled and set as specifically as possible to produce a CMYK image which matches the gamut of every output device on which the image will ultimately be printed.

File Prep Tip #72

If you need to maintain color fidelity throughout the design and creation process, calibrate your system. Calibration is best achieved through the use of a closed loop calibration process which utilizes targets with known values. These can be compared with scanned, viewed, and printed results and analyzed to create custom device-specific profiles for each component of your production system.

File Prep Tip #73

Graphic elements placed or imported into page layout documents should be manipulated (scaled, cropped, rotated, or skewed) for design iteration purposes only in those applications. Final editing choices should be applied in the original graphics application. Use publish and subscribe to speed up these updating chores.

File Prep Tip #74

In QuarkXPress use Collect for Output and Font and Picture Usage to help identify and collect document components. Extensions such as The Bundler provide even more extensive help.

File Prep Tip #75

In Pagemaker use the utility Save for Service Provider and Save as Files for remote printing to help identify and collect document components. Plug-ins such as Document Info may provide additional help.

File Prep Tip #76

Use the Link Options menu choice under the Elements menu to prevent Pagemaker from automatically including high resolution versions of graphic images in its documents.

File Prep Tip #77

Create all blends in bitmapped editing applications like Photoshop. You have more control, and they will be of higher quality and will print faster. Use Dithering and add noise and Gaussian blur to blends to prevent banding on output.

File Prep Tip #78

When creating clipping paths in Photoshop, be sure to create simple paths with few control nodes by setting tolerance at 2.0 and above during the creation of the path from a selection. Also set the flatness ratio to 3.0 or above to facilitate output at high resolution.

File Prep Tip #79

Use Levels and Curves in Photoshop instead of Levels to adjust midtone areas for gray map adjustments.

File Prep Tip #80

When adjusting the resolution of a contone image in Photoshop, do not merely add resolution to a file. This procedure will destroy your image. You can safely increase the resolution of a contone image by reducing its dimension while holding the file size constant in the image size dialog box.

File Prep Tip #81

When scanning, always use a two-step scanning process which includes an initial low resolution prescan to analyze and adjust settings which will be applied during a second high resolution scan.

File Prep Tip #82

Before converting bitmapped images to vectors using Streamline, set the tolerance to a high number, usually 4 –5, to reduce the number of nodes generated by Streamline.

File Prep Tip #83

Construct complex images in layers in both painting and drawing applications. This practice makes both initial construction and subsequent editing and troubleshooting of these images much easier. Save native copies of the original layered images prior to export as printable TIFFs and EPSs.

File Prep Tip #84

Convert type set in drawing documents to graphic outlines prior to exporting the file as an EPS document. It is also advisable to limit the amount of type which is set in any document slated for conversion to an EPS. Avoid converting small ($\leq$ 20 pts) and serif typefaces.

File Prep Tip #85

In all vector-based documents be sure to remember to split long paths and set path flatness ratios to at least 3 prior to export as an EPS.

File Prep Tip #86

In general, use applications for the purposes for which they were intended. Perform layout and typesetting with applications like QuarkXPress and Pagemaker, draw with applications like Illustrator, Freehand, or CorelDraw, and paint with applications like Photoshop and Painter.

File Prep Tip #87

For highly complex paths, use your drawing application's ability to decrease the path complexity by reducing the number of control points which occur along the paths.

File Prep Tip #88

Learn a small number of applications very well, rather than trying to learn several varieties of each kind. Become expert at one page layout, one drawing, and one painting application. Experiment with others after you are well grounded in your primary applications.

File Prep Tip #89

Remember that your color images will be separated into individual pieces of film and plates for printing. Be sure to assign your colors properly and print test or proof separations to check your color breaks. Printing separations is really the only way to check to see if your colors will separate properly.

File Prep Tip #90

Be sure that your individual spot colors are assigned different screen angles, particularly if those colors will be overlapped, or moiré patterns will likely result. If you consistently have trouble with moiré patterns when printing colored patterns and images, consider trying an FM screening method rather than conventional AM halftoning.

File Prep Tip #91

Be sure to adjust for dot gain before you send a contone image to press; otherwise, your images will look darker and have lower contrast than you expected. Use Curves or Transfer Functions to adjust for dot gain in grayscale images. For color contones, apply dot gain adjustment during the RGB to CMYK conversion process.

File Prep Tip #92

Contone images and other patterns with tonal values will be printed as a pattern of dots called a screen. Visualize how your image will print as a screen and avoid pattern assignments which cannot be effectively screened. Avoid assigning grayscale values or patterns to thin lines because they will only be imaged as a discontinuous series of dots when printed.

File Prep Tip #93

Choose a screening technology which matches the kinds of images you are trying to reproduce. We will increasingly have choices of different screening technology. Also know which technologies work best on the print device you will be using. Contone images often look better when reproduced with FM screening technology, particularly when printed on desktop banner printers, while solid area images reproduce better with AM screening technologies.

File Prep Tip #94

You can avoid the need for trapping between adjacent colored areas when you are working with process colors if you build adjacent touching elements with colors which have at least 15 percent of one dominant common color, either Cyan or Magenta.

File Prep Tip #95

As a general rule, move lighter colors into darker colors when you trap. This practice creates fewer noticeable problems in the overlap area or trap zone.

File Prep Tip #96

If you set chokes and spreads in a drawing application, be aware that most drawing application stroke lines and outlines symmetrically; that is, they put half the stroke on either side of the line or outline. If you assign a 1 pt. stroke to line in your drawing application, you are really creating only a 0.5 pt overlap or trap.

File Prep Tip #97

Note the trapping capability of your program to flag those areas which may require traditional methods. Some examples of trouble traps: trapping on top of indeterminate (multiple) background colors; and trapping items such as type on top of color imported graphics in a page layout application.

File Prep Tip #98

Avoid spreading type, especially small serif type faces; the enlargement of the characters will ruin the geometry of the typeface. In fact, it is a good idea to try and avoid either spreading or choking small type at all. Overprint type whenever possible to retain the typeface's original geometric integrity.

File Prep Tip #99

In general, you will probably want to leave the trapping chores to your printing company. Always consult your printing company prior to building in traps to make sure you know how to build them properly and that you use trap values appropriate for the film and presses. Improperly assigned traps can be more of a problem than assigning no traps at all.

File Prep Tip #100

Create composite and color-separated laser proofs of the most recent version of your documents. Use these lasers as your proofing tool. Your proofs replace the mechanical boards of old as visual guides for how you want your jobs to print. The proofs you send to your printer should be of the final corrected versions because they will be used to proof screen and film versions of your files.

File Prep Tip #101

Plan time in your production schedule for proofing. No one can proof his own work, so provide time for others to proof the jobs. Use a proofing checklist so that a complete job is done.

File Prep Tip #102

The registration color is a composite black which should be assigned only to document elements which should appear on all separations such as crop, trim, fold, and registration marks.

File Prep Tip #103

For publications which will be reused with only type changes, consider designing them with replaceable type areas and assigning a separate color to changeable text which will print on its own separation. This procedure reduces the need to reprint all plates for a copy-only change.

File Prep Tip #104

Create printer spreads on separate pages. Do not create side-by-side pages on a single sheet, e.g., two 8.5" x 11" pages on an 11" x 17" sheet. Create two separate 8.5" x 11" sheets.

File Prep Tip #105

Mark up your proofs. Indicate bleeds, FPO, and live images, and the percentage of scaling at which the proof was printed, if any, as well as crop, trim, fold, and registration marks.

File Prep Tip #106

Prior to converting an RGB image to a CMYK in Photoshop, you need to first configure the printing ink setup and separation setup dialog boxes. Is is imperative to choose the correct set of inks as well as the appropriate dot gain values for the inks, paper, and press with which your documents will be printed. Also, prior to the gamut conversion, you need to designate which kind of black generation curve will be used (UCR or GCR), as well as assign ink percent values. Call your printing company for guidance in configuring these two dialog boxes and configure them before you complete the mode/gamut change.

File Prep Tip #107

It is extremely important to fill out your EFIS prior to sending your file out to be processed. Your EFIS contains crucial information about what your file contains and how it was constructed. This information is an important aid in helping your service bureau output your document. Remember, no one can see what is on your disk and your proofs, and EFISs provide the service company with the guidelines and information they need to process your files properly. When you fill out your EFIS, be sure to indicate the number of colors/separations which you expect. Indicate whether you have a spot color job, a four-color job, or a combination of four-color plus spot colors. Always clearly indicate the spot colors to be used.

File Prep Tip #108

Organize the files you send out so that your page layout file and its associated graphics are in one folder and your fonts (both screen and printer) are in another folder. Place your screen fonts in a suitcase if possible.

File Prep Tip #109

Keep an empty suitcase, labeled with your name, in your fonts folder on your hard drive. This empty suitcase will be available to copy to your traveling disks quickly and easily, and will serve as a readily available traveling font collection site during font gathering chores.

File Prep Tip #110

Place original, fully editable parent files, such as non-split Illustrator documents with editable type and unflattened Photoshop format files, in a separate folder labeled Parent Documents. Place the original unaltered application documents in this folder. If text, path, or layer troubleshooting or editing needs to be performed on an image, the printer has the option of using these fully editable documents.

File Prep Tip #111

To test your file collection, collect files to a folder on the Desktop and launch your collected files using only the collected fonts and graphics. This simulates what your printer will do when launching your documents.

File Prep Tip #112

Label your disks with your name, company, job ID, and even your phone and fax number. Disks can get misplaced; make yours easy to identify.

File Prep Tip #113

If you send a Postscript file to your printer, make very sure that it is well prepared and that no changes will be necessary. Select your printer's PPD instead of yours prior to creating the Postscript file. A Postscript file is essentially uneditable, so what you send is what you get.

File Prep Tip #114

While it is better to work with uncompressed files, if you do send in compressed graphic files, be sure to indicate this on your EFIS and send in a decompression utility along with your disk.

File Prep Tip #115

Create a separate "PRINT" file for complex drawing documents which you may want to edit later. Keep the original or parent document as is. Simplify, split paths, adjust flatness, and remove colors from the PRINT version before you export it to the EPS. Send all three files to the printer.

File Prep Tip #116

Fill out your printer's EFIS (Electronic File Information Sheet) completely and send it along with your job and proof prints. A properly completed EFIS greatly improves the chances that your file will print quickly and easily, thereby allowing your printer to get your job done on time and on budget.

File Prep Tip #117

Develop a good working relationship with your printer or service bureau. The creation and printing of Postscript files is a joint effort between you and your printing company. It is better to establish a good relationship with one or two printers so that you each learn each other's requirements and characteristics. Negotiate year-long contracts at attractive prices. You will save money and so will the printer. Choose printing companies which have well trained digitally and Postscript-savvy sales, customer service, and production staffs. Visit the company and tour the production facility.

File Prep Hint #118

Use preflight utilities such as FlightCheck for Markzware or PreflightPro for Extensis to help you troubleshoot your documents and collect and organize your page layout files and their associated fonts and graphics.

Appendixes

APPENDIX A: BITS & BYTES

Computerese defined:

The basics of bits, Bytes, & ASCII

bit (b): The smallest unit of the digital or binary computer language, restricted to either a 0 or a 1

Byte (B): A binary number which defines a computer character such as the number "1" = 8 bits

Kilobit (Kb): One thousand (1,000) bits or 1000, 0's or 1s

Megabit (Mb): = One million (1,000,000) bits = 125,000 bytes (1,000,000 bits ÷ 8 bits/bytes = 125,000 bytes)

KiloByte (KB): One thousand (1,000) bytes or characters

MegaByte (MB): One million (1,000,000) bytes or characters

ACSII (American Standard Code for Information Interchange)

A code which translates binary numbers into number, letter, symbol, or control characters: "a" = 01100001, "1" = 00110001 ASCII or "text only" files a a format in which text files can be saved and be nearly universally translated and read on a wide variety of computer platforms and operating systems and applications.

EXAMPLES OF ASCII CODE TRANSLATIONS:

Binary	Char/Key	Binary	Char/Key	Binary	Char/Key	Binary	Char/Key
1000001 =	A	111001 =	9	1010110 =	V	1110011 =	s
1100001 =	a	111010 =	:	1010111 =	W	1110100 =	t
0110001 =	1	111011 =	;	1011000 =	X	1110101 =	u
0100001 =	!	111100 =	<	1011001 =	Y	1110110 =	v
100000 =	space	111101 =	=	1011010 =	Z	1110111 =	w
100001 =	!	111110 =	>	1011011 =	[	1111000 =	x
100010 =	"	111111 =	?	1011100 =	\	1111001 =	y
100011 =	#	1000000 =	@	1011101 =	]	1111010 =	z
100100 =	$	1000001 =	A	1011110 =	^	1111011 =	{
100101 =	%	1000010 =	B	1011111 =		1111100 =	l
100110 =	&	1000011 =	C	1100000 =		1111101 =	}
100111 =	'	1000100 =	D	1100001 =	a	1111110 =	~
101000 =	(	1000101 =	E	1100010 =	b	1111111 =	delete
101001 =	)	1000110 =	F	1100011 =	c		
101010 =	*	1000111 =	G	1100100 =	d		
101011 =	+	1001000 =	H	1100101 =	e		
101100 =	,	1001001 =	I	1100110 =	f		
101101 =	-	1001010 =	J	1100111 =	g		
101110 =	.	1001011 =	K	1101000 =	h		
101111 =	/	1001100 =	L	1101001 =	i		
110000 =	0	1001101 =	M	1101010 =	j		
110001 =	1	1001110 =	N	1101011 =	k		
110010 =	2	1001111 =	O	1101100 =	l		
110011 =	3	1010000 =	P	1101101 =	m		
110100 =	4	1010001 =	Q	1101110 =	n		
110101 =	5	1010010 =	R	1101111 =	o		
110110 =	6	1010011 =	S	1110000 =	p		
110111 =	7	1010100 =	T	1110001 =	q		
111000 =	8	1010101 =	U	1110010 =	r		

APPENDIX B: FONT REVIEW

POSTSCRIPT TYPE 1 FONTS

Screen   Printer

Truetype Fonts

Combined Screen & Printer

Characteristics	
Bitmapped	Outline
Low resolution	High resolution
Specific point size	Scalable
For screen display	For printing

Characteristics
Bitmapped & outline
Low and high resolution
Scalable
For screen display and printing

Screen Font Files

☐ B Futura Bold 10
☐ B Futura Bold 12
☐ BO Futura BoldOblique 10
☐ BO Futura BoldOblique 12
☐ Futura 10
☐ Futura 12
☐ O Futura Oblique 10
☐ O Futura Oblique 12

Printer Font Files

☐ Futur   32K PostScript™ font
☐ FuturBol   32K PostScript™ font
☐ FuturBolObl 48K PostScript™ font
☐ FuturObl   40K PostScript™ font

TrueType Font Files Examples

☐ AppleGaramond Bd
☐ AppleGaramond BdIt
☐ AppleGaramond Bk
☐ AppleGaramond BkIt

Screen Font Icon View

Printer Font Icon View

FuturBolObl   FuturObl

Futur   FuturBol

TrueType Font Icon View

AppleGaramond Bd   AppleGaramond E

ppleGaramond BdIt   AppleGaramond Bl

Full Name With Point Size

☐ B Futura Bold 10
☐ B Futura Bold 12
☐ BO Futura BoldOblique 10
☐ BO Futura BoldOblique 12

Abbreviated Name

☐ FuturBol
☐ FuturBolObl

TrueType Font Naming

Full Name But With No Point Size

☐ AppleGaramond Bd
☐ AppleGaramond BdIt
☐ AppleGaramond Bk
☐ AppleGaramond BkIt

Note: Be careful of using icons for font identification. Printer font icons vary dramatically from one manufacturer to another, while the naming conventions discussed above remain the same

Font Types and Their Characteristics

PostScript Screen fonts have point sizes included in their names because they are bitmapped graphic files and are specific sizes. PostScript Printer fonts have abbreviated names with no point sizes because they are scalable Postscript files TrueType font names have characteristics of both the screen and printer font names. They have full names like the screen fonts, but no point sizes because they are scalable like the printer fonts.

APPENDIX C: WINDOWS FONT FILES

Windows Type 1 (.pfb) Font Files

WINDOWS .PFB FILES

• these fundamental font files are stored in a separate folder called ps fonts. This also contains another folder which contains the .pfm files

• .pfb files contain both screen font data, as well as high resolution printer font information

• these need to accompany the font metric (.pfm) files when you send a file to a service bureau or printing company

Windows Type 1 Font Metric (.pfm) Font Files

WINDOWS .PFM FILES

• font metric files are stored in a separate subdirectory of the ps fonts directory, labeled .pfm

• .pfm files contain information which controls character spacing of text on a document page

• these need to accompany the outline (.pfb) font files, shown above, when you send a file to a service bureau or printer. Collection of these font files can be aided by the use of file collection utilities like Marksware's FlightCheck.

APPENDIX D: EFIS EXAMPLE

MORGAN PRESS MORGAN PRESS, INC.
© 1994

60 Buckley Circle / Manchester, New Hampshire 03109-5217
Phone 603/624-8660
603/624-2770 FAX

LETTER-HEAD
ENVELOPE
BIZ
Annual Report
'93

ELECTRONIC FILE INFORMATION SHEET

Company/Customer Name

Contact Name

Contact Telephone

Contact Fax No.

Project Name

Date/Time Submitted   Job No.

MorganPress Sales Rep.

☐ Quote Only   ☐ OK to Edit Files   ☐ Do Not Edit Files

JOB INFORMATION

Job Name:

Job Description:

Media Used:

Quantity

☐ Floppies

☐ 44/88 Syquest

Platform: ☐ Macintosh ☐ IBMPC

Output Information:

All items will print to film (negatives) at 2400 dpi, 150 lpi, emulsion down, unless otherwise noted here.

FILE INFORMATION

Composite (Page Layout) File

Name:

Application (w/version used).

Page Size:
☐ 8.5" x 11"   ☐ 11" x 17"
☐ Other:

Page Range to be Printed:

Page Orientation:
☐ Portrait(tall) ☐
Landscape (wide)

Compression Used:
☐ Disk Doubler ☐ Stuffit
☐ Other:

GRAPHIC INFORMATION

File Name   Type   Application (version)

Compressed

Note : Send Parent file as well as the Exported Freehand EPS files.

FONT INFORMATION

A b C d E f

☐ Adobe
☐ Bitstream
☐ Monotype
☐ Truetype
☐ Other

Note: Please send both screen and printer fonts. If you use TrueType fonts, use them exclusively or not at all.

COLOR INFORMATION

Color Separations: (check (√) only one)

☐ Spot Colors ☐ 4/C Process only

☐ 4/Color Process and Spot Colors

List of all spot colors and varnishes:

Traps: ☐ MorganPress to Trap
       ☐ Traps set by Customer
Bleeds: ☐ Included ☐ Not Included

PRINTS / PROOFS

Check (√) the Items Enclosed:

☐ Composite of Final Version
☐ Color Separated Print
☐ Note ____ % Reduction (if not 100%)
☐ All Images Marked FPO or Live
☐ FPO Originals Sent
☐ Bleeds Noted on Composite
☐ Changes to be made by Morgan Press marked on Composite

Special Instructions

Sales Rep. Initials

Date

HEADLINE

PROCESS CYAN PROCESS MAG PROCESS YELO PROCESS BLCK

APPENDIX E: FILE PREP UTILITIES

Packing for traveling made easy:

The following utilities will help simplify and/or facilitate your file creation and preparation chores. A brief description of the use of each application is included. The prices in parenthesis are approximate.

- ATM Deluxe (Mac and Windows) ($125): font management utility which helps organize and access large numbers of fonts
- PostScript Level 2 reference card from Merrit ($7.00): Postscript error code information
- PinPoint XT ($85.00): for troubleshooting Quark Files
- LaserCheck from Merrit ($149.00): file troubleshooting and imagesetter emulation utility
- PreFlight Pro: ($99 -350): preflight utility which troubleshoots s as well as gathers all components
- Flight Check ($99–$350): file prep utility which troubleshoots s as well as gathers all components
- Bureau Manager ($129): Quark extension for gathering file components including fonts
- Collect for Output (Free): document and graphic file collection in Quark 3.2 and above
- Save for Service Provider (Free): PageMaker 6.5+ content preflight and collection utility
- QuarkPrint ($195.00): expands Quark's print capabilities
- CheckList ($180.00): used to check and get info on both Quark and PM Postscript files
- Display Pub Info (Free): document info; addition included with Pagemaker 5.0 and above
- Blender ZiffNet Mac (Free): used to help calculate the number of blend steps required
- ATM (Free with several adobe applications): a required utility which helps provide W.Y.S.I.W.Y.G. views of scaled characters
- Suitcase – Mac ($125): font management utility which helps organize and access your fonts
- MasterJuggler– Mac ($125): font management utility which helps organize and access your fonts
- Font Chameleon ($125): allows you to change one font architecture into another
- Metamorphosis ($95): allows you to change one font architecture into another
- Font Corral ($75): provides for the collection of fonts from Pagemaker and XPress documents
- Font Sneak ($50): allows the collection of fonts from a variety of applications
- Fontographer ($195): the ultimate font creation and conversion tool
- ScanXpress Calculator (Free): helps to determine input scanning resolutions
- Color Compass ($300): color assignment and management utility
- The Fondler($75): font troubleshooting utility
- DeBabelizer ($64–$250): the ultimate file format conversion utility
- Intellihance by Extensis ($99): photo enhancement plug-in for photoshop
- ScanPrep Pro ($600): automated scanning application
- Binuscan ColorPro ($500 – $2000): comprehensive scanning, color correction, and separation suite of application.

APPENDIX F: INFORMATION RESOURCES

BOOKS

Beyond The Mac Is Not A Typewriter, Robin Williams, Peachpit Press, 1996, 1-201-88598-0

CREF Computer Ready Electronic Files 2, Scitex Graphic Arts Users Association, Brentwood TN

Design For Non-Designers, Robin Williams,
Santa Fe NM, http://www.zumacafe.com

GRACOL General Requirements For Applications In Commercial Offset Lithography V. 2.0,
Graphic Arts Communication Association, 1998, 703.519.8160

How to Make Sure What You See is What You Get,
Peter Fink, phone 800.551.5921

One-Minute Designer, Revised Edition,
Roger C. Parker, MIS: Press, 1997, 1-55828-593-8

Photoshop In Black And White, 2nd Edition,
Jim Rich and Sandy Bozek, Peachpit Press, 1995, 1-56609-189-6

Pocket Guide to Color Reproduction, Miles Southworth and Donna Southworth, Graphic
Arts Publishing, 1994, 0-933600-09-7

Pocket Guide To Digital Prepress, Frank Romano, Delmar Publishers, 1996, 0-8273-7198-5

Pocket Guide To Digital Printing, Frank Cost, Delmar, 1997, 0-8273-7592-1

Pocket Pal: A Graphics Arts Production Handbook, International Paper, 1963-1997, Memphis TN

Postscript: A Visual Approach, Ross Smith, Peachpit Press, 0-938-151-12-6

QuarkXPress: Tips & Tricks, David Blatner and Eric Taub, Peachpit Press 1992, 0-938151-79-7

Real World Photoshop, David Blatner and Bruce Fraser, Peachpit Press, 1996, 1-56609-169-1

Real World Scanning and Halftones, David Blatner and Steve Roth, Peachpit Press, 1995

The Art & Technology of Typography, Agfa Corp, 1988, Wilmington, MA

The Color Resource Complete Color Glossary, Miles Southworth, Thad McIlroy, and Donna
Southworth, The Color Resource, 1992, 1-879847-01-9

The Color Scanning Success Handbook, Michael Kieran, Desktop Publishing Associates,
1997, 1-896097-01-4

The Complete Guide To Trapping, 2nd Edition,
Brian Lawler, Hayden Books, 1995, 1-56830-098-0

The Mac (PC) Is Not A Typewriter, Robin Williams, Peachpit Press, 1990, 0-938151-31-2

The Photoshop WOW Book,(series) Linnea Dayton and Jack Davis, Peachpit Press, 1995, 1-56609-178-0

Thinking In Postscript, Glenn C. Reid, Addison–Wesley, 1990, 0-201-52372-8

Understanding Desktop Color, 2nd Edition, Michael Kieran, Desktop Publishing Associates, 1994, 1-56609-164-0

PERIODICALS

Design Tools Monthly, Boulder CO, 303.543.8300 (my favorite)

Step by Step Electronic Design, Dynamic Graphics, Peoria, ILL, 800.255.8800

Dynamic Graphics,The Idea Guide to Quick Desktop Success, Dynamic Graphics, Peoria, ILL, 800.255.8800

DTP Journal, Journal of the NADP (National Association Of Desktop Publishers) 508.887.7900

Adobe Magazine, Adobe Systems Mountain View CA 415-961-4400, www.adobe.com

Graphic Arts Monthly, Graphic Arts Communication Association, Alexandria, VA

GATF: Graphic Arts Technical Foundation, Various technical publications, Pittsburgh PA

HOW: The Bottomline Design Magazine, Cincinnati, OH, 800.333.1115

Publish, Integrated Media, San Francisco, CA, 415.243.0600

Seybold Reports, Media PA, 800.325.3830, www.seyboldreport.com

WEB RESOURCES

Viacom's Information Super Library: http://www.mcp.com _ General, broad topics electronic publishing information

Apple Computer: http://www.Apple.com _ Apple computer information

Microsoft: http://www.microsoft.com _ Microsoft information

Adobe Plug-in Source Catalog: http://www.imageclub.com/aps/ _ Plug-in resources for Adobe products

Extensis Phototools info: http://www.extensis.com _ Extension technologies for many products

Macromedia: http://www.macromedia.com: _ Freehand and super Web-based product information and help

Netscape Color Info: http://www.connect.hawaii.com/hc/webmasters/ _ Web color information and resources

Pantone: http://www.pantone.com/whatsnew.html _ Pantone-specific and general color information

Shareware: http://shareware.com _ Wild and wooly world of shareware. Bring your virus protection

Design Tools Creaticity: http://www.creaticity.com _ Wonderful update and problem solving information for wide variety of DTP issues

Amazon Books: http://www.amazon.com/exec/obidos/subst/home/home.html/002-0754583-8019430 _ Online book reviews and ordering

Adobe Publications: http://www.adobe.com/publications/adobemag _ Access old versions of Adobe Magazine and other Adobe educational information

Apple Education Site: http://www.education.apple.com _ Access Apple's extensive education; library

Apple Information/Support: http://info.apple.com _ Apple troubleshooting infomation

Digital Media: http://www.digitalmedia.net _ Excellent multimedia training

TazTally Seminars: http://www.tazseminars.com _ Seminar training topics and schedules

Quark Updates: http://www.quark.com/files/update_select.html _ Get Quark updates

For PDF files and Acrobat technology in general, consult these info sites:

• *PDF for Prepress:* www.prepress.ch/pdf_wp.pdf

• *PDF Bug List on Seybold Web site:* www.seyboldseminars.com. Includes a list of bugs and fixes and has an up-to-date list of PDF extensions

• *PDF devoted sites:* www.pdfzone.com

• *Adobe PDF info:* www.Adobe.com

Index

#s

A

B

C

D

E

F

G

H

Q

R

S

T

U

V–Z

COLOPHON

This book was constructed on a Macintosh G3 PowerBook with 160MB of RAM and a 5.0 GB hard drive with no external monitor. Scans were performed initially on an Apple ColorOne scanner. Final scans were performed on a UMAX PowerLook 2000 with Magicscan software. Final page layout was done in QuarkXPress version 4.0. Line art images were converted form pixel to vector format through Adobe Streamline and were edited and exported from Adobe illustrator 6.0 All pixel based image editing, both line art and contone, was accomplished using Adobe Photoshop.3.0.5, 4.0 and 5.0. Composite and color separate proofs were done with an Apple LaserWriter 16/600. Table of contents generation was done in QuarkXPress 4.0 and index creation was done using Sonar TOC, a QuarkXPress Xtension. Preflighting and file component gathering were accomplished with the the aid of FlightCheck, from Markzware.

All fonts used in the construction of this document are PostScript® Type 1 fonts. The primary fonts used in this document include version of Minion and GillSans typefaces from Adobe.

Macintosh®, LaserWriter® are registered trade marks of Apple Computer Inc.QuarkXPress® is a registered trade mark of Quark Inc. Illustrator®, Streamline® and Photoshop® PostScript® are registered trade marks of Adobe Inc. Pantone is a registered trade mark of Pantone Inc. TruMatch is a registered trade mark of TruMatch Corp. The Sonar TOC, is a registered trade mark of Virginia Systems. FlightCheck is a registered trade mark of Markzware. Minion and GillSans are fonts registered with Adobe Corp.

Document design and production were performed by the author, Taz Tally and Jazmine Saige as well as the publisher Prentice Hall.7

SPECIAL CALIBRATION TARGET OFFER

Improve the quality of your scanned images by calibrating your scanner. As discussed in Chapter 12, "Taming Your Scanner," calibration of your scanner is one of the key variables to improving the quality and consistency of your scanned images.

Get your copy of Taz's calibration target specifically designed by Taz for use with desktop scanners.

Order your target today at a special book purchaser's discount price.

Standard Calibration Target

Target list price $19.95
Your Price $14.95!

▼ Calibrated vs Uncalibrated Scanned Images
On the left is an image scanned on an uncalibrated scanner. On the right is the same image scanned on the same scanner with the same settings, but this time after linearization. Notice how overall image brightness, contrast, and shadow details are improved through calibration.

This target can be used with the step by step procedure provided in Chapter 12 "Taming Your Scanner."

Advanced Calibration Kit
with target and enhanced step-by-step calibration procedures is also available for those who want even more control over their scanners and scanned images.

Advanced Calibration Kit list price $34.95
Your price $29.95!

Phone Orders: 888-421-2103
Fax Orders: 816-471-4570
Web Orders www.tazseminars.com
Mail Orders To: Taz Tally Seminars
Richardson Printing P.O. Box 270225
Kansas City, MO 64127-0225

__ Standard target $14.95 each ____
__ Advanced Kit $29.95 each ____
   Shipping & Handling   **$3.00**
           Total _____

Ship To: Name_____
Company_____
Address_____
City_____State____Zip_____
Phone_____Fax_____
eMail_____
Payment Method: ❑ Check, ❑ Money Order
Credit Card: ❑ MC ❑ Visa
Card #_____
Expiration date_____